1st Edition

NBCOT® Study Guide

for the COTA® Certification Examination

Certified Occupational Therapy Assistant

Mission

Serving the public interest by advancing client care and professional practice through evidence-based certification standards and the validation of knowledge essential for effective practice in occupational therapy.

Vision

Certified occupational therapy professionals providing effective evidence-based services across all areas of practice worldwide.

Accreditation

NBCOT certification programs have received and maintained accreditation from the American National Standards Institute (ANSI) and the National Commission for Certifying Agencies (NCCA).

All rights reserved. No part of this publication may be reproduced, stored in a retrieval system, or transmitted in any form or by any means (electronic, mechanical, photocopying, recording, or otherwise) without prior written permission of the copyright owners.

This study guide is one of a number of NBCOT study tools designed to assist candidates with their exam preparation. NBCOT does not guarantee enhanced performance on the NBCOT certification exams for those using these products.

Foreward

Letter From the President

Like many candidates, as you aspire to reach your certification goal, you probably wonder, "How can I best prepare for the NBCOT certification exam?" With the numerous options available, deciding which study tools to use can be a challenge.

Well, there is no magic answer. You are the only person who can make that decision by considering your personal learning style, current academic strengths and weaknesses, fieldwork experiences, and resources. However, one thing is certain: following a realistic and well-planned study schedule can help you feel more prepared for the certification exam.

This study guide provides an overview of what to expect on the Certified Occupational Therapy Assistant COTA® exam, options on how to prepare, and practice-focused sample items grouped under the major domain areas of the certification exam content outline. Feedback, answer keys, and references are provided to enhance test preparation strategies.

We hope the information in this guide supports and augments your overall exam preparation activities. We know the practice of occupational therapy is constantly evolving. The National Board for Certification in Occupational Therapy, Inc. (NBCOT) includes only current information in exam items used for certification purposes. Although the information contained in this guide is current at the time of publication, you should refer to the most recent editions of references when studying for the NBCOT COTA® Certification Exam. The information and sample items in this guide can assist your overall study efforts; however, they will not ensure or guarantee a passing score on the certification exam.

Best of luck as you pursue your professional career as a COTA.

Paul Grace

Paul Grace, MS, CAE
President/CEO

Introduction

How to Use This Guide

Historically, regulation of the health professions in the United States began with a necessity to protect the public from the under-educated and under-trained professional. Over time, licensure, credentialing, and certification have continued the tradition of protecting the public; they have also increased their scope of activity to continuously improve the quality of practice in the profession.

NBCOT uses a formal process to grant the certification credential to an individual who:

1. Meets academic and fieldwork experience requirements,
2. Successfully completes a comprehensive exam to assess knowledge and skills for practice, and
3. Agrees to adhere to the NBCOT Candidate/Certificant Code of Conduct.

How This Study Guide Is Organized

SECTIONS

We have divided the study guide into sections to make it easier for you to find the information you are looking for. There are four sections:

Section 1
NBCOT COTA Exam

In this section, we discuss the specifics of the NBCOT COTA exam and provide information and resources for you to be informed as you prepare for the exam. You will find an overview of the format of the multiple choice and multi-select questions used on the COTA exam, and a summary of what happens after you have completed the exam. In addition, the NBCOT Navigator® Competency Assessment Platform and other benefits of earning and maintaining your COTA credential are outlined for you.

Section 2
Preparing for the Exam

Here, we provide you with tools and methods to self-reflect on your perception of your test readiness and to develop a personalized study plan that you feel will work for you. We have included multiple resources, including the *NBCOT Illustrated Description of Entry-Level COTA® Practice*, the *COTA® Entry-Level Self-Assessment*, and a worksheet for you to develop your own personalized study plan. We hope you take the time to review the NBCOT Exam StudyPack and NBCOT Aspire exam prep tools to determine if you think these tools fit into your overall study plan.

Section 3
Time to Practice

In the *Time to Practice* section, we provide you with multiple choice practice test questions organized by the domains of the COTA exam content outline.

COTA DOMAIN DESCRIPTIONS

DOMAIN 01	**COLLABORATING AND GATHERING INFORMATION** Assist the OTR to acquire information regarding factors that influence occupational performance on an ongoing basis throughout the occupational therapy process.
DOMAIN 02	**SELECTING AND IMPLEMENTING INTERVENTIONS** Implement interventions under the supervision of the OTR in accordance with the intervention plan and level of service competence to support client participation in areas of occupation throughout the occupational therapy process.
DOMAIN 03	**UPHOLDING PROFESSIONAL STANDARDS AND RESPONSIBILITIES** Uphold professional standards and responsibilities by achieving service competence and applying evidence-based interventions to promote quality in practice.

Multiple Choice Items

Each chapter in this section of the study guide starts with a multiple choice practice test. An answer key is provided after each practice test—one option is to answer all the questions, then use the answer key to determine your total score on the practice test. Or, you may decide you want to answer each item one at a time and use the answer key as a reference to learn the correct response. How you approach using these practice tests to study is up to you! After the answer key in each chapter are the rationales for the correct answers and the references for each multiple choice question.

Section 4
Appendices

To help streamline the information in the study guide, the following supporting documents and information are included in the Appendices:

APPENDIX A
Content Outline for the COTA Examination

APPENDIX B
An Illustrated Description of Entry-Level COTA® Practice

APPENDIX C
Worksheet: *Illustrated Guide*

APPENDIX D
COTA® Entry-Level Self-Assessment

APPENDIX E
References used during the development of this COTA Study Guide

Callout Boxes Used in This Study Guide

We have used distinct callout boxes throughout the study guide to make different types of content stand out. Callout boxes used in this study guide are as follows:

ⓘ Tips

These are ideas or suggestions for you to consider and think about when you are preparing for the NBCOT exam.

🔑 Key Points

A summary of information that is presented in a list.

❗ Important

Important information that you will want to repeat to yourself a few times.

🔍 Learn More

These callout boxes will provide you with the location of additional information in case you want to access and learn more about the topic.

📄 Note

Provides you with new information to clarify a particular topic.

👍 Remember

This is information that may be repeated a couple of times to draw attention to it.

Important Information for You to Know

This study guide is one of a number of NBCOT Aspire study tools designed to assist candidates with their exam preparation. NBCOT does not administer, approve, endorse, or review preparatory courses relating to the NBCOT certification exams or study materials produced by other vendors.

Table of Contents

Section 1
NBCOT COTA Exam

2 **Chapter 1**
Where to Start
Being informed

5 **Chapter 2**
All About the Exam
The development and the format of the COTA exam

10 **Chapter 3**
Format of the Test Items
Single-response multiple choice items and six-option multi-select items

13 **Chapter 4**
After the Exam
Scoring, score reports, and more

16 **Chapter 5**
Certification Renewal
Your COTA credential and benefits of maintaining certification

Section 2
Preparing for the Exam

22 **Chapter 6**
NBCOT Illustrated Description to Entry-Level COTA® Practice
Critical thinking and self-reflection

26 **Chapter 7**
NBCOT COTA® Entry-Level Self-Assessment
Identifying your strengths and learning needs

30 **Chapter 8**
Personalized Study Plan
A method for developing a study plan that works for you

35 **Chapter 9**
Exam Day
Planning for exam day and test-taking tips

Section 3
Time to Practice

40   **Chapter 10**
Domain 1: Multiple Choice Sample Questions
Practice questions with answer key and references

104   **Chapter 11**
Domain 2: Multiple Choice Sample Questions
Practice questions with answer key and references

212   **Chapter 12**
Domain 3: Multiple Choice Sample Questions
Practice questions with answer key and references

Section 4
Appendices

284   **Appendix A**
Content Outline for the COTA Examination

294   **Appendix B**
An Illustrated Description of Entry-Level COTA® Practice

328   **Appendix C**
Worksheet: Illustrated Guide

330   **Appendix D**
NBCOT COTA® Entry-Level Self-Assessment

343   **Appendix E**
References

Section 1
NBCOT COTA Exam

Chapter 1

Where to Start

Being informed

Earning a passing score on the NBCOT COTA® Certification Exam is an important milestone in your certification journey. The COTA credential is representative of practitioners who have satisfied national standards in education, experience, and professional conduct. Certification as a COTA indicates to the public that you have demonstrated the knowledge and skills necessary to provide occupational therapy services. Currently, all 50 states, the District of Columbia, Guam, and Puerto Rico require NBCOT certification as a COTA as a component for becoming licensed to practice.

🔍 Learn More

As you prepare for the certification exam, review the *NBCOT Certification Exam Handbook* available at www.nbcot.org/Students/get-certified.

Being Informed

As you embark on the journey to certification, it is important to be informed about the resources available to you. Information about the NBCOT COTA® Certification Exam, initial certification, and certification renewal as a COTA is available to you at www.nbcot.org.

NBCOT Certification Exam Handbook

The *NBCOT Certification Exam Handbook* is an important resource to refer to on your journey to certification. The Handbook was developed to provide information on how to complete and successfully submit a certification exam application. Be sure to locate the Exam Application Procedures Checklist in the Handbook, which can guide you through the exam application process.

📄 Note

The *NBCOT Certification Exam Handbook* is your go-to resource for information on how to successfully submit a certification exam application.

MyNBCOT Account

A required step to register for the NBCOT COTA® Certification Exam is to create a MyNBCOT account. This is a necessary step in the exam application process, and also allows you to access the Aspire study tools. When you log in to your MyNBCOT account, you will be able to view details about the status of your application on your personalized Student Dashboard. You will continue to use your MyNBCOT account after you earn your certification to view information related to your certification status and to access many benefits provided to you by NBCOT for use throughout your certification journey.

⊕ Learn More

Register for a MyNBCOT account at
www.nbcot.org/Students/get-certified

Begin your certification journey by creating a **MyNBCOT account**. With an account you can:

Apply for the Exam

Apply for the exam and track your application status and service order status.

⊕ Learn More

Access Aspire study tools at
www.nbcot.org/Students/Study-Tools.

Use Aspire Study Tools

Access and use your Aspire study tools to prepare for the exam.

Stay Informed

Receive notifications on the latest NBCOT news and update your information.

Staying Informed

This study guide provides information about the NBCOT COTA® Certification Exam and strategies for developing a personalized study plan. Answers to many of the questions you may have about the exam are available in the *NBCOT Certification Exam Handbook*, on the NBCOT website (www.nbcot.org), and on your personalized dashboard in your MyNBCOT account.

🔑 Key Points

- Explore the NBCOT website: www.nbcot.org
- Read the *NBCOT Certification Exam Handbook*.
- Register for a MyNBCOT account.

Chapter 2

All About the Exam

The development and the format of the COTA exam

NBCOT COTA Certification Exam

The primary purpose of the exam is to protect the public interest by certifying only those candidates who have the necessary knowledge of occupational therapy to practice as a COTA.

The current COTA certification exam is constructed from a content outline that will be described in this chapter.

NBCOT conducted a COTA practice analysis study in 2017. The results from this study were used to revalidate the exam content outline for the COTA exams that will be administered from January 2019 onward. In line with certification industry standards, NBCOT certification exams are constructed based on the results of practice analysis studies. A practice analysis study is a large-scale survey administered to entry-level COTA practitioners who are asked to evaluate job requirements on criticality and frequency rating scales. The results of the practice analysis study are used to:

- understand and classify the job requirements as the domains, tasks, and knowledge required for current occupational therapy practice
- develop a valid and defensible content outline for the exam
- determine content for the COTA certification exam
- ensure that there is a representative linkage of the test content to practice

⊕ Learn More

To learn more about this important study, view the *Practice Analysis of the Certified Occupational Therapy Assistant—Executive Summary*: www.nbcot.org/en/Students/Study-Tools/Exam-Outline.

NBCOT COTA Exam Development at a Glance

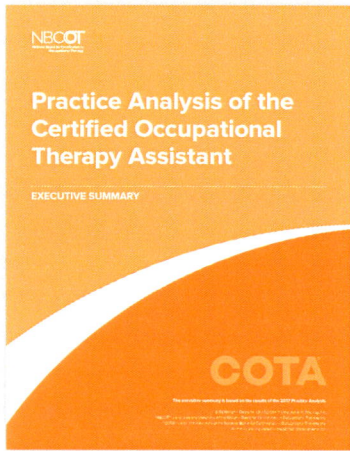

A practice analysis study validates the domain, task, and knowledge areas that are critical to and frequently used in occupational therapy practice.

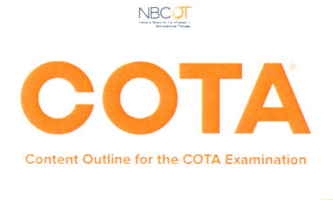

Items on the exam are based on the validated domain, task, and knowledge statements from the practice analysis study.

All COTA exam items meet:

- ✓ **BLUEPRINT SPECIFICATIONS**
- ✓ **CERTIFICATION INDUSTRY STANDARDS**
- ✓ **PSYCHOMETRIC AND SCORING STANDARDS**

Validated Domain, Task, and Knowledge Statements

From the results of this practice analysis study, the content outline for the COTA exam is developed. The results from the practice analysis identified three major domain areas for COTA practice. Within each of the three domain areas, there are a number of tasks and accompanying knowledge statements that were defined from the study results.

All items on the NBCOT exams are classified according to these domain, task, and knowledge statements.

Domains
Broadly define the major job components of the profession.

DOMAIN 01 — COLLABORATING AND GATHERING INFORMATION
Assist the OTR to acquire information regarding factors that influence occupational performance on an ongoing basis throughout the occupational therapy process.

Task 0101
Recognize the influence of development; body functions and body structures; and values, beliefs, and spirituality on a client's occupational performance.

	KNOWLEDGE OF:
010101	Impact of typical development and aging on occupational performance, health, and wellness across the life span
010102	Expected patterns, progressions, and prognoses associated with conditions that limit occupational performance
010103	Impact of body functions, body structures, and values, beliefs, and spirituality on occupational performance

Tasks
Describe activities that are performed in each domain (i.e., things that practitioners do).

Knowledge Statements
Describe the information required to perform each task competently.

🔍 Learn More

To learn more about the development and construction of the COTA exam, review the Foundations of the NBCOT Certification Examinations at www.nbcot.org/Educators/Foundations.

See Appendix A to read the Content Outline for the COTA Examination.

COTA Exam Specifications

From the results of the practice analysis study, the COTA exam specifications were developed. The exam specification table shows the percentage of exam items that appear in each domain area of the exam. The percentage of items in each domain area is shown in **Table 2.1**. The percentage of items in each domain area remain constant on each COTA exam form.

Table 2.1:
COTA content outline specifications based on the *2017 Practice Analysis Study* (effective for COTA exams administered January 2019 onward)

DOMAIN	COTA DOMAIN DESCRIPTIONS	% OF EXAM
DOMAIN 01	**COLLABORATING AND GATHERING INFORMATION** — Assist the OTR to acquire information regarding factors that influence occupational performance on an ongoing basis throughout the occupational therapy process.	28%
DOMAIN 02	**SELECTING AND IMPLEMENTING INTERVENTIONS** — Implement interventions under the supervision of the OTR in accordance with the intervention plan and level of service competence to support client participation in areas of occupation throughout the occupational therapy process.	55%
DOMAIN 03	**UPHOLDING PROFESSIONAL STANDARDS AND RESPONSIBILITIES** — Uphold professional standards and responsibilities by achieving service competence and applying evidence-based interventions to promote quality in practice.	17%

Percentage of items in each domain area

Format of the COTA Exam

The COTA exams are delivered by computers at testing centers located throughout the United States and internationally. You can schedule to take the exam during the business hours of the testing center at a time that is optimal for you. Scheduling instructions are provided in your Authorization to Test (ATT) letter that is sent to you after your exam application is complete.

You are allotted 4 hours to complete the exam. The COTA exam contains 200 questions comprised of four- and three-option single-response multiple choice items and six-option multi-select items.

Key Points

- You are given 4 hours to complete the NBCOT COTA® Certification Exam.
- The COTA exam contains 200 questions.
- Exam questions include four- and three-option single-response multiple choice items and six-option multi-select items.

Remember

You are given 4 hours to complete the NBCOT COTA® Certification Exam.

Optional Tutorial

You may take an optional tutorial about the functionality of the test screens at the beginning of the exam. This tutorial demonstrates the functionality of the exam in the computer-based testing environment. The tutorial does not count against the overall time you are allotted for the exam.

Learn More

To view the optional tutorial, visit https://sites.nbcot.org/prometricstutorial/cota/

Features of the Exam

During the exam, you will be able to highlight text that you believe is important to refer to as you decide on an answer. A strike out feature is also available to help you visually eliminate possible options from consideration, and you can mark an item to review at a later time.

Tips

- You can mark items to review later and change their responses if time allows.
- If time runs out before you review the marked items, the selected response will be submitted for scoring.
- No credit will be given to a marked item that has no response option selected.

Chapter 3

Format of the Test Items

Single-response multiple choice items and six-option multi-select items

The COTA exam consists of single-response multiple choice items and six-option multi-select items.

Single-Response Multiple Choice Items

Each single-response multiple choice item begins with a stem or premise. This is typically in the form of a written statement or question. Listed below the stem are either four (see Sample A) or three (see Sample B) possible response options. There is only one correct response, and you must select the best response based on the information provided in the stem.

SAMPLE A

ITEM STEM:

1. An OTR and a COTA, who has established service competence, are collaborating to evaluate a kindergarten student who has autism spectrum disorder. Which task can the COTA complete as part of the **INITIAL** data-gathering process?

RESPONSE OPTIONS:

    A. Score a sensory integration assessment.

    B. Select a developmental assessment to administer.

    C. Document evaluation outcomes of a classroom observation.

    D. Administer a standardized developmental checklist.

> 📄 **Note**
>
> For this sample question, the correct answer is D.
>
> To assist in your studies, the correct answers are bolded and highlighted in the Answers and Rationales section in Section 3 of this guide.

SAMPLE B

ITEM STEM:

2. A patient in an acute care facility had an uncomplicated total hip replacement, anterolateral approach, one week ago. What movement of the affected hip is typically **CONTRAINDICATED** based on standard hip precautions?

RESPONSE OPTIONS:

   A. Internal rotation

   B. External rotation

   C. Flexion to 90°

Some items may include a picture or chart in the stem. The picture or chart contains information needed to answer the question (see Sample C).

SAMPLE C

ITEM STEM:

3. A COTA is working with a client who has rheumatoid arthritis. During meal preparation, the client cuts fruit as pictured below. During the intervention session, the COTA plans to teach the client strategies to prevent deforming forces. Which type of strategy would be **MOST BENEFICIAL** for supporting this objective?

RESPONSE OPTIONS:

   A. Energy conservation

   B. Joint protection

   C. Pain management

Six-Option Multi-Select Items

Six-option multi-select items include a question stem followed by six possible response options. Of the options provided, three are correct responses and three are incorrect responses. You must select three response options in order to proceed to the next question on the exam.

SAMPLE D

ITEM STEM:

4. A client has right homonymous hemianopsia secondary to a CVA several months ago. Deficits in the client's right visual field interfere with the client's ability to participate in meal preparation. One of the client's goals is to cook meals using recipes from a favorite cookbook. Which adaptive strategies should the COTA teach the client to use in order to achieve this goal?

Select the 3 best choices.

RESPONSE OPTIONS:

A. **Place boundary markers on the right side of the printed page.**

B. Use a fluorescent pen to highlight key words in the recipe instruction.

C. **Place a ruler under each line of print that is being read on the recipe.**

D. Scan the page to search for the first letter of each word in the recipe.

E. Direct eye gaze toward the left margin of the recipe instruction page.

F. **Mark off each step of the recipe instructions as it is completed.**

👍 Remember

Six-option multi-select items have three correct responses.

📄 Note

For this sample question, the correct answers are A, C and F.

To assist in your studies, the correct answers are bolded and highlighted in the Answers and Rationales section in Section 3 of this guide.

🔑 Key Points

- Multiple choice items have only ONE correct response.
- Six-option multi-select items have THREE correct responses.

Chapter 4

After the Exam

Scoring, score reports, and more

Scoring

All NBCOT certification exams are criterion-referenced. In order to pass the exam, you must obtain a score equal to or higher than the minimum passing score. The minimum passing score represents an absolute standard and does not depend on the performance of other candidates taking the same exam. The minimum passing score for the COTA exam is set by content experts using widely recognized standard setting methodologies.

NBCOT uses a scaled scoring procedure to determine a candidate's final score. The scaled score is not a "number correct" or "percent correct" score. Raw scores are converted to scaled scores that represent equivalent levels of achievement regardless of test form. The passing point for the COTA exam is set at 450 points, with the lowest possible score set at 300 points and the highest possible score set at 600 points.

👍 Remember

Candidates must obtain a scaled score of at least 450 points to pass the exam.

Score Reports

After you complete and submit your exam, it will be scored by NBCOT. Exam scores are released on a predetermined schedule indicated on the scoring calendar. Information about scoring dates can be accessed on the NBCOT website.

When your score is released, you can view it in your MyNBCOT account. If you pass the exam, you will receive in the mail a packet containing a congratulatory letter with your overall score, an official NBCOT certificate, an identification card for your wallet, and information regarding your NBCOT benefits. Remember that by taking the exam, you have agreed not to share any information regarding the exam to others.

🔍 Learn More

Review the Foundations of the NBCOT Certification Examinations at www.nbcot.org/foundations to learn more about psychometric principles used by NBCOT for certification exam development and scoring.

🔍 Learn More

Access the scoring calendar at www.nbcot.org/Students/get-certified#Schedule.

Score Transfer

Note that completion of the NBCOT Certification Exam Application is not the same as applying for state licensure. Sending a score transfer to a state regulatory board does not automatically initiate the process to obtain a license or permit to work in that state. Certification by NBCOT is independent and different from any state or jurisdiction's law/licensure. Almost all jurisdictions, including the District of Columbia and Puerto Rico, have some form of regulation for occupational therapists and occupational therapy assistants. Before a candidate begins practicing in any state or comparable jurisdiction, it is essential that all requirements for that jurisdiction are met. To practice without a license or permit is against the law.

Retaking the Exam

Not every candidate who takes the NBCOT COTA® Certification Exam will achieve a passing score.

Candidates who receive a failing score will be notified via email when their exam result has been posted in their MyNBCOT account. The downloadable PDF feedback report will include the overall score along with domain-level performance information and an explanation of the overall and domain-level performance. The feedback report also includes answers to frequently asked questions about the feedback report and preparation needed to retake the exam. While it is very disappointing to receive notification indicating failure to meet the passing requirement, it is essential to address the consequences of this occurrence. Not passing the COTA exam may impact your plans to begin an occupational therapy job. If you do not successfully pass the NBCOT certification exam and are negotiating with an employer about a COTA position, you must inform your potential employer of your need to retake the certification exam. Additionally, you should contact state regulatory entities for specific information regarding temporary licenses.

Preparing to Retake the Certification Exam

There are various reasons why a candidate might fail the COTA exam. Reflecting on potential reasons is an important first step in preparing to retake the exam. These reasons may include:

- Poor test-taking strategies
- Inadequate study habits
- Lack of preparation
- Test anxiety
- External stresses

Note

Refer to the "Retaking the Exam" section of the *NBCOT Certification Exam Handbook* for additional information about reapplying to take the exam.

Chapter 5

Certification Renewal

Your COTA credential and benefits of maintaining certification

⊕ Learn More

Review the *Certification Renewal Handbook* at www.nbcot.org/-/media/NBCOT/PDFs/Renewal_Handbook to learn more about certification renewal.

⊕ Learn More

You can access the Certification Renewal Activities Chart at www.nbcot.org/-/media/NBCOT/PDFs/Renewal_Activity_Chart.ashx?la=en to learn more about the required units for certification.

📄 Note

If you complete all the certification renewal requirements by your scheduled renewal date, you will be granted **Active in Good Standing** certification status for another 3-year period.

After earning your initial NBCOT certification, your COTA credential will be valid for a period of 3 years. The certification renewal season occurs annually between January and March, regardless of the month your initial certification was received.

Certification renewal is required to maintain active certification. Your initial certification as a COTA is highly valued by you, the public, and your employers. NBCOT is your lifelong partner as you continue to grow and develop as a certified professional.

The requirements for certification renewal are:

- Accrue 36 units in the 3 years between your initial certification date and the date you renew your certification
- Abide by the NBCOT Practice Standards/Code of Conduct
- Complete a Certification Renewal Application
- Submit the appropriate renewal application fee

Benefits of Certification Renewal

COTA CREDENTIAL

One of the benefits of certification is having the privilege to use the COTA certification mark. It is necessary to maintain an **Active in Good Standing** certification status to use the COTA certification mark.

Fulfilling the certification renewal requirements entitles you to continue using the COTA credential.

NBCOT Navigator® Competency Assessment Platform

If you have earned a passing score on the COTA exam and have maintained an Active in Good Standing certification status, you will continue to have access to the latest evidence-based research through the NBCOT Navigator® suite.

The NBCOT Navigator is a suite of online tools designed to help you assess your competency across all areas of occupational therapy. All tools were created based on current practice and evidence-based literature. You can complete the tools to earn Competency Assessment Units (CAU) toward renewal, develop your occupational therapy knowledge and skills, and stay current in your practice.

The tools are available, at no charge, to individuals currently certified as a Certified Occupational Therapy Assistant COTA® and can be accessed through your MyNBCOT account. Competency Assessment Units (CAU) are awarded for successful completion of tools. You can accrue up to a maximum of 14 CAU per renewal period by completing tools in the NBCOT Navigator suite to use toward your NBCOT certification renewal requirements.

Note

The NBCOT Navigator is only available to active COTA certificants.

NBCOT Navigator® Tools

There is a wide range of competency assessment tools available on the NBCOT Navigator for the COTA, including: PICO, Case Simulations, Mini Games, Mini Practice Quizzes, and the OT Knowledge Library.

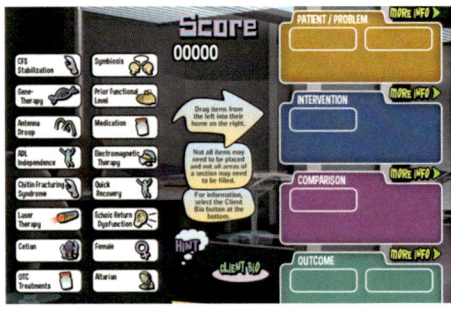

PICO

PICO is a tool that contains a series of simulated games that introduce you to the process of evaluating appropriate, evidence-based research in order to make informed decisions about OT practice.

CASE SIMULATIONS

Case simulations bring OT practice to life with a focus on clinical reasoning. Each case simulation starts with an opening scene that provides background information about the scenario. This is followed by a series of modules that engage you in providing OT services to a virtual client. Modules may include: client interviews and chart reviews; interprofessional team discussions; selecting intervention activities; provision of intervention services; and discharge planning.

🔍 Learn More

For more information on the Navigator suite, visit www.nbcot.org/navigator.

MINI GAMES

A mini game assesses specific practice knowledge and is uniquely designed for its specific topic.

Orthotic Builder
Assess your competency to work collaboratively with the OTR to select the optimal orthosis and make best-practice fabrication decisions to support recovery from a range of hand injuries and conditions.

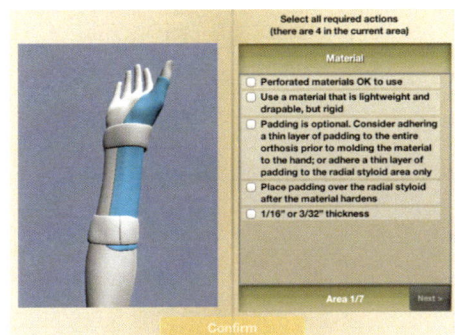

MINI PRACTICE QUIZZES

Mini Practice Quizzes are short, multiple choice quizzes grounded in evidence-based literature that are designed to assess knowledge of contemporary OT practice. Topic quizzes cover the major practice areas identified in the *NBCOT Certification Renewal Practice Analysis Study*, which include: pediatrics, school system, administration/management, acute care, rehabilitation, education/research, work/industry, wellness, and home health.

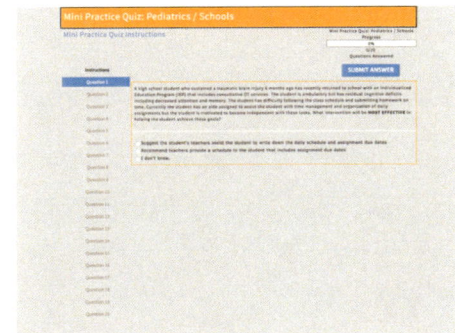

OT KNOWLEDGE LIBRARY

The OT Knowledge Library is a stylized matching tool that covers a broad range of occupational therapy knowledge.

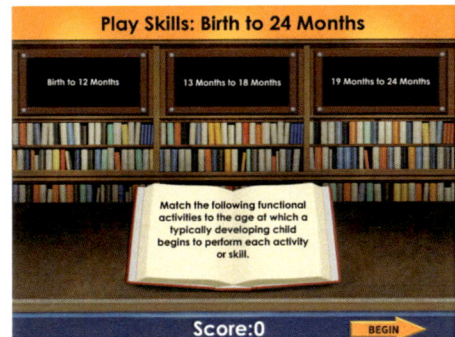

Section 2
Preparing for the Exam

Chapter 6

NBCOT Illustrated Description to Entry-Level COTA® Practice

Critical thinking and self-reflection

Critical Thinking

Critical thinking is a core skill for all successful occupational therapy practitioners. It is through critical thinking that the occupational therapy practitioner effectively completes the occupational therapy process. You can use your critical thinking skills to frame how you study for the NBCOT COTA® Certification Exam.

Define what you want to learn

For example, you may be familiar with the anatomical implications of ulnar nerve palsy but want to know more about how it impacts thumb mobility and the challenges this condition poses to a homemaker caring for a young child. You can use critical thinking to help you understand the perspective of this homemaker. Define your learning using simple questions, such as:

- How does the impairment affect the homemaker's ability to button the baby's clothes?
- How might this impact the homemaker's ability to perform grooming tasks?
- Are adaptations needed to help the homemaker open packets of formula?

Consider what you already know about the subject

Critical thinking will help you identify strengths and gaps in your knowledge. Tapping into your previous experiences from fieldwork, labs, case studies, and readings will give you a foundation upon which to build your personalized study plan based on your learning needs.

> **Note**
>
> The critical thinking skills that you use to make practice decisions can help when you are developing a personalized study plan.

Identify resources

Critical thinking is about recognizing and using all the resources available to you. Consider resources in the widest possible context; have an open mind.

Here are a few resources you may consider. Expand on these and design your own list.

- **People**—professors, fieldwork educators, mentors, peer group, community members
- **Materials**—textbooks, journal readings, reflective journals, class notes, lab exercises, exam prep tools
- **Environments**—fieldwork, community facilities, specialist clinics, adaptive workplaces, inpatient services

Challenge yourself and ask questions

Use your critical thinking skills to enhance your understanding and application of knowledge to various situations. For example:

- What interventions are beneficial and effective during the acute phase of a condition versus during the rehabilitation phase?
- Why would a client respond differently to the same intervention when it is applied in different practice settings?
- How would I document change in functional abilities in the school setting versus an older adult resident in a skilled nursing facility?

 Tip

Use creative problem-solving strategies to identify topics you want to learn more about and to trigger new learning experiences.

Organize the information you have gathered

Your critical thinking skills can help you examine patterns and make connections across your learning. For example, you can further your understanding of ulnar nerve palsy by reviewing your class notes, talking to an occupational therapy practitioner who has provided services to people who have this condition, discussing with your peers about the variety of ways this condition may affect household occupations, and identifying possible short-term and long-term treatment goals from key textbooks. **Figure 6.1** below shows the areas of learning you may choose to consult to enhance your knowledge of ulnar nerve palsy.

Figure 6.1
Areas of learning to enhance your knowledge of ulnar nerve palsy

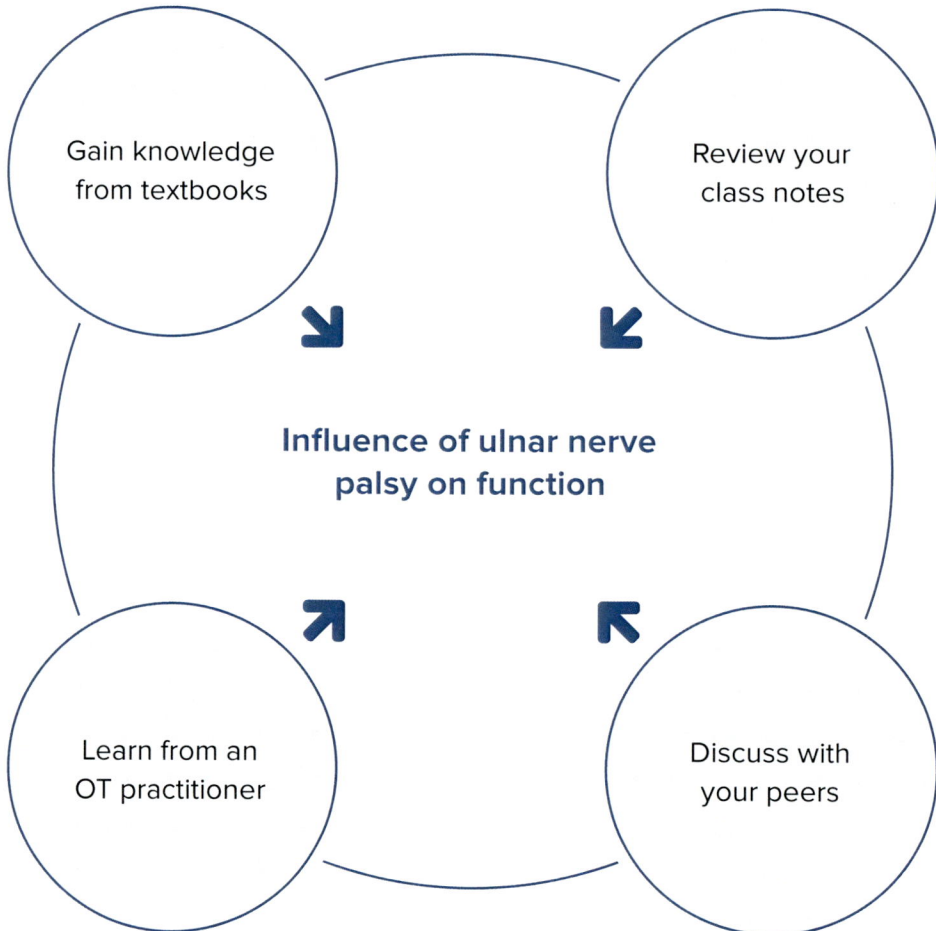

NBCOT's Illustrated Description of Entry-Level COTA® Practice

The *Illustrated Description of Entry-Level COTA® Practice* details the results of the *2017 NBCOT Practice Analysis Study*. It presents sample scenarios across a variety of practice settings that depict the tasks COTA practitioners complete in practice. Alongside each scenario is a description of how the knowledge required to competently perform a task is applied throughout the occupational therapy process. You can use the sample scenarios and associated application to practice to support your understanding of entry-level practice, as described in the practice analysis study, and to prepare for the COTA certification exam.

 See Appendix B to read the Illustrated Description of Entry-Level COTA® Practice.

The *Illustrated Description of Entry-Level COTA® Practice* is a useful tool to jump-start a self-reflective process about your level of experience and knowledge in various areas of occupational therapy practice. As you read each scenario and application to practice, think about a similar client you encountered during fieldwork or knowledge you have that relates to the scenario.

 Access the Illustrated Guide Worksheet in Appendix C to support your self-reflection process.

When using the worksheet, consider what additional information you want to learn, or brainstorm other scenarios that align with the class code of the exam. You can also bring the *Illustrated Description of Entry-Level COTA® Practice* to a study group to discuss the scenarios and the strengths and gaps in your associated knowledge.

> **❗ Important**
>
> Determine what content YOU need to review and study when preparing for the NBCOT COTA® Certification Exam.

Chapter 7

NBCOT COTA® Entry-Level Self-Assessment

Identifying your strengths and learning needs

 Note

The NBCOT COTA® Entry-Level Self-Assessment enables you to self-assess how prepared you are for the COTA certification exam.

NBCOT COTA® Entry-Level Self-Assessment

The NBCOT COTA® Entry-Level Self-Assessment is a free resource that can help you determine your overall perceived competency for entry-level practice. The self-assessment is built in relation to the validated domain, task, and knowledge statements of the NBCOT exam content outline, and it sorts practice skills by the overarching domains of entry-level practice. The feedback report provided at the end of the self-assessment is designed to help you develop or adjust your personalized study plan.

The self-assessment can be used more than once. Some students complete the self-assessment at certain points during their OTA program, while others do so before and after fieldwork. See **Figure 7.1**, which shows options for when to complete the NBCOT COTA® Entry-Level Self-Assessment.

 The NBCOT COTA® Entry-Level Self-Assessment is available in Appendix D.

⊕ Learn More

Visit www.nbcot.org/en/Students/Study-Tools/Self-Assessments to access the NBCOT COTA® Entry-Level Self-Assessment.

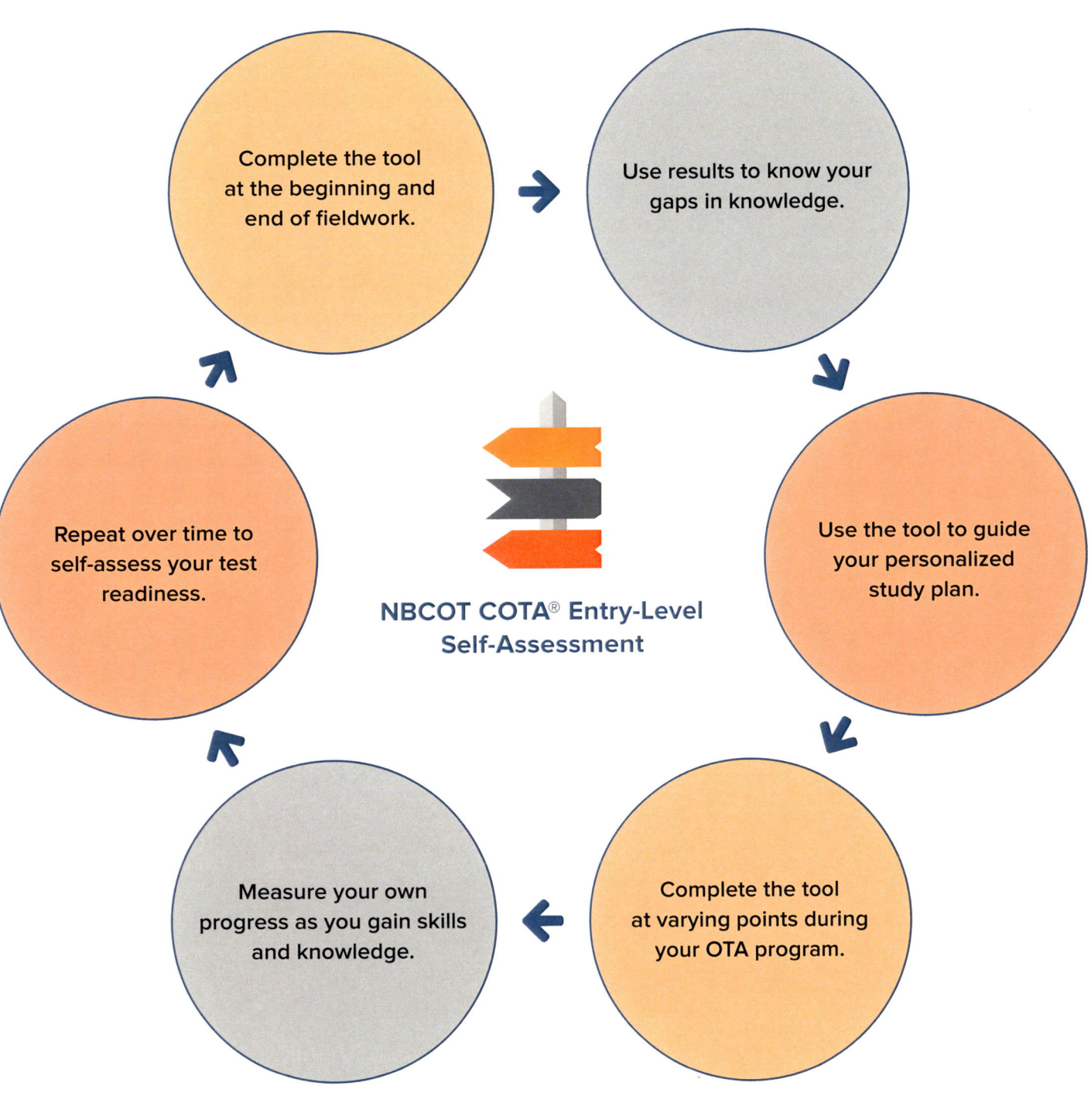

Figure 7.1
Options for using NBCOT COTA® Entry-Level Self-Assessment

How to Complete the Self-Assessment

Step 1

To complete the self-assessment, consider your competence for each skill statement based on the following question:

What knowledge and experience do you have related to these entry-level COTA skills?	Ratings
Methods for selecting, preparing, and adapting the intervention technique and environment to support optimal engagement in the intervention and promote goal achievement	○ 0 ○ 1 ○ 2 ○ 3
Technical level indications, contraindications, and precautions associated with wound management, considering the characteristics of a wound, the stage of wound healing, and the influence of the wound on engagement in occupation as guided by evidence, best practice standards, scope of practice, and state licensure practice acts in order to support functional outcomes	○ 0 ○ 1 ○ 2 ○ 3
Technical level indications, contraindications, precautions, and appropriate clinical application of superficial thermal agents as guided by evidence, best practice standards, scope of practice, and state licensure practice acts	○ 0 ○ 1 ○ 2 ○ 3
Technical level indications, contraindications, precautions, and appropriate clinical application of deep thermal, mechanical, and electrotherapeutic physical agent modalities as guided by evidence, best practice standards, scope of practice, and state licensure practice acts	○ 0 ○ 1 ○ 2 ○ 3

Tip

After completing the self-assessment, take some time to reflect on areas in which you feel competent and areas in which you need more knowledge.

Step 2

Determine a rating for your knowledge and skills in the featured practice area by using the following rating scale:

0	**No knowledge or skills:** Unfamiliar with concept or practice of the skill
1	**General knowledge through observation and academic learning:** Familiar with general knowledge related to the skill through academic learning and observation but did not have an opportunity to apply this during fieldwork
2	**General clinical skills under supervision:** Familiar with general clinical application of the skill and occasionally applied this under direct supervision during Level II fieldwork
3	**Entry-level competence:** Implemented the skill across routine situations within guidelines of Level II fieldwork practice setting

Step 3

Review your results. If you complete the online version of the NBCOT COTA® Entry-Level Self-Assessment, you will receive a feedback report containing a visual key that allows you to view your results. You can develop or adjust your personalized study plan based on these results and assess your perceived knowledge and learning needs based on the validated domain, task, and knowledge statements.

❗	**No knowledge or skills:** You are unfamiliar with concept or practice of the skill
➕	**General knowledge through observation and academic learning:** You are familiar with general knowledge related to the skill through academic learning and observation but have had limited opportunities to apply this during fieldwork. You should focus on strategies for gaining more knowledge about this skill and ways to demonstrate this knowledge in clinical situations.
🚩	**General clinical skills under supervision:** You are familiar with general clinical application of this skill and have occasionally applied the skill under direct supervision. You may want to collaborate with an experienced OTR clinician to plan independent practice-based learning activities requiring these skills.
⭐	**Entry-level competence:** You have implemented the skill across routine situations within guidelines of Level II fieldwork practice setting. Your responses indicate you have experience associated with entry-level competence.

Chapter 8

Personalized Study Plan

A method for developing a study plan that works for you

The sample planning tool on the following pages may be useful in helping you develop a personalized study plan to structure your studying. The tool allows you to pull various pieces of information together into one place.

NBCOT COTA® CERTIFICATION EXAM

Personalized STUDY PLAN

> **ⓘ Tip**
>
> Use this STUDY PLAN worksheet to reflect on the details of a personalized study plan that will work for you.

S — Start by completing the self-assessment.

T — Target a date to sit for the **NBCOT COTA®** Certification Exam.

U — Understand your personal life circumstances.

D — Develop a realistic study schedule.

Y — You need to determine where you study best.

P — Pick a method to track your progress.

L — List available resources and study tools.

A — Ask yourself how you will stick to your plan.

N — Note additional actions you need to take to prepare for exam day.

Personalized Study Plan

S — Start by completing the self-assessment.
Write down your key learning needs based on the results of the self-assessment.

T — Target a date to sit for the NBCOT COTA® Certification Exam.
Think about the length of time you need to study.

U — Understand your personal life circumstances.
Think about the commitments in your life (e.g., family responsibilities, work, personal needs) that will influence your ability to commit to your study plan.

D — Develop a realistic study schedule.
Use a calendar to map out a study schedule that includes the number of hours per day you will dedicate to studying.

Y — You need to determine where you study best.
Write down where you like to study and key features of that environment.

P

Pick a method to track your progress.

Brainstorm options, such as taking practice tests or measuring change with a self-assessment, and pick methods that work for you.

L

List available resources and study tools.

Think about the resources (e.g., textbooks, class notes, case studies) and study tools (e.g., practice tests, flashcards) you will need.

A

Ask yourself how you will stick to your plan.

Determine how to pace your study and think of methods for rewarding yourself for committing to your study schedule.

N

Note additional actions you need to take to prepare for exam day.

Keep an ongoing "to do" list, for example: review my Authorization to Test (ATT) letter, watch exam tutorials at www.nbcot.org, plan the route to the test center, research state licensure requirements, etc.

Exam Preparation Tools

In addition to this study guide, NBCOT offers a variety of test preparation resources. NBCOT's Aspire study tools are designed using the validated domain, task, and knowledge statements on which the COTA certification exams are based.

NBCOT Aspire is a suite of tools to help you prepare for the certification exam.

 Learn More

To learn more about the NBCOT Aspire study tools, go to: www.nbcot.org/en/Students/Study-Tools.

The NBCOT Exam StudyPack

The NBCOT Exam StudyPack is a comprehensive exam prep platform to support you as you prepare for the exam. The StudyPack is filled with exam prep tools and easy-to-access resources to challenge your knowledge and assist you in meeting your goal for the certification exam! You can follow a guided study pathway or self-navigate from study tool to study tool in whichever way suits your studying style and needs.

> **❗ Important**
>
> The NBCOT Exam StudyPack is a comprehensive exam prep platform with expanded content that is only available in the StudyPack.

Flashcards

Study for the certification exam anywhere, at any time. The online flashcards are easy to use and filled with practice-relevant content.

Knowledge Match Games

Test your OT knowledge in a fun and interactive online environment with the Knowledge Match Game. Use your speed and recall ability to match statements to corresponding categories.

Practice Tests

Test your readiness by simulating the computer-based format and flow of the real exam.

🔍 Learn More

Find more information on the NBCOT Aspire study tools at www.nbcot.org/aspire.

Chapter 9

Exam Day

Planning for exam day and test-taking tips

Take some time to think of strategies that can help you feel relaxed in the days leading up to your test day. Remind yourself of the progress you have made to date: you completed an occupational therapy assistant program, you took many academic courses, you successfully completed assignments, and you passed several major tests. Think back to how much you knew about occupational therapy at the start of your program compared to how much you know now.

The night before the test:

- Remind yourself that you have been preparing for this day for a long time.
- Think about where the test center is located and how long it will take you to get there.
- Make sure you have all the documents you must take to the test site—refer to the latest copy of the *NBCOT Certification Exam Handbook* at www.nbcot.org for details about the documents you need to bring.
- Decide what clothes you plan to wear: comfortable, layered clothes are key considerations.
- Have a plan for what you want to do the night before—such as exercise or spend time with friends—to alleviate pretest nerves.
- Try to get a good night's sleep and remember to set your alarm.

> **❗ Important**
>
> Review your Authorization to Test (ATT) letter and follow the instructions.

⊕ Learn More

To prepare for your test day, you can access and watch the video *What to Expect on Test Day* at www.nbcot.org/Students/get-certified#testday.

Test-Taking Tips

It's test day! This is the day you have been preparing for since the beginning of your journey to become a Certified Occupational Therapy Assistant. Your NBCOT COTA® Certification Exam will be administered at the Prometric test center you selected at the time you scheduled your exam.

ⓘ Tips

- Arrive at the test site early.
- Follow the instructions in your ATT letter.
- Use strategies to feel calm.

❗ Important

Plan to arrive at least 30 minutes before your scheduled appointment time.

⊕ Learn More

To learn more read the *Certification Exam Handbook* at www.nbcot.org/-/media/NBCOT/PDFs/Cert_Exam_Handbook.

Remember that you have 4 hours to take the exam, but your scheduled appointment time at the test center is for 5 hours and 15 minutes to allow you to complete all administrative requirements.

Prometric employs biometric-enabled check-in services at all of its test sites. This procedure consists of a number of steps to verify your eligibility to test, including taking an electronic record of your ID, photo imaging, and a digital fingertip record. You are required to undergo fingertip analysis any time you leave and re-enter the testing room for validation purposes. There is video surveillance in all candidate-accessible areas of the testing center.

A common question asked is: "Can I eat/drink in the testing room?" The answer to this question is: No, however beverages and snacks can be stored in lockers located in the testing center waiting area. You may eat or drink in the waiting area only.

After you are assigned a workspace at the testing site, familiarize yourself with the computer and make certain you can see the clock on the screen. You may request headphones if you will be distracted by others working around you. You may also ask the proctor for a marker board to use during your test time. Advise the test proctor of any problems or concerns you have regarding the test environment prior to beginning the exam.

Test-Taking Strategies

Manage Your Time

Make a plan for managing your test time. You have 4 hours to take the exam, and there are 200 questions on the COTA exam.

Exam Tutorial

An optional tutorial precedes the exam.

Organize Your Thinking

Use the marker board to help you organize and clarify your thinking.

Maintain Good Posture

Manage your posture and change your position regularly. Sit in an upright position. If you feel tension, stretch, drop your shoulders, open and close your fingers, or shift in your chair.

Read the Instructions

Be sure to read the instructions before answering each item type.

Stay Calm

If you feel anxious during the exam, take some deep, slow breaths. Don't worry if other people in the room finish before you do. You do not need to leave the room until you have used all your allotted time. If you experience a technical problem during the exam, inform the test center proctor.

> **Remember**
>
> Time spent using a tutorial is NOT deducted from the 4-hour testing time.

> **Remember**
>
> **When answering multiple choice items:**
>
> - Use the "Mark" button on the computer screen to review items later if time permits.
>
> - Only change an answer you initially selected if you are sure it is an incorrect response. The answer that comes to mind first is often correct.
>
> - Rely on your knowledge and do not watch for patterns. The test answers are randomized.

> **ⓘ Tips**
>
> **After the exam:**
>
> - Resist the urge to discuss the test items and potential answers with your peer group. You have completed the exam and it is too late to change your answers.
>
> - Resist the urge to open your study notes, texts, and review guides for the same reason given above.
>
> - Remember, it is against the NBCOT Candidate/Certificant Code of Conduct to discuss test items with other candidates or to record test information from memory.
>
> - Relax. You have completed the exam. Reward yourself for accomplishing this stage.

Section 3
Time to Practice

Chapter 10

Domain 1: Multiple Choice Sample Questions

Practice questions with answer key and references

The following multiple choice items are samples related to Domain 1.

Collaborating and Gathering Information

Assist the OTR to acquire information regarding factors that influence occupational performance on an ongoing basis throughout the occupational therapy process.

1. Which type of grasp involves holding an object with the tip of the thumb, index, and middle fingers and is a **TYPICAL** grasp used to hold a crayon to draw on paper?

   A. Pincer

   B. Tripod

   C. Hook

2. A 5-year-old student has immature prewriting skills secondary to a mild developmental delay. Currently, the student can use a wide barrel pencil to imitate vertical and horizontal strokes on a piece of paper. Using the normal sequence of writing readiness as a guide, which prewriting skills would the student be expected to acquire during the **NEXT** phase of development?

   Select the 3 best choices.

   A. Copy a diagonal line on wide-ruled paper.

   B. Draw a 6-inch (15.24 cm) vertical line using a crayon.

   C. Trace over a line with minimal deviation from the line.

   D. Copy a cross with intersecting perpendicular lines.

   E. Trace a variety of geometric shapes using a template.

   F. Write letters of their first name on vertically positioned paper.

3. A COTA is preparing to assess light touch sensation of a client who has an acute radial nerve palsy. Based on the **TYPICAL** pattern of sensory impairment for this condition, where on the dorsum of the affected hand should the COTA expect to detect diminished light touch?

   A. Fingertips of the index and middle fingers

   B. Area over the first dorsal interossei

   C. Entire length of the fifth digit

4. Which symptoms associated with a diagnosis of schizophrenia would typically have the **MOST** influence on a client's functional performance?

   A. Disorganized speech and loose association of ideas

   B. Free floating anxiety and onset of sudden acute fear

   C. Fluctuating mood ranging from elation to depression

5. Which developmentally appropriate activity is **TYPICAL** for a 3-year-old child?

    A. Coloring within the lines of a coloring book

    B. Snipping paper using blunt scissors

    C. Assembling a 15-piece picture puzzle

6. Which hand posturing is **TYPICAL** of a median nerve palsy?

    A. Clawing

    B. Benedictine

    C. Ape hand

7. A client who had a CVA several months ago is baking cookies during an OT session. The client uses the correct amount of dough for each cookie but places the dough only on the right side of the cookie sheet before stating the pan is ready to be placed in the oven. Which sensory processing deficit could be attributed to this behavior?

    A. Figure-ground neglect

    B. Homonymous hemianopsia

    C. Diminished depth perception

    D. Right-left disorientation

8. A COTA is teaching a client, who has rheumatoid arthritis, techniques for modifying activities that typically apply lateral pinch forces against the thumb and fingers. What is the purpose of providing this type of instruction?

    A. Minimize boutonnière posturing of the thumb and index finger.

    B. Prevent factors that cause swan-neck deformity.

    C. Promote dexterity and strength for fine motor control.

    D. Reduce the risk of developing MCP joint ulnar drift.

9. A COTA observes that a resident of a skilled nursing facility sits in a wheelchair in a posterior pelvic tilt and increased kyphosis of the thoracic spine. Based on this posture of the trunk and pelvic girdle, what functional activity would be **MOST** difficult for this resident?

   A. Crossing one leg over the other to put on compression socks and shoes

   B. Reaching upward to retrieve a towel hanging on a hook in the bathroom

   C. Scooting forward in the chair in preparation for transferring to a shower bench

10. An OTR and a COTA who work in an outpatient pain management clinic are collaborating to gather information about an adolescent who has a history of joint pain secondary to a connective tissue disorder. Which method is **MOST BENEFICIAL** for obtaining information about the influence of the adolescent's pain on daily routines?

    A. Complete a motivational interview with the adolescent.

    B. Obtain pain ratings using a standardized visual analog scale.

    C. Review the adolescent's medication schedule and routines.

11. A COTA recently provided a neoprene short thumb opponens orthosis to a 3-year-old child who has spastic hemiplegia. Which activity would provide the **MOST BENEFICIAL** information about the effectiveness of this orthosis?

    A. Observing the child pushing a toy shopping cart

    B. Asking the child to bring a drinking cup to the mouth

    C. Seeing if the child can hold a cracker without breaking it

12. A COTA is working with a client who has substance use disorder and was recently admitted to an outpatient rehabilitation center. A screening indicates the client lives alone and started a new job a month ago. What information would be **MOST BENEFICIAL** to gather to contribute to the client's occupational profile?

    A. List of previous jobs

    B. Concerns about the new job

    C. Educational background

13. A COTA working in the outpatient department of a children's hospital is scheduled to begin intervention with a 5-year-old child who has osteogenesis imperfecta. One of the intervention objectives is for the child to achieve age-appropriate developmental milestones for bathing and dressing. The occupational profile indicates that the child's family recently immigrated to the United States. What information is **MOST IMPORTANT** for the COTA to obtain from the child's parents during the initial session with the child?

    A. ADL routines they typically use with their child

    B. Financial ability to purchase assistive devices

    C. Willingness to make in-home modifications

14. An older adult client has vertigo associated with a recent cerebellar infarct. Which functional task would be **MOST BENEFICIAL** to have the client complete as part of a screening to gather information about the influence of this condition on ADL?

    A. Reaching overhead to get a blanket from an upper shelf in the bedroom closet

    B. Washing dishes while standing at the sink in a single-leg stance for 20 seconds on each leg

    C. Turning the head from right to left to look for food items in an above counter kitchen cabinet

15. A young adult client has mild cognitive impairment, poor attention span, and limited frustration tolerance secondary to a TBI. One of the client's goals is to resume work in a restaurant. The COTA is gathering information to contribute to the client's initial work readiness evaluation. Which data gathering method would be **BEST** for the COTA to use for this purpose?

   A. Administer a standardized vocational interest inventory.

   B. Interview the employer about the client's previous work habits.

   C. Assess cognitive-perceptual skills using simulated job tasks.

   D. Determine the client's physical capacity for work.

16. A COTA is completing a manual muscle test on the biceps of a client who has full elbow range of motion with palm-up and palm-down, and can hold the elbow flexed against moderate resistance. Which muscle strength grade is **MOST CONSISTENT** with this response?

   A. Good (4/5)

   B. Fair (3/5)

   C. Poor (2/5)

17. A COTA is administering a standardized test to assess perceptual skills of a client who had a recent CVA. After reading the instructions to the client, the client has difficulty initiating the task as requested. What action should the COTA take in response to this observation?

   A. Continue the test as indicated in the protocol manual.

   B. Ask the client to repeat back the protocol instructions.

   C. Repeat the test protocol instructions while demonstrating the task.

18. An OTR and a COTA who work in a rehabilitation hospital are collaborating to evaluate an inpatient who had a CVA. As part of the evaluation process, the OTR asks the COTA to administer a standardized assessment. In addition to following the test procedures as outlined in the test manual, which of the following actions is **MOST IMPORTANT** for the COTA to take to support the evaluation process?

    A. Rephrase test directions to the patient in easy-to-understand terms.

    B. Accurately document and communicate the results to the OTR.

    C. Explain the purpose of the test to the patient and to the patient's family.

19. An inpatient with major depression was admitted to an acute psychiatric facility one day ago. A screening indicates the patient lives alone at home and recently retired after having worked as clergy in a church for the past 35 years. What action is **MOST BENEFICIAL** for the COTA to take when gathering information to contribute to the patient's occupational profile?

    A. Explore potential part-time vocational or volunteer opportunities in the area.

    B. Determine the patient's willingness to participate in a retirement support group.

    C. Ask the patient about options for contributing to church-sponsored activities.

    D. Use open-ended questions related to the patient's feelings about retirement.

20. A client who has schizophrenia recently transitioned from living at home with parents to residing in a group home. The client is having difficulty adjusting to this new transition. The COTA is interviewing the client and the client's parents as part of the intervention planning process. What is the **PRIMARY** purpose for conducting this interview?

    A. To learn about the client's emotional needs

    B. To determine the client's developmental stage

    C. To become aware of the client's unconscious conflicts

    D. To identify the client's typical performance patterns

21. A patient was admitted to a rehabilitation facility due to a recent decline in function secondary to amyotrophic lateral sclerosis. One of the patient's goals is to live at home as long as possible. The COTA is gathering information about the patient to contribute to the initial discharge planning meeting. What information would be **MOST IMPORTANT** to gather for this purpose?

    A. Patient's vocational and leisure history

    B. Current ROM and strength measurements

    C. Assisted living option for the patient to consider

    D. Durable medical equipment needs for ADL

22. Which of the following cardiac risk factors is **MOST IMPORTANT** for the COTA to address during an intervention session with an inpatient who has coronary artery disease?

    A. Family history

    B. Blood sugar level

    C. Sedentary lifestyle

23. A client who had a nondisplaced distal radius fracture to the right-dominant upper extremity works as a hairstylist. The client reports persistent wrist and finger stiffness that makes it difficult to comb and style hair at work. Which intervention represents a biomechanical approach and should be included as part of the client's **INITIAL** intervention for maximizing long-term functional performance?

    A. Modifications to the client's work station and work tools

    B. Active-resistive ROM and strengthening exercises

    C. Dynamic orthotic wear during hours of sleep

24. A client who has multiple sclerosis works as an administrative assistant in a large corporation. Fatigue and weakness interfere with the client's ability to complete job tasks. The corporate physician is requesting a job site analysis for this client. What is the **PRIMARY** purpose of this type of analysis?

    A. To observe the client interacting with co-workers within the office environment

    B. To determine the critical work demands in relation to the client needs

    C. To assess the client's vocational interests in relation to work assignments

    D. To identify the management's willingness to provide special accommodations

25. Which of the following homemaking activities uses the **GREATEST** range of bilateral shoulder flexion and elbow extension?

    A. Ironing shirts and placing them on a hanger

    B. Washing dishes in a sink and drying pots and pans

    C. Folding sheets and hanging towels on a clothesline

    D. Dusting tabletops and vacuuming carpets

26. A client has sensory-perceptual deficits secondary to a mild CVA. Motor skills remain intact. Which task would be **BEST** to ask the patient to complete when screening for tactile agnosia?

    A. Picking up objects from a tabletop

    B. Turning a water faucet on and off

    C. Distinguishing a key from a coin in a pocket

    D. Holding an eating utensil in the dominant hand

27. Which of the following craft activities provides the **MOST** structure for a client who has bipolar 1 disorder and is in a manic phase?

    A. Watercolor painting activity

    B. Leather stamping project

    C. Magazine picture collage

28. A client with bilateral elbow contractures has 45° active extension and 90° active flexion of both elbows and 5° supination/pronation. Upper extremity muscle strength is Normal (5/5). Which activity would be **MOST DIFFICULT** for the client to perform without using compensatory movements?

    A. Putting a belt through pants belt loops

    B. Tying shoelaces

    C. Using a spoon to eat soup

29. A 4-year-old child with pervasive developmental delay requires maximum assistance for toileting. The COTA is teaching the child's parents strategies for improving the child's independence with these tasks. During a session, the parents indicate that over the past several months, the child typically does not have a bowel movement for several days at a time due to constipation. Which recommendation should the COTA provide the parents in response to this comment?

    A. Ask a pharmacist to recommend a non-prescription children's stool softener for the child.

    B. Consult with a dietitian to learn how to increase the amount of fiber in the child's diet.

    C. Schedule an appointment with the child's primary physician to rule out gastrointestinal issues.

30. A COTA working in a long-term care facility is responsible for teaching the residents strategies for supporting their independence with BADL. During BADL sessions over the past week, several of the residents reported that the assistive devices used during the sessions are not available to them when completing routine BADL with the nursing aides. What action would be **MOST BENEFICIAL** for the COTA to take in response to these reports?

    A. Submit an incident report about the nursing aides to the appropriate supervisor.

    B. Advise the residents to ask for the assistive devices prior to starting BADL.

    C. Present in-service training to nursing staff about the benefits and uses of BADL devices.

    D. Ensure the assistive devices are in a visible location and labeled with the residents' names.

31. A COTA working in an elementary school setting attends students' annual Individualized Education Program (IEP) planning meetings. What information would be within the scope of practice for the COTA to report during these meetings?

  A. Age-appropriate leisure activities the students should be able to complete

  B. Progress the students have made in school-related activities over the past year

  C. Receptive and expressive communication skills the students currently use

32. An outpatient had a moderate TBI 6 weeks ago and was recently discharged from an inpatient rehabilitation setting. Currently, the patient requires supervision for BADL and reports a goal of returning to high school with a part-time schedule. What action should the COTA take in collaboration with the OTR to support progress toward this goal?

  A. Assist the patient in accessing and completing incomplete school assignments

  B. Discuss special accommodations available to students who have disabilities

  C. Refer the patient to the school-based interprofessional team at the school

33. An inpatient sustained a transfemoral amputation 2 days ago. The COTA is scheduled to represent OT at the interprofessional team meeting to discuss care management for this patient. What information should the COTA communicate with the team during this meeting?

    A. Advice on how nursing staff should include scar massage into daily dressing changes

    B. Methods nursing staff can use during routine care to assist the patient in managing phantom limb sensations

    C. Specific techniques that will be used during OT sessions to facilitate the patient's adjustment to the loss of a limb

    D. Initial steps and techniques for putting on and taking off the prosthesis

34. An inpatient had a CVA 3 weeks ago and is preparing for discharge to live alone at home. The COTA learns that the patient intends to resume driving short distances to the grocery store and to church after discharge. The COTA does not think the patient has the ability to drive at this time. What action should the COTA take in response to learning this information?

    A. Administer a screening to identify the patient's pre-driving skills.

    B. Initiate a referral to a comprehensive driver education program.

    C. Talk with the patient about the implications of this decision.

35. A COTA is preparing to teach breathing strategies to an inpatient who has COPD and mild cognitive impairment. At the start of the session, the COTA plans to gather information to understand the patient's level of health literacy. Which question would be **BEST** to ask the patient as part of the screening process to learn about the patient's level of health literacy?

    A. How confident do you feel about explaining your medical history to the doctor?

    B. Do you read information about the side effects of your prescribed medications?

    C. Are you able to sign the consent forms for your medical treatment in the hospital?

36. A COTA is working with the Individualized Education Program (IEP) team to determine a student's eligibility for school-based OT intervention. What information does the team rely upon to make final eligibility determinations?

    A. Physician's referral and diagnosis severity

    B. Standardized test scores and documented disability

    C. Classroom performance and curriculum-based needs

    D. Birth history and previous early intervention services

37. A client who has schizophrenia is participating in a day treatment program at a community-based mental health center. During an OT group, the client admits to "forgetting" to take prescribed medications. After discussing the importance of taking the prescribed medication with the client, what is the **NEXT** action the COTA should take in response to this comment?

    A. Contact the referring physician and report the client's nonadherence.

    B. Alert the client's family or significant other to monitor adherence.

    C. Teach the client to use a smart phone application for medication management.

38. A COTA is providing intervention for an inpatient diagnosed with Guillain-Barré syndrome 3 days ago. The patient requires a ventilator for respiratory support and has complete paralysis of the upper and lower extremities. Which interventions should be included in the treatment sessions during this phase of the patient's rehabilitation?

    A. Daily strengthening routine with resistive exercise and instruction in strategies to adjust to long-term disability

    B. Positioning program, caregiver education in passive ROM, and recommendations for low-tech electronic aids for daily living

    C. Gradual increase in self-care activities and guidelines to perform a progressive resistive exercise regimen

39. An inpatient who has congestive heart failure has had a recent decline in function and now requires a wheelchair for mobility. A COTA is completing a home visit in preparation for the patient's discharge to live with family. The family lives in an apartment on the second level of a multi-level apartment building. During the home visit, the COTA identifies several areas in the apartment that are not accessible by a wheelchair. What is the **NEXT** action the COTA should take based on this information?

    A. Collaborate with the patient and family to discuss the patient's needs.

    B. Suggest ways the furniture should be arranged for wheelchair access.

    C. Have family members notify the apartment manager of needed changes.

40. An outpatient client, whose primary insurance is Medicare, sustained a wrist fracture 8 weeks ago and has been participating in OT 3 times per week for the past 2 weeks. ROM and strength of the affected extremity are improving, and the client has returned to limited work in a department store. However, the client is still reluctant to use the hand. At the end of a session, the client refuses to schedule more OT visits, citing "transportation problems." What is the **FIRST** action the COTA should take in this situation?

    A. Talk with the client to determine a solution.

    B. Teach the client an independent home program.

    C. Refer the client to a home health agency.

    D. Encourage scheduling a monthly reevaluation.

41. An older adult patient who had a recent CVA was admitted to an inpatient rehabilitation facility 2 days ago. The patient is scheduled to participate in an initial self-care session. A records review indicates the patient immigrated to the United States several years ago and is living with family members. What **INITIAL** action should the COTA take to support the patient's participation in the intervention sessions?

    A. Gather information about the patient's cultural values regarding self-care.

    B. Ensure a translator is available for each of the patient's scheduled sessions.

    C. Administer a standardized evaluation to determine the patient's current function.

42. A COTA is selecting activities to include in a homemaking skills session with a client who has an anxiety disorder. A review of the occupational profile indicates the client immigrated to the United States with a spouse and two children one year ago. Stress of the relocation and symptoms of the anxiety disorder are interfering with the ability to complete simple daily tasks. One of the client's goals is to fully participate in family roles and routines. What activities should the COTA include in the session in order to support the client's goal?

    A. Incorporate the client's culture and values into the session activities.

    B. Provide instruction about using appliances typically found in homes in the U.S.

    C. Teach the client about the family value system in the United States.

43. Which behavioral cues exhibited during intervention are **TYPICAL** of a client with low health literacy?

    Select the 3 best choices.

    A. Glancing at educational handouts

    B. Asking clarifying questions during a session

    C. Demonstrating a new skill learned during therapy

    D. Avoiding written questionnaires and forms

    E. Providing a detailed summary of new information

    F. Missing several scheduled appointments

44. A COTA working in an outpatient setting is preparing a home program for a client who has mild hemiplegia and neurobehavioral deficits secondary to a CVA several months ago. What information would be **MOST IMPORTANT** for the COTA to verify prior to teaching the client the program?

    A. Extent to which the client has a detailed understanding of the program rationale

    B. Client's learning needs for independent follow-through of the prescribed program

    C. Client's capacity to verbalize the home program instructions

    D. Amount of family support available to the client on a daily basis

45. An inpatient who has moderately severe cognitive decline secondary to Alzheimer's disease has been undergoing medical treatment for pneumonia. Currently, the patient has difficulty sequencing steps for self-care activities and becomes easily frustrated. The patient will be discharged in one week to live at home with adult children. What action should the COTA include as part of the overall intervention in preparation for the patient's transition to home?

   A. Advise the family to hire a home health aide to assist the patient with daily BADL tasks.

   B. Provide the family with behavioral strategies for supporting the patient's function at home.

   C. Recommend the family purchase assistive devices for the patient to use during BADL tasks at home.

   D. Instruct the family to adjust medication routines to prevent agitation and support the patient's function.

46. A COTA, who works in a hospital setting, is teaching precautions to an inpatient who recently had open-heart surgery. Which of the following would be the **MOST EFFECTIVE** communication methods for the COTA to use in the education session to promote the patient's understanding of the information presented?

   Select the 3 best choices.

   A. Be approachable and allow the patient to ask questions.

   B. Explain the information thoroughly using evidence and medical language.

   C. Present small amounts of information at a time and give the patient time to respond.

   D. Make eye contact during the intervention session.

   E. Provide detailed instructions to the patient and the caregiver.

   F. Fill quiet moments with conversation and additional information.

47. An inpatient has neurobehavioral deficits secondary to a CVA one month ago. At the time of the initial evaluation, the patient required moderate verbal cues to complete oral hygiene and grooming. Currently, the patient is able to complete these tasks independently during self-care sessions. This occurs one week earlier than the time frame listed in the intervention plan for achieving this goal. What action should the COTA take prior to the **NEXT** scheduled BADL session with this patient?

   A. Revise the intervention plan with new short-term goals.

   B. Administer a standardized functional assessment.

   C. Collaborate with the OTR to review the intervention goals.

48. A client had a partial hand amputation secondary to an industrial accident 3 months ago. The client has been attending OT at least three times weekly since the date of injury. Until recently, the client has been compliant with the home exercise program. Now the client is canceling appointments and seems less motivated to complete prescribed daily exercises and splinting. Which **INITIAL** action should the COTA take in response to the client's behaviors?

   A. Decrease the frequency and intensity of the overall intervention plan.

   B. Discuss these observations and concerns with the client.

   C. Review the treatment plan and the long-term goals with the OTR.

49. A COTA working in a community-based mental health program has been working with a client who has a substance use disorder. Based on observation of the client's performance and a review of the client's goals, the COTA concludes that the client has attained maximum benefits from attending a vocational skills group. Which action should the COTA take based on this information?

    A. Discuss the client's status with the supervising OTR.

    B. Reevaluate the client prior to the next group session.

    C. Discharge the client from this particular group.

50. An inpatient has hemiplegia secondary to a recent TBI and is functioning at Level V (Confused-inappropriate, Non-agitated) on the Rancho Los Amigos scale. A COTA is planning an initial dressing session to teach the patient lower body dressing techniques. Which intervention environment would be **MOST CONDUCIVE** for supporting the patient's success during this session?

    A. Quiet room in the rehabilitation department away from other patients

    B. Bathroom in the patient's room so the patient can sit on the tub bench

    C. Patient's private room with the patient seated in a bedside chair

Answer Key

Domain 1 Sample Items

Item Number	Key	Item Number	Key
1.	B	26.	C
2.	A, C, D	27.	B
3.	B	28.	C
4.	A	29.	C
5.	B	30.	C
6.	C	31.	B
7.	B	32.	C
8.	D	33.	B
9.	B	34.	C
10.	A	35.	A
11.	B	36.	C
12.	B	37.	A
13.	A	38.	B
14.	C	39.	A
15.	A	40.	A
16.	A	41.	A
17.	A	42.	A
18.	B	43.	A, D, F
19.	D	44.	B
20.	D	45.	B
21.	D	46.	A, C, D
22.	C	47.	C
23.	B	48.	B
24.	B	49.	A
25.	C	50.	C

Multiple Choice Answers, Rationales, and References

1. Which type of grasp involves holding an object with the tip of the thumb, index, and middle fingers and is a **TYPICAL** grasp used to hold a crayon to draw on paper?

    A. Pincer

    B. Tripod

    C. Hook

Correct Answer: B

RATIONALE:
A tripod grasp involves holding a writing utensil or an object with the tip of the thumb, index, and middle fingers.

Reference:
Solomon, J. W., & O'Brien, J. C. (2016). *Pediatric skills for occupational therapy assistants* (4th ed., pp. 428-429). St. Louis, MO: Mosby Elsevier.

2. A 5-year-old student has immature prewriting skills secondary to a mild developmental delay. Currently, the student can use a wide barrel pencil to imitate vertical and horizontal strokes on a piece of paper. Using the normal sequence of writing readiness as a guide, which prewriting skills would the student be expected to acquire during the **NEXT** phase of development?

Select the 3 best choices.

A. Copy a diagonal line on wide-ruled paper.

B. Draw a 6-inch (15.24 cm) vertical line using a crayon.

C. Trace over a line with minimal deviation from the line.

D. Copy a cross with intersecting perpendicular lines.

E. Trace a variety of geometric shapes using a template.

F. Write letters of their first name on vertically positioned paper.

Correct Answers: A, C, D

RATIONALE:
In the developmental sequence of prewriting skills, a student who has mastered the ability to imitate vertical and horizontal strokes on a piece of paper would be expected to progress to performing these options **NEXT**.

Reference:
Solomon, J. W., & O'Brien, J. C. (2016). *Pediatric skills for occupational therapy assistants* (4th ed., pp. 428-429). St. Louis, MO: Mosby Elsevier.

3. A COTA is preparing to assess light touch sensation of a client who has an acute radial nerve palsy. Based on the **TYPICAL** pattern of sensory impairment for this condition, where on the dorsum of the affected hand should the COTA expect to detect diminished light touch?

    A. Fingertips of the index and middle fingers

    B. **Area over the first dorsal interossei**

    C. Entire length of the fifth digit

Correct Answer: B

RATIONALE:
The area over the first dorsal interossei falls within the sensory distribution of the radial nerve.

References:
Early, M. B. (2013). *Physical dysfunction practice skills for the occupational therapy assistant* (3rd ed., pp. 159-160). St. Louis, MO: Mosby Elsevier.

Radomski, M. V., & Trombly Latham, C. A. (Eds.). (2014). *Occupational therapy for physical dysfunction* (7th ed., pp. 281-283). Philadelphia, PA: Lippincott Williams & Wilkins.

4. Which symptoms associated with a diagnosis of schizophrenia would typically have the **MOST** influence on a client's functional performance?

    A. **Disorganized speech and loose association of ideas**

    B. Free floating anxiety and onset of sudden acute fear

    C. Fluctuating mood ranging from elation to depression

Correct Answer: A

RATIONALE:
Symptoms of schizophrenia that impact functional performance include disorganized speech and loose association of ideas.

Reference:
Early, M. B. (2017). *Mental health concepts & techniques for the occupational therapy assistant* (5th ed., pp. 153-159). Philadelphia, PA: Lippincott Williams & Wilkins.

5. Which developmentally appropriate activity is **TYPICAL** for a 3-year-old child?

   A. Coloring within the lines of a coloring book

   B. Snipping paper using blunt scissors

   C. Assembling a 15-piece picture puzzle

Correct Answer: B

RATIONALE:
The development of fine motor and manipulation skills in children will enable a typically developing 3-year-old child to cut paper using blunt scissors.

Reference:
Case-Smith, J., & O'Brien, J. C. (2015). *Occupational therapy for children and adolescents* (7th ed., p. 88). St. Louis, MO: Mosby Elsevier.

6. Which hand posturing is **TYPICAL** of a median nerve palsy?

   A. Clawing

   B. Benedictine

   C. Ape hand

Correct Answer: C

RATIONALE:
An ape hand deformity is characterized by an inability to abduct the thumb and is caused by a complete laceration to the median nerve or a median nerve palsy.

References:
Cooper, C. (2014). *Fundamentals of hand therapy: Clinical reasoning and treatment guidelines for common diagnoses of the upper extremity* (2nd ed., p. 292). St. Louis, MO: Mosby Elsevier.

Early, M. B. (2013). *Physical dysfunction practice skills for the occupational therapy assistant* (3rd ed., pp. 609-610). St. Louis, MO: Mosby Elsevier.

Radomski, M. V., & Trombly Latham, C. A. (Eds.). (2014). *Occupational therapy for physical dysfunction* (7th ed., p. 1147). Philadelphia, PA: Lippincott Williams & Wilkins.

7. A client who had a CVA several months ago is baking cookies during an OT session. The client uses the correct amount of dough for each cookie but places the dough only on the right side of the cookie sheet before stating the pan is ready to be placed in the oven. Which sensory processing deficit could be attributed to this behavior?

   A. Figure-ground neglect

   B. Homonymous hemianopsia

   C. Diminished depth perception

   D. Right-left disorientation

Correct Answer: B

RATIONALE:
Homonymous hemianopsia is a visual field impairment involving both eyes where the client only sees either to the right or left of midline.

Reference:
Early, M. B. (2013). *Physical dysfunction practice skills for the occupational therapy assistant* (3rd ed., pp. 442-443). St. Louis, MO: Mosby Elsevier.

8. A COTA is teaching a client, who has rheumatoid arthritis, techniques for modifying activities that typically apply lateral pinch forces against the thumb and fingers. What is the purpose of providing this type of instruction?

   A. Minimize boutonnière posturing of the thumb and index finger.

   B. Prevent factors that cause swan-neck deformity.

   C. Promote dexterity and strength for fine motor control.

   D. Reduce the risk of developing MCP joint ulnar drift.

Correct Answer: D

RATIONALE:
Rheumatoid arthritis is an autoimmune condition that may result in ulnar deviation deformities. Modifying activities that typically apply lateral pinch forces against the thumb and fingers reduces the risk of developing MCP joint ulnar drift.

Reference:
Early, M. B. (2013). *Physical dysfunction practice skills for the occupational therapy assistant* (3rd ed., pp. 572-574). St. Louis, MO: Mosby Elsevier.

9. A COTA observes that a resident of a skilled nursing facility sits in a wheelchair in a posterior pelvic tilt and increased kyphosis of the thoracic spine. Based on this posture of the trunk and pelvic girdle, what functional activity would be **MOST** difficult for this resident?

   A. Crossing one leg over the other to put on compression socks and shoes

   B. Reaching upward to retrieve a towel hanging on a hook in the bathroom

   C. Scooting forward in the chair in preparation for transferring to a shower bench

Correct Answer: B

RATIONALE:
Kyphosis and a posterior pelvic tilt result in a biomechanical disadvantage for upward reaching and limits the maximum available range of motion for shoulder flexion.

Reference:
Keough, J. L., Sain, S. J., & Roller, C. L. (2017). *Kinesiology for the occupational therapy assistant: Essential components of function and movement* (2nd ed., pp. 104-105, 116.). Thorofare, NJ: SLACK, Inc.

10. An OTR and a COTA who work in an outpatient pain management clinic are collaborating to gather information about an adolescent who has a history of joint pain secondary to a connective tissue disorder. Which method is **MOST BENEFICIAL** for obtaining information about the influence of the adolescent's pain on daily routines?

   A. Complete a motivational interview with the adolescent.

   B. Obtain pain ratings using a standardized visual analog scale.

   C. Review the adolescent's medication schedule and routines.

Correct Answer: A

RATIONALE:
Motivational interviewing is a client-centered method that can help this adolescent identify personal goals and assist the COTA in determining the client's desire to adopt a new approach to managing chronic pain.

Reference:
Brown, C., & Stoffel V. C. (2011). *Occupational therapy in mental health: A vision for participation* (pp. 361-362). Philadelphia, PA: F.A. Davis Company.

11. A COTA recently provided a neoprene short thumb opponens orthosis to a 3-year-old child who has spastic hemiplegia. Which activity would provide the **MOST BENEFICIAL** information about the effectiveness of this orthosis?

   A. Observing the child pushing a toy shopping cart

   B. Asking the child to bring a drinking cup to the mouth

   C. Seeing if the child can hold a cracker without breaking it

Correct Answer: B

RATIONALE:
One of the objectives for having the child wear a neoprene short thumb opponens orthosis is to encourage active thumb opposition. Asking the child to bring a drinking cup to the mouth allows the COTA to observe if the child moves the thumb into opposition during a functional activity.

References:
Case-Smith, J., & O'Brien, J. C. (2015). *Occupational therapy for children and adolescents* (7th ed., pp. 233-235). St. Louis, MO: Mosby Elsevier.

Jacobs, M., & Austin, N. (2014). *Orthotic intervention for the hand and upper extremity: Splinting principles and process* (2nd ed., pp. 167-169). Philadelphia, PA: Lippincott Williams & Wilkins.

12. A COTA is working with a client who has substance use disorder and was recently admitted to an outpatient rehabilitation center. A screening indicates the client lives alone and started a new job a month ago. What information would be **MOST BENEFICIAL** to gather to contribute to the client's occupational profile?

    A. List of previous jobs

    B. **Concerns about the new job**

    C. Educational background

Correct Answer: B

RATIONALE:
To contribute to the occupational profile, it is **MOST BENEFICIAL** to learn possible concerns the client has about the new job in order to assist the OTR in developing a client-centered intervention plan.

Reference:
Early, M. B. (2013). *Physical dysfunction practice skills for the occupational therapy assistant* (3rd ed., p. 84). St. Louis, MO: Mosby Elsevier.

13. A COTA working in the outpatient department of a children's hospital is scheduled to begin intervention with a 5-year-old child who has osteogenesis imperfecta. One of the intervention objectives is for the child to achieve age-appropriate developmental milestones for bathing and dressing. The occupational profile indicates that the child's family recently immigrated to the United States. What information is **MOST IMPORTANT** for the COTA to obtain from the child's parents during the initial session with the child?

    A. **ADL routines they typically use with their child**

    B. Financial ability to purchase assistive devices

    C. Willingness to make in-home modifications

Correct Answer: A

RATIONALE:
To develop a client-centered intervention plan, it is important to obtain information specific to this family and their culture.

Reference:
Wagenfeld, A., Kaldenberg, J., & Honaker, D. (Eds.). (2017). *Foundations of pediatric practice for the occupational therapy assistant* (2nd ed., p. 228). Thorofare, NJ: SLACK, Inc.

14. An older adult client has vertigo associated with a recent cerebellar infarct. Which functional task would be **MOST BENEFICIAL** to have the client complete as part of a screening to gather information about the influence of this condition on ADL?

    A. Reaching overhead to get a blanket from an upper shelf in the bedroom closet

    B. Washing dishes while standing at the sink in a single-leg stance for 20 seconds on each leg

    C. Turning the head from right to left to look for food items in an above counter kitchen cabinet

Correct Answer: C

RATIONALE:
Screening for vertigo involves asking the client to move the head from side to side.

References:
Early, M. B. (2013). *Physical dysfunction practice skills for the occupational therapy assistant* (3rd ed., p. 409). St. Louis, MO: Mosby Elsevier.

Gillen, G. (2016). *Stroke rehabilitation: A function-based approach* (4th ed., p. 421). St. Louis, MO: Elsevier.

15. A young adult client has mild cognitive impairment, poor attention span, and limited frustration tolerance secondary to a TBI. One of the client's goals is to resume work in a restaurant. The COTA is gathering information to contribute to the client's initial work readiness evaluation. Which data gathering method would be **BEST** for the COTA to use for this purpose?

    A. **Administer a standardized vocational interest inventory.**

    B. Interview the employer about the client's previous work habits.

    C. Assess cognitive-perceptual skills using simulated job tasks.

    D. Determine the client's physical capacity for work.

Correct Answer: A

RATIONALE:
Information gathered about the client's vocational interests should be included in the initial work readiness evaluation and used as the basis for further evaluation and intervention planning.

Reference:
Early, M. B. (2017). *Mental health concepts & techniques for the occupational therapy assistant* (5th ed., pp. 531-532). Philadelphia, PA: Lippincott Williams & Wilkins.

16. A COTA is completing a manual muscle test on the biceps of a client who has full elbow range of motion with palm-up and palm-down, and can hold the elbow flexed against moderate resistance. Which muscle strength grade is **MOST CONSISTENT** with this response?

    A. **Good (4/5)**

    B. Fair (3/5)

    C. Poor (2/5)

Correct Answer: A

RATIONALE:
Based on the Manual Muscle Testing grading system, full ROM against moderate resistance is rated as Good (4/5).

Reference:
Keough, J. L., Sain, S. J., & Roller, C. L. (2017). *Kinesiology for the occupational therapy assistant: Essential components of function and movement* (2nd ed., p. 91). Thorofare, NJ: SLACK, Inc.

17. A COTA is administering a standardized test to assess perceptual skills of a client who had a recent CVA. After reading the instructions to the client, the client has difficulty initiating the task as requested. What action should the COTA take in response to this observation?

   A. Continue the test as indicated in the protocol manual.

   B. Ask the client to repeat back the protocol instructions.

   C. Repeat the test protocol instructions while demonstrating the task.

Correct Answer: A

RATIONALE:
When administering a standardized assessment, the established administration procedures must be strictly followed. If the protocols are not followed, the assessment results are not reliable.

Reference:
Early, M. B. (2013). *Physical dysfunction practice skills for the occupational therapy assistant* (3rd ed., p. 60). St. Louis, MO: Mosby Elsevier.

18. An OTR and a COTA who work in a rehabilitation hospital are collaborating to evaluate an inpatient who had a CVA. As part of the evaluation process, the OTR asks the COTA to administer a standardized assessment. In addition to following the test procedures as outlined in the test manual, which of the following actions is **MOST IMPORTANT** for the COTA to take to support the evaluation process?

    A. Rephrase test directions to the patient in easy-to-understand terms.

    B. **Accurately document and communicate the results to the OTR.**

    C. Explain the purpose of the test to the patient and to the patient's family.

Correct Answer: B

RATIONALE:
It is critical for the COTA to accurately document and report results from the standardized assessment so that the OTR can then interpret the results.

Reference:
Early, M. B. (2013). *Physical dysfunction practice skills for the occupational therapy assistant* (3rd ed., pp. 59-60). St. Louis, MO: Mosby Elsevier.

19. An inpatient with major depression was admitted to an acute psychiatric facility one day ago. A screening indicates the patient lives alone at home and recently retired after having worked as clergy in a church for the past 35 years. What action is **MOST BENEFICIAL** for the COTA to take when gathering information to contribute to the patient's occupational profile?

   A. Explore potential part-time vocational or volunteer opportunities in the area.

   B. Determine the patient's willingness to participate in a retirement support group.

   C. Ask the patient about options for contributing to church-sponsored activities.

   D. **Use open-ended questions related to the patient's feelings about retirement.**

Correct Answer: D

RATIONALE:
Asking open-ended questions is a nondirective method for encouraging the patient's active participation and input in the information gathering process.

Reference:
Early, M. B. (2017). *Mental health concepts & techniques for the occupational therapy assistant* (5th ed., pp. 39-40). Philadelphia, PA: Lippincott Williams & Wilkins.

20. A client who has schizophrenia recently transitioned from living at home with parents to residing in a group home. The client is having difficulty adjusting to this new transition. The COTA is interviewing the client and the client's parents as part of the intervention planning process. What is the **PRIMARY** purpose for conducting this interview?

   A. To learn about the client's emotional needs

   B. To determine the client's developmental stage

   C. To become aware of the client's unconscious conflicts

   D. To identify the client's typical performance patterns

Correct Answer: D

RATIONALE:
The **PRIMARY** reason for interviewing the parents is to identify the client's typical performance patterns, including safety issues, current skills and abilities, and functional limitations. This information is important for facilitating the client's transition from a supervised home environment to a group home setting.

Reference:
Early, M. B. (2017). *Mental health concepts & techniques for the occupational therapy assistant* (5th ed., pp. 412-413). Philadelphia, PA: Lippincott Williams & Wilkins.

21. A patient was admitted to a rehabilitation facility due to a recent decline in function secondary to amyotrophic lateral sclerosis. One of the patient's goals is to live at home as long as possible. The COTA is gathering information about the patient to contribute to the initial discharge planning meeting. What information would be **MOST IMPORTANT** to gather for this purpose?

A. Patient's vocational and leisure history

B. Current ROM and strength measurements

C. Assisted living option for the patient to consider

D. **Durable medical equipment needs for ADL**

Correct Answer: D

RATIONALE:
Amyotrophic lateral sclerosis is a progressive degenerative neuromuscular disease. Disease progression is rapid, resulting in significant mobility deficits and eventual paralysis. Information about durable medical equipment (DME) needs for the home environment is **MOST IMPORTANT** given the patient's goal to live at home as long as possible.

Reference:
Early, M. B. (2013). *Physical dysfunction practice skills for the occupational therapy assistant* (3rd ed., pp. 55, 68, 525-527). St. Louis, MO: Mosby Elsevier.

22. Which of the following cardiac risk factors is **MOST IMPORTANT** for the COTA to address during an intervention session with an inpatient who has coronary artery disease?

    A. Family history

    B. Blood sugar level

    C. **Sedentary lifestyle**

Correct Answer: C

RATIONALE:
Having an inactive lifestyle is considered a modifiable or changeable cardiac risk factor that can be influenced through occupational therapy intervention.

Reference:
Early, M.B. (2013). *Physical dysfunction practice skills for the occupational therapy assistant* (3rd ed., p. 679). St. Louis, MO: Elsevier Mosby.

23. A client who had a nondisplaced distal radius fracture to the right-dominant upper extremity works as a hairstylist. The client reports persistent wrist and finger stiffness that makes it difficult to comb and style hair at work. Which intervention represents a biomechanical approach and should be included as part of the client's **INITIAL** intervention for maximizing long-term functional performance?

    A. Modifications to the client's work station and work tools

    B. **Active-resistive ROM and strengthening exercises**

    C. Dynamic orthotic wear during hours of sleep

Correct Answer: B

RATIONALE:
Improving strength, ROM, and muscle endurance are typically the focus of intervention when using a biomechanical approach.

Reference:
Early, M. B. (2013). *Physical dysfunction practice skills for the occupational therapy assistant* (3rd ed., p. 214). St. Louis, MO: Mosby Elsevier.

24. A client who has multiple sclerosis works as an administrative assistant in a large corporation. Fatigue and weakness interfere with the client's ability to complete job tasks. The corporate physician is requesting a job site analysis for this client. What is the **PRIMARY** purpose of this type of analysis?

    A. To observe the client interacting with co-workers within the office environment

    B. To determine the critical work demands in relation to the client needs

    C. To assess the client's vocational interests in relation to work assignments

    D. To identify the management's willingness to provide special accommodations

Correct Answer: B

RATIONALE:
The **PRIMARY** purpose of this type of analysis is to observe the client performing job tasks in a natural environment. This will provide objective information for determining the impact of the disease in relation to the critical demands of the job.

Reference:
Early, M. B. (2013). *Physical dysfunction practice skills for the occupational therapy assistant* (3rd ed., pp. 344-345). St. Louis, MO: Mosby Elsevier.

25. Which of the following homemaking activities uses the **GREATEST** range of bilateral shoulder flexion and elbow extension?

   A. Ironing shirts and placing them on a hanger

   B. Washing dishes in a sink and drying pots and pans

   C. Folding sheets and hanging towels on a clothesline

   D. Dusting tabletops and vacuuming carpets

Correct Answer: C

RATIONALE:
The results of a task analysis of each of these activities indicate that folding sheets and reaching to hang clothes on a clothesline requires the **GREATEST** amount of bilateral shoulder flexion and elbow extension.

Reference:
Early, M. B. (2013). *Physical dysfunction practice skills for the occupational therapy assistant* (3rd ed., pp. 119-123, 209-210). St. Louis, MO: Mosby Elsevier.

26. A client has sensory-perceptual deficits secondary to a mild CVA. Motor skills remain intact. Which task would be **BEST** to ask the patient to complete when screening for tactile agnosia?

   A. Picking up objects from a tabletop

   B. Turning a water faucet on and off

   C. Distinguishing a key from a coin in a pocket

   D. Holding an eating utensil in the dominant hand

Correct Answer: C

RATIONALE:
Tactile gnosis is the ability to recognize familiar objects by touch with vision occluded. A client with tactile agnosia would not be able to find a key in a pocket since the client would not be able to distinguish the object's characteristics without the aid of visual cues.

Reference:
Early, M. B. (2013). *Physical dysfunction practice skills for the occupational therapy assistant* (3rd ed., p. 461). St. Louis, MO: Mosby Elsevier.

27. Which of the following craft activities provides the **MOST** structure for a client who has bipolar 1 disorder and is in a manic phase?

    A. Watercolor painting activity

    B. Leather stamping project

    C. Magazine picture collage

Correct Answer: B

RATIONALE:
The results of a task analysis of each of these activities indicate that a leather stamping project is the most structured as it requires the least amount of creative input and has specific steps to complete.

Reference:
Early, M. B. (2017). *Mental health concepts & techniques for the occupational therapy assistant* (5th ed., p. 322). Philadelphia, PA: Lippincott Williams & Wilkins.

28. A client with bilateral elbow contractures has 45° active extension and 90° active flexion of both elbows and 5° supination/pronation. Upper extremity muscle strength is Normal (5/5). Which activity would be **MOST DIFFICULT** for the client to perform without using compensatory movements?

    A. Putting a belt through pants belt loops

    B. Tying shoelaces

    C. Using a spoon to eat soup

Correct Answer: C

RATIONALE:
The results of a task analysis of each of these activities indicate that using a spoon to eat soup requires supination and would be **MOST DIFFICULT** for the client to perform without using compensatory movements.

Reference:
Early, M. B. (2013). *Physical dysfunction practice skills for the occupational therapy assistant* (3rd ed., p. 118). St. Louis, MO: Mosby Elsevier.

29. A 4-year-old child with pervasive developmental delay requires maximum assistance for toileting. The COTA is teaching the child's parents strategies for improving the child's independence with these tasks. During a session, the parents indicate that over the past several months, the child typically does not have a bowel movement for several days at a time due to constipation. Which recommendation should the COTA provide the parents in response to this comment?

    A. Ask a pharmacist to recommend a non-prescription children's stool softener for the child.

    B. Consult with a dietitian to learn how to increase the amount of fiber in the child's diet.

    C. Schedule an appointment with the child's primary physician to rule out gastrointestinal issues.

Correct Answer: C

RATIONALE:
A referral to the primary physician is warranted to determine if there is a medical cause for the child's constipation.

Reference:
Smith-Gabai, H., & Holm, S. (Eds.). (2017). *Occupational therapy in acute care* (2nd ed., p. 102). Bethesda, MD: AOTA Press.

30. A COTA working in a long-term care facility is responsible for teaching the residents strategies for supporting their independence with BADL. During BADL sessions over the past week, several of the residents reported that the assistive devices used during the sessions are not available to them when completing routine BADL with the nursing aides. What action would be **MOST BENEFICIAL** for the COTA to take in response to these reports?

    A. Submit an incident report about the nursing aides to the appropriate supervisor.

    B. Advise the residents to ask for the assistive devices prior to starting BADL.

    C. Present in-service training to nursing staff about the benefits and uses of BADL devices.

    D. Ensure the assistive devices are in a visible location and labeled with the residents' names.

Correct Answer: C

RATIONALE:
Providing in-service training to the nursing staff will allow the opportunity to teach information about the benefits and use of BADL devices and to facilitate a collaborative approach in supporting each resident to meet their goals.

Reference:
Lohman, H., Byers-Connon, S., & Padilla, R. L. (2019). *Occupational therapy with elders: Strategies for the COTA* (4th ed., p. 147). Maryland Heights, MO: Mosby Elsevier.

31. A COTA working in an elementary school setting attends students' annual Individualized Education Program (IEP) planning meetings. What information would be within the scope of practice for the COTA to report during these meetings?

A. Age-appropriate leisure activities the students should be able to complete

B. Progress the students have made in school-related activities over the past year

C. Receptive and expressive communication skills the students currently use

Correct Answer: B

RATIONALE:
The COTA is responsible for reporting students' progress during school-related activities.

Reference:
Solomon, J. W., & O'Brien, J. C. (2016). *Pediatric skills for occupational therapy assistants* (4th ed., pp. 51-52). St. Louis, MO: Elsevier Mosby.

32. An outpatient had a moderate TBI 6 weeks ago and was recently discharged from an inpatient rehabilitation setting. Currently, the patient requires supervision for BADL and reports a goal of returning to high school with a part-time schedule. What action should the COTA take in collaboration with the OTR to support progress toward this goal?

   A. Assist the patient in accessing and completing incomplete school assignments

   B. Discuss special accommodations available to students who have disabilities

   C. **Refer the patient to the school-based interprofessional team at the school**

Correct Answer: C

RATIONALE:
Referring the patient to a school-based team is a proactive approach to ensure appropriate services are in place to support a successful transition back to school.

Reference:
Case-Smith, J., & O'Brien, J. C. (2015). *Occupational therapy for children and adolescents* (7th ed., p. 844). St. Louis, MO: Mosby Elsevier.

33. An inpatient sustained a transfemoral amputation 2 days ago. The COTA is scheduled to represent OT at the interprofessional team meeting to discuss care management for this patient. What information should the COTA communicate with the team during this meeting?

   A. Advice on how nursing staff should include scar massage into daily dressing changes

   B. **Methods nursing staff can use during routine care to assist the patient in managing phantom limb sensations**

   C. Specific techniques that will be used during OT sessions to facilitate the patient's adjustment to the loss of a limb

   D. Initial steps and techniques for putting on and taking off the prosthesis

Correct Answer: B

RATIONALE:
In the post-operative phase, OT intervention following a transfemoral amputation includes strategies to manage phantom limb sensations. Team communication regarding effective interventions will promote a collaborative, client-centered approach to care.

Reference:
Radomski, M. V., & Trombly Latham, C. A. (Eds.). (2014). *Occupational therapy for physical dysfunction* (7th ed., pp. 1267-1272). Philadelphia, PA: Lippincott Williams & Wilkins.

34. An inpatient had a CVA 3 weeks ago and is preparing for discharge to live alone at home. The COTA learns that the patient intends to resume driving short distances to the grocery store and to church after discharge. The COTA does not think the patient has the ability to drive at this time. What action should the COTA take in response to learning this information?

    A. Administer a screening to identify the patient's pre-driving skills.

    B. Initiate a referral to a comprehensive driver education program.

    C. Talk with the patient about the implications of this decision.

Correct Answer: C

RATIONALE:
The COTA should gather additional information from the client and collaborate with the OTR before taking action.

Reference:
Early, M. B. (2013). *Physical dysfunction practice skills for the occupational therapy assistant* (3rd ed., p. 320). St. Louis, MO: Mosby Elsevier.

35. A COTA is preparing to teach breathing strategies to an inpatient who has COPD and mild cognitive impairment. At the start of the session, the COTA plans to gather information to understand the patient's level of health literacy. Which question would be **BEST** to ask the patient as part of the screening process to learn about the patient's level of health literacy?

   A. **How confident do you feel about explaining your medical history to the doctor?**

   B. Do you read information about the side effects of your prescribed medications?

   C. Are you able to sign the consent forms for your medical treatment in the hospital?

Correct Answer: A

RATIONALE:
Asking an open-ended question encourages the patient to discuss difficulties or concerns about communicating health information and contributes to the COTA's understanding of the patient's level of health literacy. Close-ended questions that require a Yes/No response limit the potential amount of information obtained during this screening process.

Reference:
Mahle, A. J., & Ward, L. W. (2019). *Adult physical conditions: Intervention strategies for occupational therapy assistants* (pp. 59-60). Philadelphia, PA: F.A. Davis.

36. A COTA is working with the Individualized Education Program (IEP) team to determine a student's eligibility for school-based OT intervention. What information does the team rely upon to make final eligibility determinations?

   A. Physician's referral and diagnosis severity

   B. Standardized test scores and documented disability

   C. Classroom performance and curriculum-based needs

   D. Birth history and previous early intervention services

Correct Answer: C

RATIONALE:
The Individuals with Disabilities Education Act (IDEA) mandates that eligibility requirements for IEP services are based on a student's classroom needs and performance in relation to curriculum-based objectives.

Reference:
Solomon, J. W., & O'Brien, J. C. (2016). *Pediatric skills for occupational therapy assistants* (4th ed., pp. 48-50). St. Louis, MO: Mosby Elsevier.

37. A client who has schizophrenia is participating in a day treatment program at a community-based mental health center. During an OT group, the client admits to "forgetting" to take prescribed medications. After discussing the importance of taking the prescribed medication with the client, what is the **NEXT** action the COTA should take in response to this comment?

   A. **Contact the referring physician and report the client's nonadherence.**

   B. Alert the client's family or significant other to monitor adherence.

   C. Teach the client to use a smart phone application for medication management.

Correct Answer: A

RATIONALE:
The COTA needs to report the client's nonadherence; abruptly stopping medication can have negative consequences and put the client at risk of relapse.

Reference:
Early, M. B. (2017). *Mental health concepts & techniques for the occupational therapy assistant* (5th ed., pp. 268-269.). Philadelphia, PA: Lippincott Williams & Wilkins.

38. A COTA is providing intervention for an inpatient diagnosed with Guillain-Barré syndrome 3 days ago. The patient requires a ventilator for respiratory support and has complete paralysis of the upper and lower extremities. Which interventions should be included in the treatment sessions during this phase of the patient's rehabilitation?

   A. Daily strengthening routine with resistive exercise and instruction in strategies to adjust to long-term disability

   B. Positioning program, caregiver education in passive ROM, and recommendations for low-tech electronic aids for daily living

   C. Gradual increase in self-care activities and guidelines to perform a progressive resistive exercise regimen

Correct Answer: B

RATIONALE:
These interventions are a priority during the acute phase of Guillain-Barré syndrome.

Reference:
Radomski, M. V., & Trombly Latham, C. A. (Eds.). (2014). *Occupational therapy for physical dysfunction* (7th ed., pp. 1094-1095). Philadelphia, PA: Lippincott Williams & Wilkins.

39. An inpatient who has congestive heart failure has had a recent decline in function and now requires a wheelchair for mobility. A COTA is completing a home visit in preparation for the patient's discharge to live with family. The family lives in an apartment on the second level of a multi-level apartment building. During the home visit, the COTA identifies several areas in the apartment that are not accessible by a wheelchair. What is the **NEXT** action the COTA should take based on this information?

    A. **Collaborate with the patient and family to discuss the patient's needs.**

    B. Suggest ways the furniture should be arranged for wheelchair access.

    C. Have family members notify the apartment manager of needed changes.

Correct Answer: A

RATIONALE:
Prior to providing recommendations, the COTA should first discuss options with the client and the family to establish client-centered priorities.

Reference:
Early, M. B. (2013). *Physical dysfunction practice skills for the occupational therapy assistant* (3rd ed., pp. 243-248). St. Louis, MO: Mosby Elsevier.

40. An outpatient client, whose primary insurance is Medicare, sustained a wrist fracture 8 weeks ago and has been participating in OT 3 times per week for the past 2 weeks. ROM and strength of the affected extremity are improving, and the client has returned to limited work in a department store. However, the client is still reluctant to use the hand. At the end of a session, the client refuses to schedule more OT visits, citing "transportation problems." What is the **FIRST** action the COTA should take in this situation?

    A. **Talk with the client to determine a solution.**

    B. Teach the client an independent home program.

    C. Refer the client to a home health agency.

    D. Encourage scheduling a monthly reevaluation.

Correct Answer: A

RATIONALE:
The COTA should initially collaborate with the client regarding barriers to participation in OT and potential solutions.

Reference:
Early, M. B. (2013). *Physical dysfunction practice skills for the occupational therapy assistant* (3rd ed., pp. 31-32). St. Louis, MO: Mosby Elsevier.

41. An older adult patient who had a recent CVA was admitted to an inpatient rehabilitation facility 2 days ago. The patient is scheduled to participate in an initial self-care session. A records review indicates the patient immigrated to the United States several years ago and is living with family members. What **INITIAL** action should the COTA take to support the patient's participation in the intervention sessions?

A. Gather information about the patient's cultural values regarding self-care.

B. Ensure a translator is available for each of the patient's scheduled sessions.

C. Administer a standardized evaluation to determine the patient's current function.

Correct Answer: A

RATIONALE:
Information about the patient's cultural values should be used to guide intervention plans and activities.

Reference:
Early, M. B. (2017). *Mental health concepts & techniques for the occupational therapy assistant* (5th ed., pp. 205-206). Philadelphia, PA: Lippincott Williams & Wilkins.

42. A COTA is selecting activities to include in a homemaking skills session with a client who has an anxiety disorder. A review of the occupational profile indicates the client immigrated to the United States with a spouse and two children one year ago. Stress of the relocation and symptoms of the anxiety disorder are interfering with the ability to complete simple daily tasks. One of the client's goals is to fully participate in family roles and routines. What activities should the COTA include in the session in order to support the client's goal?

    A. Incorporate the client's culture and values into the session activities.

    B. Provide instruction about using appliances typically found in homes in the U.S.

    C. Teach the client about the family value system in the United States.

Correct Answer: A

RATIONALE:
The COTA should gather information about the client's values, routines, habits, and expectations. When teaching homemaking skills, the COTA should respect and support the client's cultural preferences.

Reference:
Early, M. B. (2017). *Mental health concepts & techniques for the occupational therapy assistant* (5th ed., pp. 205-206, 512). Philadelphia, PA: Lippincott Williams & Wilkins.

43. Which behavioral cues exhibited during intervention are **TYPICAL** of a client with low health literacy?

    Select the 3 best choices.

    A. **Glancing at educational handouts**

    B. Asking clarifying questions during a session

    C. Demonstrating a new skill learned during therapy

    D. **Avoiding written questionnaires and forms**

    E. Providing a detailed summary of new information

    F. **Missing several scheduled appointments**

    Correct Answers: A, D, F

    RATIONALE:
    These behavioral cues are suggestive of low health literacy.

    Reference:
    Jacobs, K. (2016). *Management and administration for the OTA: Leadership and application skills.* (pp. 122-123). Thorofare, NJ: SLACK, Inc.

44. A COTA working in an outpatient setting is preparing a home program for a client who has mild hemiplegia and neurobehavioral deficits secondary to a CVA several months ago. What information would be **MOST IMPORTANT** for the COTA to verify prior to teaching the client the program?

   A. Extent to which the client has a detailed understanding of the program rationale

   B. **Client's learning needs for independent follow-through of the prescribed program**

   C. Client's capacity to verbalize the home program instructions

   D. Amount of family support available to the client on a daily basis

Correct Answer: B

RATIONALE:
The client's ability to follow through with a self-directed program impacts functional outcomes and is **MOST IMPORTANT** to consider.

Reference:
Early, M. B. (2013). *Physical dysfunction practice skills for the occupational therapy assistant* (3rd ed., pp. 181-182). St. Louis, MO: Mosby Elsevier.

45. An inpatient who has moderately severe cognitive decline secondary to Alzheimer's disease has been undergoing medical treatment for pneumonia. Currently, the patient has difficulty sequencing steps for self-care activities and becomes easily frustrated. The patient will be discharged in one week to live at home with adult children. What action should the COTA include as part of the overall intervention in preparation for the patient's transition to home?

A. Advise the family to hire a home health aide to assist the patient with daily BADL tasks.

B. Provide the family with behavioral strategies for supporting the patient's function at home.

C. Recommend the family purchase assistive devices for the patient to use during BADL tasks at home.

D. Instruct the family to adjust medication routines to prevent agitation and support the patient's function.

Correct Answer: B

RATIONALE:
To minimize caregiver stress and to promote a safe discharge environment, the COTA should provide the family with behavioral strategies prior to discharge.

Reference:
Early, M. B. (2013). *Physical dysfunction practice skills for the occupational therapy assistant* (3rd ed., pp. 528-529). St. Louis, MO: Mosby Elsevier.

46. A COTA, who works in a hospital setting, is teaching precautions to an inpatient who recently had open-heart surgery. Which of the following would be the **MOST EFFECTIVE** communication methods for the COTA to use in the education session to promote the patient's understanding of the information presented?

    Select the 3 best choices.

    A. **Be approachable and allow the patient to ask questions.**

    B. Explain the information thoroughly using evidence and medical language.

    C. **Present small amounts of information at a time and give the patient time to respond.**

    D. **Make eye contact during the intervention session.**

    E. Provide detailed instructions to the patient and the caregiver.

    F. Fill quiet moments with conversation and additional information.

Correct Answers: A, C, D

RATIONALE:
These options represent effective communication methods that result in enhanced health literacy of the patient.

Reference:
Lohman, H., Byers-Connon, S., & Padilla, R. L. (2019). *Occupational therapy with elders: Strategies for the COTA* (4th ed., p. 147). Maryland Heights, MO: Mosby Elsevier.

47. An inpatient has neurobehavioral deficits secondary to a CVA one month ago. At the time of the initial evaluation, the patient required moderate verbal cues to complete oral hygiene and grooming. Currently, the patient is able to complete these tasks independently during self-care sessions. This occurs one week earlier than the time frame listed in the intervention plan for achieving this goal. What action should the COTA take prior to the **NEXT** scheduled BADL session with this patient?

    A. Revise the intervention plan with new short-term goals.

    B. Administer a standardized functional assessment.

    C. Collaborate with the OTR to review the intervention goals.

    Correct Answer: C

    RATIONALE:
    It is the responsibility of the COTA to collaborate with the OTR when there is a change in the patient's status and to discuss options for modifying the intervention plan.

    Reference:
    Early, M. B. (2013). *Physical dysfunction practice skills for the occupational therapy assistant* (3rd ed., pp. 54-55, 72). St. Louis, MO: Mosby Elsevier.

48. A client had a partial hand amputation secondary to an industrial accident 3 months ago. The client has been attending OT at least three times weekly since the date of injury. Until recently, the client has been compliant with the home exercise program. Now the client is canceling appointments and seems less motivated to complete prescribed daily exercises and splinting. Which **INITIAL** action should the COTA take in response to the client's behaviors?

A. Decrease the frequency and intensity of the overall intervention plan.

B. **Discuss these observations and concerns with the client.**

C. Review the treatment plan and the long-term goals with the OTR.

Correct Answer: B

RATIONALE:
The COTA should **INITIALLY** discuss with the client any changes in behavior that may have an impact on the client's intervention goals or overall outcomes.

Reference:
Early, M. B. (2013). *Physical dysfunction practice skills for the occupational therapy assistant* (3rd ed., pp. 62-63, 67). St. Louis, MO: Mosby Elsevier.

49. A COTA working in a community-based mental health program has been working with a client who has a substance use disorder. Based on observation of the client's performance and a review of the client's goals, the COTA concludes that the client has attained maximum benefits from attending a vocational skills group. Which action should the COTA take based on this information?

A. Discuss the client's status with the supervising OTR.

B. Reevaluate the client prior to the next group session.

C. Discharge the client from this particular group.

Correct Answer: A

RATIONALE:
It is the responsibility of the COTA to collaborate with the OTR when there is a change in the client's status and to discuss options for modifying or discontinuing the intervention plan.

Reference:
Early, M. B. (2017). *Mental health concepts & techniques for the occupational therapy assistant* (5th ed., p. 467). Philadelphia, PA: Lippincott Williams & Wilkins.

50. An inpatient has hemiplegia secondary to a recent TBI and is functioning at Level V (Confused-inappropriate, Non-agitated) on the Rancho Los Amigos scale. A COTA is planning an initial dressing session to teach the patient lower body dressing techniques. Which intervention environment would be **MOST CONDUCIVE** for supporting the patient's success during this session?

    A. Quiet room in the rehabilitation department away from other patients

    B. Bathroom in the patient's room so the patient can sit on the tub bench

    C. **Patient's private room with the patient seated in a bedside chair**

Correct Answer: C

RATIONALE:
Based on the patient's current level of functioning, the patient's private room is **MOST CONDUCIVE** for promoting progress because it provides the fewest distractions and is most familiar to the patient.

Reference:
Early, M. B. (2013). *Physical dysfunction practice skills for the occupational therapy assistant* (3rd ed., p. 509). St. Louis, MO: Mosby Elsevier.

Chapter 11

Domain 2: Multiple Choice Sample Questions

Practice questions with answer key and references

The following multiple choice items are samples related to Domain 2.

Selecting and Implementing Interventions

Implement interventions under the supervision of the OTR in accordance with the intervention plan and level of service competence to support client participation in areas of occupation throughout the occupational therapy process.

1. A kindergarten-age student who has spastic cerebral palsy is painting while seated at a table in art class. The student can hold a paintbrush, but a dominant asymmetrical tonic neck reflex prevents the student from reaching for the paint located near the student's dominant side. Which technique would be **MOST EFFECTIVE** to use to inhibit this reflex and support the student's success with the art task?

    A. Place the paint at midline in front of the student.

    B. Provide the student with a paintbrush with a weighted handle.

    C. Adapt the tabletop to a 45° elevated angle.

    D. Have the student use a standing frame while painting.

2. A client has referred pain symptoms associated with a back injury from a fall 6 months ago. Which physical agent modality would be **MOST BENEFICIAL** to use as an adjunct to activities for pain management?

   A. Transcutaneous electrical nerve stimulation

   B. Neuromuscular electrical stimulation

   C. Nonthermal phonophoresis ultrasound

3. A COTA working at an assisted living facility is planning to take 8-10 residents on an outing to a restaurant. Several of the residents have hearing impairments. The COTA plans to contact the restaurant in advance of the outing to ask for a table arrangement conducive to the group's socialization. Which table setup would be **BEST** for this purpose?

   A. U-shaped table located close to the kitchen, so the residents are comfortable speaking loudly to each other.

   B. Rectangular table in a busy section of the restaurant so loud talking will not disturb other patrons.

   C. Round dining table that will comfortably accommodate both the residents and the COTA.

   D. Several small tables positioned directly under a fluorescent overhead light, so residents are able to read and discuss menu options.

4. A client has mild hemiparesis secondary to having a left CVA several months ago. One of the client's goals is to increase strength and fine motor control to be able to play the piano, a favorite leisure activity. Which activity would be **MOST BENEFICIAL** to include in the intervention to support progress toward this goal?

   A. Making a pinch pot using firm modeling clay

   B. Manipulating pegs of various sizes and stringing one-inch (2.54 cm) beads

   C. Practicing a repetitive program of piano keyboard drills

   D. Completing resistive exercises while listening to piano music

5. A client is working on a needlework project for a grandchild's birthday but is having difficulty finishing the project due to low vision from early stage cataracts. The client is scheduled for cataract surgery, but the surgery date is after the grandchild's birthday. Which compensatory technique should the COTA recommend to promote the client's ability to finish the needlework project in time for the birthday?

   A. Advise the client to use high-contrast colored thread.

   B. Place the project in an adjustable frame.

   C. Reduce the amount of ambient light in the room.

   D. Provide the client with a lighted, hands-free magnifier.

6. A 9-year-old child who has moderate hemiplegia often neglects to use the affected upper extremity. Which activity would be **MOST BENEFICIAL** for encouraging the child's bilateral fine motor control?

   A. Playing with a hand-held video game

   B. Tossing a beanbag at a target

   C. Playing a game of darts

   D. Drawing on a chalkboard

7. Pictured below are children putting on dress-up clothes during unstructured play time. What type of play does this represent?

A. Constructive

B. Exploratory

C. Pretend

8. A client has an intense fear of grocery shopping due to an anxiety disorder. The client is a homemaker whose goal is to be able to buy food for a family meal. Which method is **BEST** for promoting initial progress toward goal achievement?

A. Take the client on an outing to a local convenience store.

B. Teach the client to divide the grocery shopping task into manageable steps.

C. Simulate grocery shopping tasks during several sessions in the clinic.

9. An adolescent who has a conduct disorder is participating in an OT group to increase socialization skills using a skills acquisition model. While playing a familiar board game, the adolescent loses a turn, becomes frustrated, and demands to play something else. How should the COTA respond to the adolescent's behavior?

   A. Modify the game rules to promote success.

   B. Excuse the adolescent from the activity session.

   C. Encourage the adolescent to complete the activity.

   D. Allow the adolescent to select another activity.

10. A resident of a long-term care facility has moderately severe cognitive decline secondary to dementia. The resident occasionally becomes combative during morning BADL. What **INITIAL** action should the COTA take when these behaviors occur?

    A. Allow for nursing staff to complete the dressing session.

    B. Identify the possible factors that provoked the behavior.

    C. Use a firm voice to tell the resident to stop the behavior.

    D. Delay the session until later in the afternoon.

11. A resident of a long-term care facility has moderately severe cognitive decline secondary to Alzheimer's disease. Each afternoon when nursing staff change shifts, the resident becomes agitated and attempts to elope from the nursing facility, stating, "I need to go back to work." Which action would be **MOST EFFECTIVE** for redirecting the resident's attention and decreasing the risk of elopement?

    A. Have the resident participate in a simple craft activity.

    B. Take the resident outside for a walk around the facility.

    C. Encourage the resident to watch television in the day room.

    D. Begin a reminiscence activity related to something the resident likes.

12. An older adult client who has mild macular degeneration is referred to OT. The client is an avid reader and subscribes to several magazines. The client is experiencing progressive difficulty reading the magazines due to the reflective glare from the glossy paper. Which **INITIAL** adaptation should the COTA recommend to the client to support participation in this preferred leisure activity?

   A. Obtain audio and large-print books and magazines from a local library.

   B. Subscribe to satellite radio to be able to listen to books and news stories.

   C. Direct the lighting source from behind the shoulder when reading.

   D. Contact publishers for availability of non-glare print issues of the publication.

13. A client who has reduced visual acuity reports difficulty preparing meals due to the low vision. Which kitchen modification would be **MOST BENEFICIAL** to include as a recommendation for supporting the client's participation with meal preparation tasks?

   A. Label food items in large print using high-contrast colors.

   B. Use fluorescent bulbs in household light fixtures.

   C. Keep frequently used items on the countertop.

   D. Replace wooden cabinet doors with glass panels.

14. An adolescent client has an eating disorder and attends a partial hospitalization program. The client refuses to come to a scheduled OT group. What is the **FIRST** action the COTA should take based on this refusal?

   A. Respect the client's right to decline treatment.

   B. Contact the client's primary caregiver.

   C. Determine the client's reason for not participating.

15. A COTA is selecting a group intervention for an inpatient who has paranoid schizophrenia. The patient has transitioned from being self-isolative to tolerating being around several people at the same time. Which type of group would support the patient's social development?

   A. Parallel

   B. Project

   C. Egocentric-cooperative

   D. Cooperative

16. A COTA leads a variety of groups for clients participating in a community-based mental health program. What would be the **PRIMARY** role of the COTA when leading an egocentric-cooperative group in this setting?

   A. Assisting the participants in developing and discussing group norms

   B. Helping the participants select tasks for their specific skill level

   C. Providing suggestions for helping the group make a decision

   D. Setting limits for specified short-term projects or activities

17. What should be the **INITIAL** focus of an activity group for inpatients who have been undergoing treatment for major depression?

   A. Completion of a simple craft project

   B. Participation in a short-term familiar task

   C. Interaction in a structured setting

   D. Diversion from the hospital environment

18. A COTA is selecting activities for an inpatient who recently had a CVA and has tactile agnosia. The goal of the activity is to improve the patient's awareness of objects located in the affected hand. Which activity would be **MOST EFFECTIVE** for promoting progress toward this goal?

    A. Using vision to identify coins placed in the hand

    B. Sorting various coins into separate piles

    C. Picking up pennies and dropping them into a jar

19. A kindergarten student, who has a sensory modulation disorder, intentionally bumps into walls and forcefully throws objects when playing on the playground. Which sensory stimulation activity is **MOST EFFECTIVE** for promoting a reduction of these behaviors?

    A. Spinning the student in a net swing using a predictable rhythm

    B. Having the student search for objects hidden in a container of uncooked rice

    C. Allowing the student to jump up and down in an immersion pool of balls

20. During a bathing session, a client who has schizoaffective disorder begins talking about faces appearing on the wall. Which action should the COTA take in response to this observation?

    A. Provide reassurance and redirect the client to the activity.

    B. Respond using humor and offer to discuss the bugs on the wall.

    C. Use a calm voice and ask the client to stop the negative behavior.

21. A patient with Alzheimer's disease is admitted to a skilled nursing facility from home following a recent decline in function. Evaluation results indicate the patient has moderately severe cognitive decline with major memory deficits that impact completion of BADL tasks. The COTA is planning a self-care intervention session using task segmentation strategies to assist the patient with dressing tasks. Which verbal prompts would support the patient's task completion?

    Select the 3 best choices.

    A. "Pick up one sock from the bed. Place the sock on the right foot. Pull the sock up."

    B. "Pants with an elastic waistband are easier to get on than pants with a zipper."

    C. "Put the T-shirt over your head. Reach up and put one arm through the sleeve."

    D. "Choose a pair of lace-up shoes from the closet and put them on."

    E. "It's a cold day today. Why don't you put on a long-sleeved sweater?"

    F. "Undo the buttons of the shirt. I'll help you place your arm in the sleeve."

22. A student in second grade recently witnessed domestic violence in the home and has symptoms of post-traumatic stress disorder (PTSD). One of the intervention priorities is for the student to develop coping strategies to manage the symptoms associated with the condition. Which initial action would be **MOST BENEFICIAL** for the COTA to include in the intervention for this student?

    A. Develop a calm and sensory-friendly space for the student at school.

    B. Consult with the student's family about the safety of the home environment.

    C. Offer a session for all students in the classroom to learn relaxing yoga poses.

23. A student in the first grade has a mild visual perceptual deficit. The teacher reports the student is a good auditory learner but often writes letters and numbers backward when completing class assignments. Which activity would be **MOST BENEFICIAL** for improving the student's directionality when writing?

   A. Playing a game of follow-the-leader to form letters in the air

   B. Having the student repetitively practice forming letters on paper

   C. Teaching the student to use rhymes that describe how to form letters

   D. Providing the student with worksheets to trace letters of the alphabet

24. A COTA is planning a developmental activity program for preschool students. One of the students who attends the program has spina bifida. All of the students are cognitively intact and range in age from 3-4 years old. What type of group activity would maximize participation for all students?

   A. Symbolic play using a variety of puppets

   B. Tabletop board games with standard rules

   C. Imaginative play using small snap-together blocks

   D. Gross motor games that include jumping and catching

25. An adolescent client has moderate cognitive delays. The client, who is a visual learner, wants to learn to shave using an electric razor. What is the **FIRST** method the COTA should use when teaching this skill to the client?

   A. Provide the client with a step-by-step written list of instructions.

   B. Use a hand-over-hand technique and assist the client to shave.

   C. Demonstrate the task to the client while standing at the sink.

26. A patient has a visual field deficit secondary to a recent CVA. This interferes with the patient's ability to dress independently. Which task represents the **MOST EFFECTIVE** intervention method for visual field deficits to support the patient's independence with dressing?

   A. Encouraging the patient to bear weight through the affected side during dressing tasks

   B. Teaching the patient to place the non-affected extremity in a garment first when dressing

   C. Having the patient practice organized scanning patterns to find specified clothing items

27. A student with a mild intellectual disability is enrolled in a mainstream third-grade class. The student frequently asks the teacher for assistance to tie shoelaces. The COTA plans to use backward chaining techniques to help the student manage shoe laces independently. Which techniques should the COTA include as part of the intervention when using this strategy?

   Select the 3 best choices.

   A. Have the student pull the laces to tighten the loops of the bow.

   B. Teach the student to pull on the shoe lace to untie the shoe.

   C. Reinforce the student's completion of the last steps of tying laces.

   D. Start the session by having the student take both shoes off.

   E. Provide the student with pictures illustrating each step of shoe-tying.

   F. Provide hand-over-hand assistance during the initial steps of tying a shoe.

28. A resident of a skilled nursing facility who has moderate cognitive decline is beginning to have difficulty with self-feeding. Which method would be **MOST BENEFICIAL** for the COTA to teach the dining room staff to use when assisting this resident to self-feed?

   A. Backward chaining

   B. Forward chaining

   C. Hand-over-hand assistance

   D. Whole learning

29. A client has mild-moderate cognitive decline secondary to dementia. The client has difficulty remembering when to take a prescribed medicine. One of the intervention goals is for the client to independently take medications at the correct dosage times. Which compensatory technique would be **MOST BENEFICIAL** for supporting this goal?

   A. Have a caregiver place medication in a 7-day pill storage container at the beginning of each week.

   B. Advise the client to wear a voice-message alarm preprogrammed to activate at specific times of the day.

   C. Teach the client to maintain a medication diary that outlines daily prescription medication requirements and dosage history.

   D. Provide the client with a pocket day-planner that indicates which medications to take each day.

30. A client has moderate cognitive decline secondary to dementia. This influences the client's ability to independently complete BADL. Which compensatory approach would be **MOST BENEFICIAL** to use to support the client's independence with grooming tasks?

    A. Paste sequential picture cards of grooming tasks on the bathroom door.

    B. Adhere simple step-by-step instructions for grooming to the bathroom mirror.

    C. Provide a toiletry kit for the client to store frequently used grooming items.

    D. Place grooming items at eye level on a shelf by the bathroom sink.

31. An older adult client, who has rheumatoid arthritis, is able to chop vegetables but frequently experiences hand fatigue before completing the meal preparation tasks. Which is the **BEST** recommendation for improving the client's ability to complete the steps to prepare a meal?

    A. Encourage the client to purchase prepared meals to heat up in the microwave.

    B. Fabricate a hand-based orthotic to maintain joint alignment.

    C. Provide information about cooking utensils with ergonomic handles.

32. A COTA is using forward chaining to teach dressing skills to an inpatient who has hemiplegia. One of the intervention goals is for the patient to learn to put on a front-opening, button-down shirt. What is the **FIRST** task that should be initiated when using forward chaining to effectively promote goal achievement?

    A. Encourage the patient to place the affected hand in the sleeve.

    B. Ask the patient to fasten buttons of various sizes on a dressing board.

    C. Have the patient pull the buttons through each of the button holes.

33. An inpatient has severe upper extremity burn scar contractures. The patient is participating in OT to improve independence with grooming and personal hygiene. The COTA observes the patient has difficulty completing peritoneal hygiene after toileting. What actions should the COTA take based on this observation?

Select the 3 best choices.

A. Develop a strengthening program to improve task performance.

B. Identify compensatory methods needed for these tasks.

C. Determine assistive devices to improve functional outcomes.

D. Ask nursing staff to provide assistance as needed during self-care.

E. Place ADL items in the bathroom within the patient's reach.

F. Ensure the patient wears compression garments during toileting.

34. A COTA is teaching proper biomechanics to a client who has chronic low back pain. The client, who works as a garden landscaper, is required to lift and carry paving stones as part of the daily job tasks. Which technique should the COTA teach the client to use when engaging in this aspect of the job?

Select the 3 best choices.

A. Carry the stone at chest height with elbows in full flexion.

B. Position the feet close together when lowering the stone.

C. Bend at the hips and knees when picking up the stone.

D. Extend the lumbar spine slightly while carrying the stone.

E. Keep the spine in alignment when holding the stone.

F. Hold the stone as close to the body as possible.

35. An inpatient in an addiction recovery hospital has been undergoing treatment for acute alcohol poisoning and a substance use disorder. During the discharge planning meeting, the patient asks for suggestions on ways to reduce the risk of relapse and to support long-term sobriety after returning home. What suggestions should the COTA provide to the patient to support this request?

Select the 3 best choices.

A. Participate in a structured community-based recreation class.

B. Consider adopting a pet to divert attention away from any desire to use drugs or alcohol.

C. Make it a priority to routinely attend self-help and recovery support groups.

D. Sign a written contract to commit to a lifetime of long-term sobriety.

E. Engage in a daily schedule of preferred physical exercise.

F. Volunteer to be the designated driver whenever socializing with friends.

36. A client has recently been diagnosed with rheumatoid arthritis. The client works as a medical laboratory technician. Completing essential job tasks of frequently turning off equipment knobs and tightening specimen cup lids result in bilateral hand and wrist pain by the end of the work day. Which movements are **CONTRAINDICATED** for this client to use during these job tasks?

A. Wrist extension

B. MCP joint ulnar deviation

C. Wrist ulnar deviation

D. Composite finger extension

37. A patient who had a total hip replacement, anterolateral approach 2 weeks ago wants to lie on the non-affected hip while sleeping. Which adaptation should the patient use when sleeping in this position?

   A. Place a pillow under both feet.

   B. Use an abduction wedge between the legs.

   C. Sleep on memory foam or air mattress.

   D. Flex the affected hip, keeping the non-affected leg straight.

38. A client has difficulty completing home management tasks due to symptoms associated with COPD. One of the intervention goals is for the client to learn techniques for reducing the impact of the disease symptoms on occupational performance. Which intervention should be included in the **INITIAL** phase of rehabilitation for supporting this goal?

   A. Teach the client to use energy conservation techniques during BADL tasks.

   B. Provide the client with a home program of upper body strengthening exercises.

   C. Have the client attend a series of stress management classes.

   D. Instruct the client on how to use visual imagery techniques for pain reduction.

39. A COTA is teaching a client, who recently had surgery for an L_4-L_5 discectomy and fusion, to use body mechanics as pictured below. The client is planning to retrieve a cooking utensil from the drawer. What is the **NEXT** instruction the COTA should provide to the client?

A. Hold the utensil close to the body and straighten knees and hips to return to a standing position.

B. Place the utensil on the counter and then use both hands to push into a standing position.

C. Hold on to the utensil and move one leg into extension behind the other leg to stand up.

40. A client who has chronic low back pain is participating in a pain management program. One of the intervention goals is for the client to learn proper body mechanics to use during personal laundry tasks. Which strategy should the COTA teach the client to use for promoting progress toward this goal?

A. Carry one small basket of laundry at a time to the laundry area.

B. Lift one large bundle of clothes from the washer to put into the dryer.

C. Bend forward at the waist while loading clothes into the washer or dryer.

D. Keep the feet shoulder-width apart when twisting the torso to place clothes into the dryer.

41. An inpatient in a rehabilitation facility has hemiplegia, moderate short-term memory deficits, and impulsiveness secondary to a TBI 3 months ago. Currently, the patient requires moderate cueing for safety during BADL. The patient is preparing for transition to live at home with the spouse as the primary caregiver. One of the discharge goals is to teach the spouse safety techniques to use when the patient is showering in a stall shower at home. What instructions should the COTA include in the caregiver training to support this goal?

   A. Observe the patient throughout the task to be sure the patient holds onto the grab bar while standing in the shower.

   B. Have the patient sit on a bath stool with suction feet while providing stand-by assistance throughout the task.

   C. Encourage the patient to use an extended handle reacher and provide hand-over-hand assistance as needed.

   D. Respect the patient's privacy, but remain outside the bathroom door until the patient has turned off the water in the shower.

42. Which of the following actions is **MOST IMPORTANT** for the COTA to take when preparing for a self-care session with an inpatient who has COPD?

   A. Arrange ADL supplies so that they are within easy reach of the patient.

   B. Make sure the patient has adequate standing tolerance to complete the entire activity.

   C. Have the patient's preferred spray deodorants and talcum powders available for use.

   D. Place a chair just outside of the bathroom door in case the patient becomes fatigued.

43. A 3-year-old child has cerebral palsy and requires maximum assistance from a caregiver for feeding. The child has fluctuant muscle tone and a persistent asymmetrical tonic neck reflex. The child is able to swallow pureed foods when they are placed in the mouth but has a tongue thrust and poor lip closure when eating. One of the intervention goals is for the caregiver to feed the child with a spoon, with the child seated in a standard high chair. Which techniques should the COTA include as part of the caregiver instructions for feeding the child with a spoon?

Select the 3 best choices.

A. Fasten a seatbelt placed at a 45° angle on the child's hips.

B. Maintain the child's neck in slight extension beyond neutral.

C. Manually stabilize the child's neck in the midline.

D. Position the child's hips and knees at a 90° angle.

E. Sit to the right or left side of the child when feeding the child.

F. Use external supports to position the trunk in midline.

44. A 4-year-old child has hypotonia secondary to cerebral palsy. This results in poor lip closure, which makes it difficult for the child to transition from using a bottle to drinking from a cup with a spouted lid. Which intervention would be **MOST BENEFICIAL** for the child to do in order to promote initial progress toward drinking from a cup?

A. Sip a favorite fruit juice from a cup with a nose cutout.

B. Blow soap bubbles into the air at the start of the session.

C. Whistle a simple tune before each drink from a cup.

D. Suck on a piece of sour candy prior to practicing drinking from the cup.

45. A 4-year-old child has persistent asymmetrical tonic neck reflex (ATNR) and symmetrical tonic neck reflex (STNR) secondary to moderate cerebral palsy. The COTA is teaching the caregiver strategies to use when feeding the child. The COTA positions the child in a chair that provides good head and trunk control. Where should the caregiver sit to inhibit the ATNR and STNR reflexes when feeding the child?

   A. Slightly on the right side of midline and just above the child's eye level

   B. Next to the child and at the child's eye level

   C. In front of the child and slightly below the child's eye level

   D. At the child's midline and slightly above the child's eye level

46. A 5-year-old child has developmental motor delay secondary to spastic diplegia. The child is able to sit upright in a wheelchair without postural supports. Evaluation results indicate the child has age-appropriate cognition and visual perception, but fine motor skills are equivalent to a typically developing 4-year-old child. The child wants to be able to dress independently. Which developmental play activities would be beneficial to include as part of the child's intervention sessions in order to support goal attainment?

   Select the 3 best choices.

   A. Creating greeting cards using stencils and colored pencils

   B. Finger painting activity with various textured paint

   C. Cutting, gluing, and coloring alphabet letter shapes

   D. Blowing bubbles and catching them with both hands

   E. Sorting game with tweezers to pick up small items

   F. Imitating a 3-D block design using 1-inch (2.54 cm) blocks

47. A COTA is selecting an activity for a group of children who are 3 years old and have mild developmental delay. The primary purpose of the group is to promote coordinated movements of both upper extremities. Which activity would be **MOST BENEFICIAL** for supporting the group goal?

   A. Rolling a large therapy ball to each other
   B. Playing dress-up to imitate action heroes
   C. Playing prone-lying scooter board games
   D. Jumping rope in rhythm to a well-known song

48. Which interventions are **MOST BENEFICIAL** for a client who has venous insufficiency and moderate edema of the lower extremity?

Select the 3 best choices.

   A. Elevating the lower extremity above the heart
   B. Wearing compression stockings
   C. Applying pneumatic pumps
   D. Encouraging the client to work in a standing position
   E. Massaging the leg when painful
   F. Applying ice pack or cold compress

49. A client who sustained a 35% total body surface area burn involving the shoulder, elbow, and chest has just received the first set of compression garments. What information should be provided as part of the client education during the initial fitting session with the client?

Select the 3 best choices.

   A. Garment wear can be discontinued after 2 months.
   B. Wear the garments at least 23 hours per day.
   C. Loose-fitting areas around joint creases are acceptable.
   D. Avoid applying lotions to the skin prior to donning the garments.
   E. Remove the garments for bathing activities.
   F. Observe for signs of skin irritation from zippers and seams.

50. A 2-year-old child with a congenital transradial amputation of the right arm is being fitted for a prosthesis for the first time. Which caregiver instructions are important for the COTA to include in the education for proper daily care of the residual limb and prosthesis?

Select the 3 best choices.

- **A.** Apply moisturizer before donning the device.
- **B.** Change the prosthetic sock routinely.
- **C.** Check skin for signs of irritation.
- **D.** Report pressure areas immediately.
- **E.** Soak the residual limb in warm water.
- **F.** Tighten mechanical parts of the device.

51. An inpatient has hemiplegia secondary to a recent CVA and is preparing for discharge to live at home with a spouse. The patient has persistent edema of the affected upper extremity despite using proper positioning techniques. One of the intervention goals is to teach the patient methods for managing the edema after discharge. Which action would be **MOST BENEFICIAL** to include as part of the intervention for supporting this goal?

- **A.** Fabricate a resting hand splint for the patient to wear at all times.
- **B.** Instruct the patient on how to perform retrograde massage techniques.
- **C.** Provide the patient with handout instructions for preparing home paraffin baths.
- **D.** Teach the patient and caregiver to use manual lymphatic treatment techniques.

52. A client has spastic hemiplegia secondary to a left CVA several months ago. One of the intervention goals is to teach the primary caregiver proper positioning techniques for reducing the client's muscle tone and providing sensory input when the client is side lying on the affected side in bed. What instructions should the COTA provide the caregiver to properly position the client in order to achieve this goal?

Select the 3 best choices.

- **A.** Place the right scapula in full protraction with the shoulder flexed to 90°.
- **B.** Position a pillow under the left leg with the knee and hip in flexion.
- **C.** Flex the left elbow to 90° and place the affected hand in a palm down position.
- **D.** Avoid using a pillow under the head, neck, and upper shoulders.
- **E.** Maintain the affected hip in extension and the knee in slight flexion.
- **F.** Use a pillow between the torso and upper arm to slightly adduct the left shoulder.

53. A client who sustained an irreversible radial nerve injury had a tendon transfer of the pronator teres to extensor carpi radialis brevis muscle 8 weeks ago. The client has difficulty activating the muscle for its newly intended function of wrist extension. Which technique would be **MOST BENEFICIAL** to use for recruiting the donor muscle to extend the wrist?

Select the 3 best choices.

- **A.** Gently tap along the antagonist muscles during ROM exercises.
- **B.** Instruct the client to simultaneously perform wrist extension with both hands.
- **C.** Apply vibration to the pronator teres prior to the start of active wrist extension exercises.
- **D.** Fabricate an immobilization orthosis to support the wrist and digits in extension.
- **E.** Encourage the client to extend the wrist in an ulnar direction as much as possible.
- **F.** Ask the client to imagine completing a simple task using the involved hand.

54. A child who has spastic hemiplegic cerebral palsy wants to independently play with toy cars on a mat placed on the floor. Which position is **MOST EFFECTIVE** for reducing the child's muscle tone to meet this objective?

   A. Side lying on the affected side supported by pillows

   B. Long-sitting on the floor while leaning against a wall

   C. Prone over a firm cylindrical bolster

55. Which technique would be **MOST EFFECTIVE** for a client to use for managing the symptoms of COPD during a functional task at home?

   A. Breathing out when pushing items and breathing in when pulling items

   B. Inhaling through the mouth and exhaling through the nose when lifting

   C. Taking shallow, quick breaths whenever shortness of breath occurs

   D. Crossing both arms across the chest when breathing becomes difficult

56. A client with relapsing-remitting multiple sclerosis is 7 days postpartum. The client requires minimal assistance for unsupported sitting balance, has mild incoordination of the upper extremity, and is able to independently complete self-care in a seated position. The client wants to learn how to safely hold the infant. Which positions should the COTA teach the client to use for supporting this goal?

Select the 3 best choices.

A. Side lying on a bed with the client and the infant facing each other

B. Supine in a bed with the infant in a nearby baby seat secured to a raised safety frame

C. Supported in an arm chair with the infant in an over-the-shoulder sling baby carrier

D. Seated on the edge of the bed with the infant placed on a C-shaped nursing pillow

E. Propped against a 45° wedge cushion with the infant held on the chest

F. Semi-reclined in a gliding rocking chair with the infant supported in supine on the client's lap

57. A COTA is using a pediatric constraint-induced movement therapy (P-CIMT) approach during intervention for a 5-year-old child who has hemiplegic cerebral palsy. Which elements, when used together, are **MOST IMPORTANT** to incorporate into the overall intervention strategy when using the P-CIMT approach?

Select the 3 best choices.

A. Apply a mitt to the child's unaffected upper extremity at the start of an activity.

B. Engage the child in familiar play activities using only the affected upper extremity.

C. Implement the intervention activities in the clinic environment as much as possible.

D. Limit the use of the intervention approach to a maximum of 2 hours per day.

E. Provide the child's parents with activity suggestions for encouraging bilateral play.

F. Teach the child's parents how to implement this strategy as part of the child's typical daily tasks.

58. A 5-year-old child has moderate hypertonicity secondary to cerebral palsy. Increased muscle tone interferes with the child's ability to complete dressing independently. Which technique would be **MOST EFFECTIVE** for reducing the child's muscle tone prior to initiating a dressing task?

    A. Bouncing the child up and down on a large therapy ball

    B. Having the child gently rock forward and backward in quadruped

    C. Using quick tapping to the spastic muscle bellies

    D. Applying heavy joint compression to both arms

59. A COTA is preparing to fabricate a thermoplastic anti-spasticity hand orthosis for a school-age child. Which orthotic material characteristics would be **BEST** for this type of orthosis?

    A. Bonds to itself

    B. High rigidity

    C. Stretches easily

60. An OTR and a COTA are collaborating to select a thermoplastic material to use when fabricating a long-arm posterior elbow immobilization orthosis for a client who sustained a proximal radius fracture. What material characteristics are **OPTIMAL** for this type of orthosis?

    Select the 3 best choices.

    A. Low conformability

    B. High rigidity

    C. High drapability

    D. High conformability

    E. 1/8" thickness material

    F. 1/16" thickness material

61. A 5-year-old child has poor wrist stability and decreased fine motor coordination secondary to spastic cerebral palsy. One of the intervention goals is to fabricate a wrist orthosis to improve functional use of the hands to support independence with self-feeding. Which of the following options represent challenges associated with fabricating the orthosis for this child?

Select the 3 best choices.

A. Inconsistent nature of the child's hypertonicity

B. Child's fear of the unfamiliar clinic environment

C. Limitations in types and colors of thermoplastics

D. Inability to protect vulnerable areas of the hand

E. Lack of commercially available stretch resistant materials

F. Length of time to completely cool the material

62. A patient sustained a complete C_6 spinal cord injury several weeks ago. One of the intervention goals is to maximize independence with self-feeding. Which assistive device would be **MOST BENEFICIAL** for the patient to use during meals to support this goal?

A. Switch-operated feeder

B. Mobile arm support

C. Tenodesis orthosis

D. Wrist cock-up splint

63. A preschool student who has spastic diplegia cerebral palsy wants to play with peers during floor-time activities in the classroom. The COTA assists the student to sit on the floor, but tight hamstring muscles make it difficult for the student to sit comfortably. Which intervention is **MOST EFFECTIVE** for enabling the student to sit on the floor to participate in play activities with peers?

A. Positioning a triangular-shaped wedge under the knees

B. Placing lateral supports beside the student

C. Strapping a small pillow under the student's ankles

64. An OTR and a COTA are selecting a manual wheelchair for a client who has flaccid hemiplegia and will be using a wheelchair for most mobility. Which of the following features are **OPTIMAL** to include in the wheelchair specifications for this client?

Select the 3 best choices.

A. Standard sling seat

B. Detachable arm rests

C. Swing-away footrests

D. Elevating leg rests

E. Adjustable recline

F. Wheel with two hand rims

65. A COTA is working with a resident in a skilled nursing facility during mealtime in the dining room. One of the resident's goals is to independently self-feed. The COTA determines that the resident initially sits upright in the wheelchair, but throughout the meal leans laterally to one side and slides forward in the chair. Which action would be **MOST BENEFICIAL** to include as part of the positioning recommendation for supporting the self-feeding goal?

A. Use wheelchair accessories to support the resident's hips, knees, and ankles in 90° of flexion.

B. Position the resident approximately 30 inches (76.2 cm) from the plate and utensils at the table.

C. Modify the chair by measuring the width of the resident's hips and adding 2 inches (5.08 cm).

66. An adolescent sustained a C_8 spinal cord injury several months ago. One of the outpatient intervention goals is for the adolescent to be independent in functional mobility on all indoor surfaces and level outdoor terrain. What type of mobility equipment would be **MOST BENEFICIAL** for supporting this goal?

    A. Lightweight folding wheelchair with modified rims

    B. Power wheelchair with reclining back and chin control

    C. Adjustable wheeled stander with sip and puff switch

    D. Standard wheelchair with removable arms and leg rests

67. A resident has poor motor control and incoordination of the dominant upper extremity secondary to cerebellar ataxia. One of the goals is to help the resident independently self-feed. Which assistive device would be **MOST BENEFICIAL** for the resident to use for supporting this goal?

    A. Plastic-coated, angled spoon

    B. Eating utensil with a built-up handle

    C. Scoop dish with a suction cup base

68. An older adult who has osteoarthritis sits on a shower seat while in the tub but is unable to reach all body parts when bathing. Which adaptive equipment would be **MOST BENEFICIAL** to promote independence when bathing?

    Select the 3 best choices.

    A. Long-handled sponge

    B. Laminated visual cue cards

    C. Hand-held shower

    D. Anti-slip shower mat

    E. Water temperature control device

    F. Suction cup soap holder

69. A student who is in the third grade has illegible handwriting due to a mild sensory processing disorder. The student does not space letters and words uniformly on the paper. What is the **FIRST** handwriting solution the COTA should use to help improve the student's handwriting?

   A. Encourage the teacher to allow the student extra time to complete desktop activities.

   B. Provide the student with a keyboard and computer to use for written assignments.

   C. Have the student write on paper with raised lines and use a finger to guide spacing.

70. An inpatient has Fair minus (3-/5) functional muscle strength of the dominant upper extremity and of the dominant hand. One of the patient's goals is to independently brush teeth. Which assistive device would be **CONTRAINDICATED** for the patient to use for supporting this goal?

   A. Toothbrush with a built-up handle

   B. Weighted electric toothbrush

   C. Automatic toothpaste dispenser

71. During a self-feeding session, the COTA teaches a client to use the adaptive utensil pictured below. What is the **PRIMARY** reason for recommending a client use this type of device?

A. Impaired gross motor coordination

B. Weak hand and grasp strength

C. Limited upper extremity AROM

72. An inpatient sustained an incomplete T_2 spinal cord injury (ASIA C) several weeks ago. One of the intervention goals is for the patient to be independent with wheelchair transfers. The patient is able to transfer without assistive devices from the bed to the wheelchair but requires moderate assistance when completing transfers from the wheelchair to a standard toilet. What is the **NEXT** action the COTA should take to support the patient's progress with this transfer skill?

A. Encourage the patient to use a bedside commode instead of the bathroom toilet.

B. Teach the patient to use a sliding board transfer to a raised toilet seat.

C. Complete a manual muscle test to determine the patient's triceps strength.

D. Evaluate the difference in height between the wheelchair and the toilet.

73. A client in a home health setting has stage 2 Parkinson's disease. The client had a recent decline in function and is now learning to use a walker for mobility in the home. The COTA is teaching the client how to transport food items in the kitchen using the walker with an attached tray. What information should the COTA include as part of the instructions for minimizing fall risk during this task?

    A. Stand inside the frame of the walker and turn slowly.

    B. Turn the walker to the desired direction then move the legs.

    C. Move the walker to one side and use the counter for support.

    D. Place one hand on the counter and the other on the walker to move it.

74. A client sustained a complete T_2 spinal cord injury several months ago. The client is learning compensatory strategies to use for promoting independence and safety during homemaking activities. One of the client's goals is to be able to prepare family meals independently. Which environmental modification would promote progress toward this goal?

    A. Positioning an angled mirror above the stove

    B. Replacing stove knobs with larger handles

    C. Using smaller pans with extended handles

    D. Stirring hot liquids with rubber-coated cooking utensils

75. A COTA is recommending home modifications for an inpatient who has general debility secondary to pneumonia. Currently, the patient independently performs ADL but needs a rest break every 5 minutes. The patient is preparing for discharge to live with a spouse in a single-level apartment with 3 stairs to enter. Which adaptations should be included as part of the discharge recommendations?

    A. Post safety reminders on the wall in a clearly visible location.

    B. Install a ramp with no more than a 5° incline.

    C. Remove clutter and loose rugs in commonly used living areas.

Answer Key

Domain 2 Sample Items

Item Number	Key
1.	A
2.	A
3.	C
4.	C
5.	D
6.	A
7.	C
8.	B
9.	C
10.	B
11.	D
12.	C
13.	A
14.	C
15.	B
16.	A
17.	B
18.	A
19.	C
20.	A
21.	A, C, F
22.	A
23.	C
24.	A
25.	C

Item Number	Key
26.	C
27.	A, C, F
28.	C
29.	B
30.	D
31.	C
32.	A
33.	B, C, E
34.	C, E, F
35.	A, C, E
36.	B
37.	B
38.	A
39.	A
40.	A
41.	B
42.	A
43.	A, D, F
44.	B
45.	C
46.	B, C, E
47.	A
48.	A, B, C
49.	B, E, F
50.	B, C, D

Item Number	Key
51.	B
52.	A, B, E
53.	B, C, F
54.	A
55.	A
56.	A, C, E
57.	A, B, F
58.	B
59.	B
60.	A, B, E
61.	A, B, F
62.	C
63.	A
64.	B, C, F
65.	A
66.	A
67.	C
68.	A, C, F
69.	C
70.	B
71.	B
72.	D
73.	A
74.	A
75.	C

Multiple Choice Answers, Rationales, and References

DOMAIN 02

1. A kindergarten-age student who has spastic cerebral palsy is painting while seated at a table in art class. The student can hold a paintbrush, but a dominant asymmetrical tonic neck reflex prevents the student from reaching for the paint located near the student's dominant side. Which technique would be **MOST EFFECTIVE** to use to inhibit this reflex and support the student's success with the art task?

    A. Place the paint at midline in front of the student.

    B. Provide the student with a paintbrush with a weighted handle.

    C. Adapt the tabletop to a 45° elevated angle.

    D. Have the student use a standing frame while painting.

Correct Answer: A

RATIONALE:
Head movements to either side can trigger the asymmetrical tonic neck reflex (ATNR). Placing the paint in front of the student is **MOST EFFECTIVE** for minimizing side-to-side head movements.

Reference:
Solomon, J. W., & O'Brien, J. C. (2016). *Pediatric skills for occupational therapy assistants* (4th ed., pp. 80-84, 318-319, 325-326). St. Louis, MO: Mosby Elsevier.

2. A client has referred pain symptoms associated with a back injury from a fall 6 months ago. Which physical agent modality would be **MOST BENEFICIAL** to use as an adjunct to activities for pain management?

   A. Transcutaneous electrical nerve stimulation

   B. Neuromuscular electrical stimulation

   C. Nonthermal phonophoresis ultrasound

Correct Answer: A

RATIONALE:

Transcutaneous electrical nerve stimulation (TENS) is a physical agent modality used to reduce symptoms associated with chronic pain. TENS is used as an adjunct to activity or while performing an activity.

Reference:
Mahle, A. J., & Ward, L. W. (2019). *Adult physical conditions: Intervention strategies for occupational therapy assistants* (pp. 464-466, 470-471). Philadelphia, PA: F.A. Davis.

3. A COTA working at an assisted living facility is planning to take 8-10 residents on an outing to a restaurant. Several of the residents have hearing impairments. The COTA plans to contact the restaurant in advance of the outing to ask for a table arrangement conducive to the group's socialization. Which table setup would be **BEST** for this purpose?

   A. U-shaped table located close to the kitchen, so the residents are comfortable speaking loudly to each other.

   B. Rectangular table in a busy section of the restaurant so loud talking will not disturb other patrons.

   C. Round dining table that will comfortably accommodate both the residents and the COTA.

   D. Several small tables positioned directly under a fluorescent overhead light, so residents are able to read and discuss menu options.

Correct Answer: C

RATIONALE:
The social aspects of dining are enhanced if the residents who have hearing impairments are seated at a round table. This allows the residents to clearly see and make eye contact with others when talking.

Reference:
Lohman, H., Byers-Connon, S., & Padilla, R. L. (2019). *Occupational therapy with elders: Strategies for the COTA* (4th ed., pp. 238-239). Maryland Heights, MO: Mosby Elsevier.

4. A client has mild hemiparesis secondary to having a left CVA several months ago. One of the client's goals is to increase strength and fine motor control to be able to play the piano, a favorite leisure activity. Which activity would be **MOST BENEFICIAL** to include in the intervention to support progress toward this goal?

   A. Making a pinch pot using firm modeling clay

   B. Manipulating pegs of various sizes and stringing one-inch (2.54 cm) beads

   C. Practicing a repetitive program of piano keyboard drills

   D. Completing resistive exercises while listening to piano music

Correct Answer: C

RATIONALE:
This activity is **MOST BENEFICIAL** because it involves working on fine motor skills using an activity that is meaningful and important to the client.

Reference:
Early, M.B. (2013). *Physical dysfunction practice skills for the occupational therapy assistant* (3rd ed., pp. 377-378). St. Louis, MO: Elsevier Mosby.

5. A client is working on a needlework project for a grandchild's birthday but is having difficulty finishing the project due to low vision from early stage cataracts. The client is scheduled for cataract surgery, but the surgery date is after the grandchild's birthday. Which compensatory technique should the COTA recommend to promote the client's ability to finish the needlework project in time for the birthday?

   A. Advise the client to use high-contrast colored thread.
   B. Place the project in an adjustable frame.
   C. Reduce the amount of ambient light in the room.
   D. Provide the client with a lighted, hands-free magnifier.

Correct Answer: D

RATIONALE:
In the early stage of cataract development, a magnifier can be a helpful device to compensate for inadequate visual acuity.

Reference:
Lohman, H., Byers-Connon, S., & Padilla, R. L. (2019). *Occupational therapy with elders: Strategies for the COTA* (4th ed., pp. 219, 224-225). Maryland Heights, MO: Mosby Elsevier.

6. A 9-year-old child who has moderate hemiplegia often neglects to use the affected upper extremity. Which activity would be **MOST BENEFICIAL** for encouraging the child's bilateral fine motor control?

   A. **Playing with a hand-held video game**

   B. Tossing a beanbag at a target

   C. Playing a game of darts

   D. Drawing on a chalkboard

Correct Answer: A

RATIONALE:
Of the choices provided, this is the only activity that promotes bilateral hand use.

Reference:
Solomon, J. W., & O'Brien, J. C. (2016). *Pediatric skills for occupational therapy assistants* (4th ed., p. 507). St. Louis, MO: Mosby Elsevier.

7. Pictured below are children putting on dress-up clothes during unstructured play time. What type of play does this represent?

   A. Constructive
   B. Exploratory
   C. Pretend

Correct Answer: C

RATIONALE:
Pretend play is characterized by playing dress-up and make-believe games.

Reference:
Solomon, J. W., & O'Brien, J. C. (2016). *Pediatric skills for occupational therapy assistants* (4th ed., p. 421). St. Louis, MO: Mosby Elsevier.

8. A client has an intense fear of grocery shopping due to an anxiety disorder. The client is a homemaker whose goal is to be able to buy food for a family meal. Which method is **BEST** for promoting initial progress toward goal achievement?

   A. Take the client on an outing to a local convenience store.

   B. Teach the client to divide the grocery shopping task into manageable steps.

   C. Simulate grocery shopping tasks during several sessions in the clinic.

Correct Answer: B

RATIONALE:
Breaking the whole task into smaller steps is less overwhelming for the client and allows for initial progress toward the client's goal.

Reference:
Early, M. B. (2017). *Mental health concepts & techniques for the occupational therapy assistant* (5th ed., pp. 513-514). Philadelphia, PA: Lippincott Williams & Wilkins.

9. An adolescent who has a conduct disorder is participating in an OT group to increase socialization skills using a skills acquisition model. While playing a familiar board game, the adolescent loses a turn, becomes frustrated, and demands to play something else. How should the COTA respond to the adolescent's behavior?

   A. Modify the game rules to promote success.

   B. Excuse the adolescent from the activity session.

   C. Encourage the adolescent to complete the activity.

   D. Allow the adolescent to select another activity.

Correct Answer: C

RATIONALE:
Encouraging the adolescent to continue to participate in playing the board game develops and reinforces positive behaviors in the adolescent.

References:
Early, M. B. (2017). *Mental health concepts & techniques for the occupational therapy assistant* (5th ed., pp. 180, 485). Philadelphia, PA: Lippincott Williams & Wilkins.

Bonder, B. R. (2015). *Psychopathology and function* (5th ed., pp. 306-308). Thorofare, NJ: SLACK, Inc.

10. A resident of a long-term care facility has moderately severe cognitive decline secondary to dementia. The resident occasionally becomes combative during morning BADL. What **INITIAL** action should the COTA take when these behaviors occur?

    A. Allow for nursing staff to complete the dressing session.

    B. Identify the possible factors that provoked the behavior.

    C. Use a firm voice to tell the resident to stop the behavior.

    D. Delay the session until later in the afternoon.

Correct Answer: B

RATIONALE:
The COTA should **INITIALLY** consider the factors that contributed to the combative behaviors. This allows the COTA to identify effective solutions for deescalating the agitation.

Reference:
Lohman, H., Byers-Connon, S., & Padilla, R. L. (2019). *Occupational therapy with elders: Strategies for the COTA* (4th ed., pp. 285-288). Maryland Heights, MO: Mosby Elsevier.

11. A resident of a long-term care facility has moderately severe cognitive decline secondary to Alzheimer's disease. Each afternoon when nursing staff change shifts, the resident becomes agitated and attempts to elope from the nursing facility, stating, "I need to go back to work." Which action would be **MOST EFFECTIVE** for redirecting the resident's attention and decreasing the risk of elopement?

   A. Have the resident participate in a simple craft activity.

   B. Take the resident outside for a walk around the facility.

   C. Encourage the resident to watch television in the day room.

   D. Begin a reminiscence activity related to something the resident likes.

Correct Answer: D

RATIONALE:
"Sun-downing," plus the disruptions surrounding a shift change, can cause someone who has Alzheimer's disease to become agitated and confused. Engaging the resident in a reminiscence activity related to something of value to the resident would help to redirect the resident away from sources of confusion during this time of the day.

Reference:
Lohman, H., Byers-Connon, S., & Padilla, R. L. (2019). *Occupational therapy with elders: Strategies for the COTA* (4th ed., pp. 285-288). Maryland Heights, MO: Mosby Elsevier.

12. An older adult client who has mild macular degeneration is referred to OT. The client is an avid reader and subscribes to several magazines. The client is experiencing progressive difficulty reading the magazines due to the reflective glare from the glossy paper. Which **INITIAL** adaptation should the COTA recommend to the client to support participation in this preferred leisure activity?

    A. Obtain audio and large-print books and magazines from a local library.

    B. Subscribe to satellite radio to be able to listen to books and news stories.

    C. Direct the lighting source from behind the shoulder when reading.

    D. Contact publishers for availability of non-glare print issues of the publication.

Correct Answer: C

RATIONALE:
Positioning the light source behind the client's shoulder will prevent the reflective glare from glossy magazine paper from pointing into the client's eyes while reading.

Reference:
Lohman, H., Byers-Connon, S., & Padilla, R. L. (2019). *Occupational therapy with elders: Strategies for the COTA* (4th ed., p. 220). Maryland Heights, MO: Mosby Elsevier.

13. A client who has reduced visual acuity reports difficulty preparing meals due to the low vision. Which kitchen modification would be **MOST BENEFICIAL** to include as a recommendation for supporting the client's participation with meal preparation tasks?

    A. Label food items in large print using high-contrast colors.

    B. Use fluorescent bulbs in household light fixtures.

    C. Keep frequently used items on the countertop.

    D. Replace wooden cabinet doors with glass panels.

Correct Answer: A

RATIONALE:
Symptoms of decreased visual acuity include inability to see objects clearly, difficulty distinguishing visual details, and difficulty discriminating contrast and colors. Labeling food items with large-print labels and high-contrast colors would be **MOST BENEFICIAL** for enabling clients with decreased visual acuity to use the remaining vision to enhance functional performance.

Reference:
Early, M.B. (2013). *Physical dysfunction practice skills for the occupational therapy assistant* (3rd ed., p. 441). St. Louis, MO: Elsevier Mosby.

14. An adolescent client has an eating disorder and attends a partial hospitalization program. The client refuses to come to a scheduled OT group. What is the **FIRST** action the COTA should take based on this refusal?

    A. Respect the client's right to decline treatment.

    B. Contact the client's primary caregiver.

    C. Determine the client's reason for not participating.

Correct Answer: C

RATIONALE:
The COTA should **FIRST** collaborate with the client to ascertain their reason for refusal. As part of the therapeutic relationship, the COTA and client should work together to establish meaningful goals and interventions.

References:
Early, M. B. (2017). *Mental health concepts & techniques for the occupational therapy assistant* (5th ed., pp. 285-287, 297-298). Philadelphia, PA: Lippincott Williams & Wilkins.

Jacobs, K., & MacRae, N. (Eds.). (2017). *Occupational therapy essentials for clinical competence* (3rd ed., pp. 138-139). Thorofare, NJ: SLACK, Inc.

15. A COTA is selecting a group intervention for an inpatient who has paranoid schizophrenia. The patient has transitioned from being self-isolative to tolerating being around several people at the same time. Which type of group would support the patient's social development?

   A. Parallel

   B. Project

   C. Egocentric-cooperative

   D. Cooperative

Correct Answer: B

RATIONALE:
A project group would assist the patient in feeling accepted by others while engaging in valued activities that encourage cooperation and socialization.

Reference:
Early, M. B. (2017). *Mental health concepts & techniques for the occupational therapy assistant* (5th ed., pp. 374, 376-377). Philadelphia, PA: Lippincott Williams & Wilkins.

16. A COTA leads a variety of groups for clients participating in a community-based mental health program. What would be the **PRIMARY** role of the COTA when leading an egocentric-cooperative group in this setting?

    A. **Assisting the participants in developing and discussing group norms**
    B. Helping the participants select tasks for their specific skill level
    C. Providing suggestions for helping the group make a decision
    D. Setting limits for specified short-term projects or activities

Correct Answer: A

RATIONALE:
Participants in an egocentric-cooperative group are able to discuss group goals and norms and have the ability to work cooperatively with peers to meet the goals of the group.

Reference:
Early, M. B. (2017). *Mental health concepts & techniques for the occupational therapy assistant* (5th ed., pp. 374, 377). Philadelphia, PA: Lippincott Williams & Wilkins.

17. What should be the **INITIAL** focus of an activity group for inpatients who have been undergoing treatment for major depression?

    A. Completion of a simple craft project
    B. **Participation in a short-term familiar task**
    C. Interaction in a structured setting
    D. Diversion from the hospital environment

Correct Answer: B

RATIONALE:
To support progress in patients who have major depression, the **INITIAL** focus of the group should be on activities that have a high opportunity for success.

Reference:
Early, M. B. (2017). *Mental health concepts & techniques for the occupational therapy assistant* (5th ed., pp. 317-319). Philadelphia, PA: Lippincott Williams & Wilkins.

18. A COTA is selecting activities for an inpatient who recently had a CVA and has tactile agnosia. The goal of the activity is to improve the patient's awareness of objects located in the affected hand. Which activity would be **MOST EFFECTIVE** for promoting progress toward this goal?

A. Using vision to identify coins placed in the hand

B. Sorting various coins into separate piles

C. Picking up pennies and dropping them into a jar

Correct Answer: A

RATIONALE:
Tactile agnosia is the lack of ability to identify objects using the tactile system. Intervention includes teaching the client to use the visual system to compensate for the deficit.

Reference:
Mahle, A. J., & Ward, L. W. (2019). *Adult physical conditions: Intervention strategies for occupational therapy assistants* (p. 233). Philadelphia, PA: F.A. Davis.

19. A kindergarten student, who has a sensory modulation disorder, intentionally bumps into walls and forcefully throws objects when playing on the playground. Which sensory stimulation activity is **MOST EFFECTIVE** for promoting a reduction of these behaviors?

    A. Spinning the student in a net swing using a predictable rhythm

    B. Having the student search for objects hidden in a container of uncooked rice

    C. Allowing the student to jump up and down in an immersion pool of balls

Correct Answer: C

RATIONALE:
This student is demonstrating sensory-seeking behaviors that warrant proprioceptive stimulation and activities that encourage active, gross motor movements.

References:
Case-Smith, J., & O'Brien, J. C. (2015). *Occupational therapy for children and adolescents* (7th ed., pp. 271-273). St. Louis, MO: Mosby Elsevier.

Wagenfeld, A., & Kaldenberg, J. (Eds.). (2017). *Foundations of pediatric practice for the occupational therapy assistant* (3rd ed., pp. 165-166). Thorofare, NJ: SLACK, Inc.

20. During a bathing session, a client who has schizoaffective disorder begins talking about faces appearing on the wall. Which action should the COTA take in response to this observation?

    A. Provide reassurance and redirect the client to the activity.

    B. Respond using humor and offer to discuss the bugs on the wall.

    C. Use a calm voice and ask the client to stop the negative behavior.

Correct Answer: A

RATIONALE:
A client who is experiencing visual hallucinations may feel frightened or anxious. Talking in a calm voice reassures the client, and redirecting the client to a purposeful activity assists in minimizing the impact of the hallucination.

Reference:
Early, M. B. (2017). *Mental health concepts & techniques for the occupational therapy assistant* (5th ed., pp. 322-324). Philadelphia, PA: Lippincott Williams & Wilkins.

21. A patient with Alzheimer's disease is admitted to a skilled nursing facility from home following a recent decline in function. Evaluation results indicate the patient has moderately severe cognitive decline with major memory deficits that impact completion of BADL tasks. The COTA is planning a self-care intervention session using task segmentation strategies to assist the patient with dressing tasks. Which verbal prompts would support the patient's task completion?

    Select the 3 best choices.

    A. **"Pick up one sock from the bed. Place the sock on the right foot. Pull the sock up."**

    B. "Pants with an elastic waistband are easier to get on than pants with a zipper."

    C. **"Put the T-shirt over your head. Reach up and put one arm through the sleeve."**

    D. "Choose a pair of lace-up shoes from the closet and put them on."

    E. "It's a cold day today. Why don't you put on a long-sleeved sweater?"

    F. **"Undo the buttons of the shirt. I'll help you place your arm in the sleeve."**

    Correct Answers: A, C, F

    RATIONALE:
    Clients at this level of function have the most success when verbal cues are provided using a direct communication style and instructions for a multi-step task are broken down and provided one step at a time.

    References:
    Early, M.B. (2013). *Physical dysfunction practice skills for the occupational therapy assistant* (3rd ed., pp. 528-529). St. Louis, MO: Elsevier Mosby.

    Lohman, H., Byers-Connon, S., & Padilla, R. L. (2019). *Occupational therapy with elders: Strategies for the COTA* (4th ed., pp. 289-291). Maryland Heights, MO: Mosby Elsevier.

22. A student in second grade recently witnessed domestic violence in the home and has symptoms of post-traumatic stress disorder (PTSD). One of the intervention priorities is for the student to develop coping strategies to manage the symptoms associated with the condition. Which initial action would be **MOST BENEFICIAL** for the COTA to include in the intervention for this student?

   A. Develop a calm and sensory-friendly space for the student at school.

   B. Consult with the student's family about the safety of the home environment.

   C. Offer a session for all students in the classroom to learn relaxing yoga poses.

Correct Answer: A

RATIONALE:
A student who has experienced trauma benefits from a safe, sensory-friendly room or environment to manage the symptoms of PTSD.

Reference:
Manville, C. A., & Keough, J. L. (2016). *Mental health practice for the occupational therapy assistant*. (p. 70). Thorofare, NJ: SLACK Inc.

23. A student in the first grade has a mild visual perceptual deficit. The teacher reports the student is a good auditory learner but often writes letters and numbers backward when completing class assignments. Which activity would be **MOST BENEFICIAL** for improving the student's directionality when writing?

    A. Playing a game of follow-the-leader to form letters in the air

    B. Having the student repetitively practice forming letters on paper

    C. Teaching the student to use rhymes that describe how to form letters

    D. Providing the student with worksheets to trace letters of the alphabet

Correct Answer: C

RATIONALE:
Creating rhymes about school assignments is **MOST BENEFICIAL** in helping the student to process, remember, and recall information through the use of language cues.

Reference:
Solomon, J. W., & O'Brien, J. C. (2016). *Pediatric skills for occupational therapy assistants* (4th ed., p. 442). St. Louis, MO: Mosby Elsevier.

24. A COTA is planning a developmental activity program for preschool students. One of the students who attends the program has spina bifida. All of the students are cognitively intact and range in age from 3-4 years old. What type of group activity would maximize participation for all students?

    A. Symbolic play using a variety of puppets

    B. Tabletop board games with standard rules

    C. Imaginative play using small snap-together blocks

    D. Gross motor games that include jumping and catching

Correct Answer: A

RATIONALE:
Children at this developmental stage typically engage in pretend play by acting out scenarios with dolls and dress-up toys.

Reference:
Solomon, J. W., & O'Brien, J. C. (2016). *Pediatric skills for occupational therapy assistants* (4th ed., pp. 108, 110, 212-213). St. Louis, MO: Mosby Elsevier.

25. An adolescent client has moderate cognitive delays. The client, who is a visual learner, wants to learn to shave using an electric razor. What is the **FIRST** method the COTA should use when teaching this skill to the client?

A. Provide the client with a step-by-step written list of instructions.

B. Use a hand-over-hand technique and assist the client to shave.

C. **Demonstrate the task to the client while standing at the sink.**

Correct Answer: C

RATIONALE:

Visual learners acquire information best through seeing a skill or task performed.

References:
Early, M.B. (2013). *Physical dysfunction practice skills for the occupational therapy assistant* (3rd ed., pp. 455-456). St. Louis, MO: Elsevier Mosby.

Solomon, J. W., & O'Brien, J. C. (2016). *Pediatric skills for occupational therapy assistants* (4th ed., p. 442). St. Louis, MO: Mosby Elsevier.

26. A patient has a visual field deficit secondary to a recent CVA. This interferes with the patient's ability to dress independently. Which task represents the **MOST EFFECTIVE** intervention method for visual field deficits to support the patient's independence with dressing?

   A. Encouraging the patient to bear weight through the affected side during dressing tasks

   B. Teaching the patient to place the non-affected extremity in a garment first when dressing

   C. **Having the patient practice organized scanning patterns to find specified clothing items**

Correct Answer: C

RATIONALE:
Intervention methods for a visual field deficit include teaching the patient visual scanning techniques and to follow an organized scan path during ADL.

References:
Early, M.B. (2013). *Physical dysfunction practice skills for the occupational therapy assistant* (3rd ed., p. 476). St. Louis, MO: Elsevier Mosby.

Radomski, M. V., & Trombly Latham, C. A. (Eds.). (2014). *Occupational therapy for physical dysfunction* (7th ed., p. 708). Philadelphia, PA: Lippincott Williams & Wilkins.

27. A student with a mild intellectual disability is enrolled in a mainstream third-grade class. The student frequently asks the teacher for assistance to tie shoelaces. The COTA plans to use backward chaining techniques to help the student manage shoe laces independently. Which techniques should the COTA include as part of the intervention when using this strategy?

Select the 3 best choices.

A. Have the student pull the laces to tighten the loops of the bow.

B. Teach the student to pull on the shoe lace to untie the shoe.

C. Reinforce the student's completion of the last steps of tying laces.

D. Start the session by having the student take both shoes off.

E. Provide the student with pictures illustrating each step of shoe-tying.

F. Provide hand-over-hand assistance during the initial steps of tying a shoe.

Correct Answers: A, C, F

RATIONALE:
The backward chaining technique involves helping the student complete all steps of the task up to the final step. Using this technique, the COTA allows the student to independently perform the final steps of the task.

References:
Early, M.B. (2013). *Physical dysfunction practice skills for the occupational therapy assistant* (3rd ed., p. 250). St. Louis, MO: Elsevier Mosby.

Solomon, J. W., & O'Brien, J. C. (2016). *Pediatric skills for occupational therapy assistants* (4th ed., p. 359). St. Louis, MO: Mosby Elsevier.

28. A resident of a skilled nursing facility who has moderate cognitive decline is beginning to have difficulty with self-feeding. Which method would be **MOST BENEFICIAL** for the COTA to teach the dining room staff to use when assisting this resident to self-feed?

- **A.** Backward chaining
- **B.** Forward chaining
- **C. Hand-over-hand assistance**
- **D.** Whole learning

Correct Answer: C

RATIONALE:
A resident at this stage of cognitive impairment benefits from hand-over-hand assistance for ADL tasks that are difficult.

Reference:
Early, M.B. (2013). *Physical dysfunction practice skills for the occupational therapy assistant* (3rd ed., p. 250). St. Louis, MO: Elsevier Mosby.

29. A client has mild-moderate cognitive decline secondary to dementia. The client has difficulty remembering when to take a prescribed medicine. One of the intervention goals is for the client to independently take medications at the correct dosage times. Which compensatory technique would be **MOST BENEFICIAL** for supporting this goal?

    A. Have a caregiver place medication in a 7-day pill storage container at the beginning of each week.

    B. Advise the client to wear a voice-message alarm preprogrammed to activate at specific times of the day.

    C. Teach the client to maintain a medication diary that outlines daily prescription medication requirements and dosage history.

    D. Provide the client with a pocket day-planner that indicates which medications to take each day.

Correct Answer: B

RATIONALE:
A voice-message alarm can be programmed by a caregiver to alert a client, who is functioning at this cognitive level, when it is time to take a medication and which medications should be taken.

Reference:
Lohman, H., Byers-Connon, S., & Padilla, R. L. (2019). *Occupational therapy with elders: Strategies for the COTA* (4th ed., pp. 178-180). Maryland Heights, MO: Mosby Elsevier.

30. A client has moderate cognitive decline secondary to dementia. This influences the client's ability to independently complete BADL. Which compensatory approach would be **MOST BENEFICIAL** to use to support the client's independence with grooming tasks?

   A. Paste sequential picture cards of grooming tasks on the bathroom door.

   B. Adhere simple step-by-step instructions for grooming to the bathroom mirror.

   C. Provide a toiletry kit for the client to store frequently used grooming items.

   D. **Place grooming items at eye level on a shelf by the bathroom sink.**

Correct Answer: D

RATIONALE:
A client who has moderate cognitive decline will benefit from task simplification and environmental adaptations, such as placing frequently used ADL items at eye level.

Reference:
Pendleton, H. M., & Schultz-Krohn, W. (Eds.). (2018). *Pedretti's occupational therapy: Practice skills for the physical dysfunction* (8th ed., pp. 881-882). St. Louis, MO: Mosby Elsevier.

31. An older adult client, who has rheumatoid arthritis, is able to chop vegetables but frequently experiences hand fatigue before completing the meal preparation tasks. Which is the **BEST** recommendation for improving the client's ability to complete the steps to prepare a meal?

   A. Encourage the client to purchase prepared meals to heat up in the microwave.

   B. Fabricate a hand-based orthotic to maintain joint alignment.

   C. Provide information about cooking utensils with ergonomic handles.

Correct Answer: C

RATIONALE:
Ergonomic handles will ease the client's hand fatigue caused by the repetitive movements associated with chopping vegetables.

Reference:
Mahle, A. J., & Ward, L. W. (2019). *Adult physical conditions: Intervention strategies for occupational therapy assistants* (pp. 545-546). Philadelphia, PA: F.A. Davis.

32. A COTA is using forward chaining to teach dressing skills to an inpatient who has hemiplegia. One of the intervention goals is for the patient to learn to put on a front-opening, button-down shirt. What is the **FIRST** task that should be initiated when using forward chaining to effectively promote goal achievement?

   A. **Encourage the patient to place the affected hand in the sleeve.**

   B. Ask the patient to fasten buttons of various sizes on a dressing board.

   C. Have the patient pull the buttons through each of the button holes.

Correct Answer: A

RATIONALE:
The forward chaining technique involves encouraging the patient to complete the first step independently and assisting the patient to complete the subsequent steps of a task or activity.

Reference:
Early, M.B. (2013). *Physical dysfunction practice skills for the occupational therapy assistant* (3rd ed., pp. 182, 250). St. Louis, MO: Elsevier Mosby.

33. An inpatient has severe upper extremity burn scar contractures. The patient is participating in OT to improve independence with grooming and personal hygiene. The COTA observes the patient has difficulty completing peritoneal hygiene after toileting. What actions should the COTA take based on this observation?

Select the 3 best choices.

  A. Develop a strengthening program to improve task performance.

  B. Identify compensatory methods needed for these tasks.

  C. Determine assistive devices to improve functional outcomes.

  D. Ask nursing staff to provide assistance as needed during self-care.

  E. Place ADL items in the bathroom within the patient's reach.

  F. Ensure the patient wears compression garments during toileting.

Correct Answers: B, C, E

RATIONALE:
Teaching adaptive and compensatory strategies will support the client's independence in ADL.

References:
Pendleton, H. M., & Schultz-Krohn, W. (Eds.). (2018). *Pedretti's occupational therapy: Practice skills for the physical dysfunction* (8th ed., pp. 1070-1071). St. Louis, MO: Mosby Elsevier.

Radomski, M. V., & Trombly Latham, C. A. (Eds.). (2014). *Occupational therapy for physical dysfunction* (7th ed., p. 1255). Philadelphia, PA: Lippincott Williams & Wilkins.

34. A COTA is teaching proper biomechanics to a client who has chronic low back pain. The client, who works as a garden landscaper, is required to lift and carry paving stones as part of the daily job tasks. Which technique should the COTA teach the client to use when engaging in this aspect of the job?

Select the 3 best choices.

   A. Carry the stone at chest height with elbows in full flexion.

   B. Position the feet close together when lowering the stone.

   C. Bend at the hips and knees when picking up the stone.

   D. Extend the lumbar spine slightly while carrying the stone.

   E. Keep the spine in alignment when holding the stone.

   F. Hold the stone as close to the body as possible.

Correct Answers: C, E, F

RATIONALE:
Following these principles of body mechanics will reduce the risk of a work-related injury during job demands that involve lifting and carrying.

Reference:
Radomski, M. V., & Trombly Latham, C. A. (Eds.). (2014). *Occupational therapy for physical dysfunction* (7th ed., p. 817). Philadelphia, PA: Lippincott Williams & Wilkins.

35. An inpatient in an addiction recovery hospital has been undergoing treatment for acute alcohol poisoning and a substance use disorder. During the discharge planning meeting, the patient asks for suggestions on ways to reduce the risk of relapse and to support long-term sobriety after returning home. What suggestions should the COTA provide to the patient to support this request?

    Select the 3 best choices.

    A. **Participate in a structured community-based recreation class.**

    B. Consider adopting a pet to divert attention away from any desire to use drugs or alcohol.

    C. **Make it a priority to routinely attend self-help and recovery support groups.**

    D. Sign a written contract to commit to a lifetime of long-term sobriety.

    E. **Engage in a daily schedule of preferred physical exercise.**

    F. Volunteer to be the designated driver whenever socializing with friends.

    Correct Answers: A, C, E

    RATIONALE:
    These options promote positive health behaviors that support a lifestyle in recovery.

    Reference:
    Wagenfeld, A. (2016). *Foundations of theory and practice for the occupational therapy assistant* (p. 586). Baltimore, MD: Lippincott Williams & Wilkins.

36. A client has recently been diagnosed with rheumatoid arthritis. The client works as a medical laboratory technician. Completing essential job tasks of frequently turning off equipment knobs and tightening specimen cup lids result in bilateral hand and wrist pain by the end of the work day. Which movements are **CONTRAINDICATED** for this client to use during these job tasks?

    A. Wrist extension

    B. **MCP joint ulnar deviation**

    C. Wrist ulnar deviation

    D. Composite finger extension

Correct Answer: B

RATIONALE:
MCP joint ulnar drift is a characteristic deformity associated with rheumatoid arthritis. To protect the MCP joints, clients who have rheumatoid arthritis should avoid movements that place these joints in ulnar deviation.

Reference:
Early, M.B. (2013). *Physical dysfunction practice skills for the occupational therapy assistant* (3rd ed., pp. 193-194, 573-574, 581-585). St. Louis, MO: Elsevier Mosby.

37. A patient who had a total hip replacement, anterolateral approach 2 weeks ago wants to lie on the non-affected hip while sleeping. Which adaptation should the patient use when sleeping in this position?

   A. Place a pillow under both feet.

   B. Use an abduction wedge between the legs.

   C. Sleep on memory foam or air mattress.

   D. Flex the affected hip, keeping the non-affected leg straight.

Correct Answer: B

RATIONALE:
To maintain correct hip position, the affected leg must be abducted and in alignment.

Reference:
Early, M.B. (2013). *Physical dysfunction practice skills for the occupational therapy assistant* (3rd ed., pp. 624, 630). St. Louis, MO: Elsevier Mosby.

38. A client has difficulty completing home management tasks due to symptoms associated with COPD. One of the intervention goals is for the client to learn techniques for reducing the impact of the disease symptoms on occupational performance. Which intervention should be included in the **INITIAL** phase of rehabilitation for supporting this goal?

   A. **Teach the client to use energy conservation techniques during BADL tasks.**

   B. Provide the client with a home program of upper body strengthening exercises.

   C. Have the client attend a series of stress management classes.

   D. Instruct the client on how to use visual imagery techniques for pain reduction.

Correct Answer: A

RATIONALE:
COPD typically causes dyspnea, shortness of breath, and fatigue. Learning energy conservation techniques during the **INITIAL** phase of rehabilitation will promote the client's functional performance within the limitations of the COPD symptoms.

Reference:
Early, M.B. (2013). *Physical dysfunction practice skills for the occupational therapy assistant* (3rd ed., pp. 682-687). St. Louis, MO: Elsevier Mosby.

39. A COTA is teaching a client, who recently had surgery for an L_4-L_5 discectomy and fusion, to use body mechanics as pictured below. The client is planning to retrieve a cooking utensil from the drawer. What is the **NEXT** instruction the COTA should provide to the client?

A. **Hold the utensil close to the body and straighten knees and hips to return to a standing position.**

B. Place the utensil on the counter and then use both hands to push into a standing position.

C. Hold on to the utensil and move one leg into extension behind the other leg to stand up.

Correct Answer: A

RATIONALE:
This option allows the client to hold the utensil close to the center of gravity and maintain the spine in alignment while transitioning from a squat position to a standing position.

References:
Early, M.B. (2013). *Physical dysfunction practice skills for the occupational therapy assistant* (3rd ed., pp. 191-193). St. Louis, MO: Elsevier Mosby.

Smith-Gabai, H., & Holm, S. (Eds.). (2017). *Occupational therapy in acute care* (2nd ed., p. 448). Bethesda, MD: AOTA Press.

40. A client who has chronic low back pain is participating in a pain management program. One of the intervention goals is for the client to learn proper body mechanics to use during personal laundry tasks. Which strategy should the COTA teach the client to use for promoting progress toward this goal?

- **A. Carry one small basket of laundry at a time to the laundry area.**
- B. Lift one large bundle of clothes from the washer to put into the dryer.
- C. Bend forward at the waist while loading clothes into the washer or dryer.
- D. Keep the feet shoulder-width apart when twisting the torso to place clothes into the dryer.

Correct Answer: A

RATIONALE:
Carrying one small basket of clothes at a time reduces stress on the muscles in the back.

Reference:
Early, M.B. (2013). *Physical dysfunction practice skills for the occupational therapy assistant* (3rd ed., pp. 191-193). St. Louis, MO: Elsevier Mosby.

41. An inpatient in a rehabilitation facility has hemiplegia, moderate short-term memory deficits, and impulsiveness secondary to a TBI 3 months ago. Currently, the patient requires moderate cueing for safety during BADL. The patient is preparing for transition to live at home with the spouse as the primary caregiver. One of the discharge goals is to teach the spouse safety techniques to use when the patient is showering in a stall shower at home. What instructions should the COTA include in the caregiver training to support this goal?

    A. Observe the patient throughout the task to be sure the patient holds onto the grab bar while standing in the shower.

    B. Have the patient sit on a bath stool with suction feet while providing stand-by assistance throughout the task.

    C. Encourage the patient to use an extended handle reacher and provide hand-over-hand assistance as needed.

    D. Respect the patient's privacy, but remain outside the bathroom door until the patient has turned off the water in the shower.

Correct Answer: B

RATIONALE:
Memory deficits and impulsivity may compromise the patient's safety during bathing tasks. A caregiver should provide stand-by assistance in order to reduce safety risk.

Reference:
Early, M.B. (2013). *Physical dysfunction practice skills for the occupational therapy assistant* (3rd ed., p. 503). St. Louis, MO: Elsevier Mosby.

42. Which of the following actions is **MOST IMPORTANT** for the COTA to take when preparing for a self-care session with an inpatient who has COPD?

    A. Arrange ADL supplies so that they are within easy reach of the patient.

    B. Make sure the patient has adequate standing tolerance to complete the entire activity.

    C. Have the patient's preferred spray deodorants and talcum powders available for use.

    D. Place a chair just outside of the bathroom door in case the patient becomes fatigued.

Correct Answer: A

RATIONALE:
To ensure the safety of the patient throughout the session, it is **MOST IMPORTANT** to place supplies within easy reach of the patient.

Reference:
Lohman, H., Byers-Connon, S., & Padilla, R. L. (2019). *Occupational therapy with elders: Strategies for the COTA* (4th ed., pp. 332-333). Maryland Heights, MO: Mosby Elsevier.

43. A 3-year-old child has cerebral palsy and requires maximum assistance from a caregiver for feeding. The child has fluctuant muscle tone and a persistent asymmetrical tonic neck reflex. The child is able to swallow pureed foods when they are placed in the mouth but has a tongue thrust and poor lip closure when eating. One of the intervention goals is for the caregiver to feed the child with a spoon, with the child seated in a standard high chair. Which techniques should the COTA include as part of the caregiver instructions for feeding the child with a spoon?

Select the 3 best choices.

A. Fasten a seatbelt placed at a 45° angle on the child's hips.

B. Maintain the child's neck in slight extension beyond neutral.

C. Manually stabilize the child's neck in the midline.

D. Position the child's hips and knees at a 90° angle.

E. Sit to the right or left side of the child when feeding the child.

F. Use external supports to position the trunk in midline.

Correct Answers: A, D, F

RATIONALE:
These options encourage postural alignment and stability to promote effective oral motor function.

References:
DeLany, J.V., & Pendzick, M.J. (2009). *Working with children and adolescents: A guide for the occupational therapy assistant* (p. 229). Upper Saddle River, NJ: Pearson Prentice Hall.

Solomon, J. W., & O'Brien, J. C. (2016). *Pediatric skills for occupational therapy assistants* (4th ed., pp. 325, 342-344). St. Louis, MO: Mosby Elsevier.

44. A 4-year-old child has hypotonia secondary to cerebral palsy. This results in poor lip closure, which makes it difficult for the child to transition from using a bottle to drinking from a cup with a spouted lid. Which intervention would be **MOST BENEFICIAL** for the child to do in order to promote initial progress toward drinking from a cup?

   A. Sip a favorite fruit juice from a cup with a nose cutout.

   B. Blow soap bubbles into the air at the start of the session.

   C. Whistle a simple tune before each drink from a cup.

   D. Suck on a piece of sour candy prior to practicing drinking from the cup.

Correct Answer: B

RATIONALE:
Blowing soap bubbles is a motivating age-appropriate play activity that promotes lip closure and oral motor control.

References:
Case-Smith, J., & O'Brien, J. C. (2015). *Occupational therapy for children and adolescents* (7th ed., pp. 409-410). St. Louis, MO: Mosby Elsevier.

DeLany, J.V., & Pendzick, M.J. (2009). *Working with children and adolescents: A guide for the occupational therapy assistant* (pp. 226-229). Upper Saddle River, NJ: Pearson Prentice Hall.

45. A 4-year-old child has persistent asymmetrical tonic neck reflex (ATNR) and symmetrical tonic neck reflex (STNR) secondary to moderate cerebral palsy. The COTA is teaching the caregiver strategies to use when feeding the child. The COTA positions the child in a chair that provides good head and trunk control. Where should the caregiver sit to inhibit the ATNR and STNR reflexes when feeding the child?

   A. Slightly on the right side of midline and just above the child's eye level

   B. Next to the child and at the child's eye level

   C. In front of the child and slightly below the child's eye level

   D. At the child's midline and slightly above the child's eye level

Correct Answer: C

RATIONALE:
Sitting in front of the child and slightly below the child's eye level inhibits the persistent primitive reflexes, which interfere with bilateral hand skills and hand-to-mouth movements.

References:
Case-Smith, J., & O'Brien, J. C. (2015). *Occupational therapy for children and adolescents* (7th ed., pp. 409-410). St. Louis, MO: Mosby Elsevier.

DeLany, J.V., & Pendzick, M.J. (2009). *Working with children and adolescents: A guide for the occupational therapy assistant* (pp. 229, 476). Upper Saddle River, NJ: Pearson Prentice Hall.

46. A 5-year-old child has developmental motor delay secondary to spastic diplegia. The child is able to sit upright in a wheelchair without postural supports. Evaluation results indicate the child has age-appropriate cognition and visual perception, but fine motor skills are equivalent to a typically developing 4-year-old child. The child wants to be able to dress independently. Which developmental play activities would be beneficial to include as part of the child's intervention sessions in order to support goal attainment?

Select the 3 best choices.

A. Creating greeting cards using stencils and colored pencils

B. Finger painting activity with various textured paint

C. Cutting, gluing, and coloring alphabet letter shapes

D. Blowing bubbles and catching them with both hands

E. Sorting game with tweezers to pick up small items

F. Imitating a 3-D block design using 1-inch (2.54 cm) blocks

Correct Answers: B, C, E

RATIONALE:
Results of a task-focused activity analysis indicate that each of these play activities require fine motor skills. Including these activities in the child's intervention sessions will support progress toward the child's goal.

Reference:
Solomon, J. W., & O'Brien, J. C. (2016). *Pediatric skills for occupational therapy assistants* (4th ed., pp. 148, 458-459). St. Louis, MO: Mosby Elsevier.

47. A COTA is selecting an activity for a group of children who are 3 years old and have mild developmental delay. The primary purpose of the group is to promote coordinated movements of both upper extremities. Which activity would be **MOST BENEFICIAL** for supporting the group goal?

   A. **Rolling a large therapy ball to each other**

   B. Playing dress-up to imitate action heroes

   C. Playing prone-lying scooter board games

   D. Jumping rope in rhythm to a well-known song

Correct Answer: A

RATIONALE:
This activity would be **MOST BENEFICIAL** for promoting bilateral use of the upper extremities at a developmentally appropriate level.

References:
Solomon, J. W., & O'Brien, J. C. (2016). *Pediatric skills for occupational therapy assistants* (4th ed., pp. 110-111). St. Louis, MO: Mosby Elsevier.

Case-Smith, J., & O'Brien, J. C. (2015). *Occupational therapy for children and adolescents* (7th ed., p. 88). St. Louis, MO: Mosby Elsevier.

48. Which interventions are **MOST BENEFICIAL** for a client who has venous insufficiency and moderate edema of the lower extremity?

    Select the 3 best choices.

    A. **Elevating the lower extremity above the heart**

    B. **Wearing compression stockings**

    C. **Applying pneumatic pumps**

    D. Encouraging the client to work in a standing position

    E. Massaging the leg when painful

    F. Applying ice pack or cold compress

Correct Answers: A, B, C

RATIONALE:
These intervention methods assist in the prevention and progression of venous insufficiency and lower extremity edema.

Reference:
Smith-Gabai, H., & Holm, S. (Eds.). (2017). *Occupational therapy in acute care* (2nd ed., pp. 258-259). Bethesda, MD: AOTA Press.

49. A client who sustained a 35% total body surface area burn involving the shoulder, elbow, and chest has just received the first set of compression garments. What information should be provided as part of the client education during the initial fitting session with the client?

    Select the 3 best choices.

    A. Garment wear can be discontinued after 2 months.

    B. **Wear the garments at least 23 hours per day.**

    C. Loose-fitting areas around joint creases are acceptable.

    D. Avoid applying lotions to the skin prior to donning the garments.

    E. **Remove the garments for bathing activities.**

    F. **Observe for signs of skin irritation from zippers and seams.**

Correct Answers: B, E, F

RATIONALE:
Following these instructions will promote optimal effectiveness of the pressure garments to influence hypertrophic scarring.

References:
Pendleton, H. M., & Schultz-Krohn, W. (Eds.). (2018). *Pedretti's occupational therapy: Practice skills for the physical dysfunction* (8th ed., p. 1069). St. Louis, MO: Mosby Elsevier.

Radomski, M. V., & Trombly Latham, C. A. (Eds.). (2014). *Occupational therapy for physical dysfunction* (7th ed., pp. 1254-1255). Philadelphia, PA: Lippincott Williams & Wilkins.

50. A 2-year-old child with a congenital transradial amputation of the right arm is being fitted for a prosthesis for the first time. Which caregiver instructions are important for the COTA to include in the education for proper daily care of the residual limb and prosthesis?

Select the 3 best choices.

A. Apply moisturizer before donning the device.

B. Change the prosthetic sock routinely.

C. Check skin for signs of irritation.

D. Report pressure areas immediately.

E. Soak the residual limb in warm water.

F. Tighten mechanical parts of the device.

Correct Answers: B, C, D

RATIONALE:
Following these instructions will assist in maintaining skin integrity of the residual limb and integrating prosthetic use into daily habits and routines.

Reference:
Solomon, J. W., & O'Brien, J. C. (2016). *Pediatric skills for occupational therapy assistants* (4th ed., p. 199). St. Louis, MO: Mosby Elsevier.

51. An inpatient has hemiplegia secondary to a recent CVA and is preparing for discharge to live at home with a spouse. The patient has persistent edema of the affected upper extremity despite using proper positioning techniques. One of the intervention goals is to teach the patient methods for managing the edema after discharge. Which action would be **MOST BENEFICIAL** to include as part of the intervention for supporting this goal?

    A. Fabricate a resting hand splint for the patient to wear at all times.

    B. Instruct the patient on how to perform retrograde massage techniques.

    C. Provide the patient with handout instructions for preparing home paraffin baths.

    D. Teach the patient and caregiver to use manual lymphatic treatment techniques.

Correct Answer: B

RATIONALE:
Retrograde massage techniques are effective edema management methods that can be used frequently throughout the day as part of the overall home program.

Reference:
Early, M.B. (2013). *Physical dysfunction practice skills for the occupational therapy assistant* (3rd ed., p. 600). St. Louis, MO: Elsevier Mosby.

52. A client has spastic hemiplegia secondary to a left CVA several months ago. One of the intervention goals is to teach the primary caregiver proper positioning techniques for reducing the client's muscle tone and providing sensory input when the client is side lying on the affected side in bed. What instructions should the COTA provide the caregiver to properly position the client in order to achieve this goal?

Select the 3 best choices.

A. Place the right scapula in full protraction with the shoulder flexed to 90°.

B. Position a pillow under the left leg with the knee and hip in flexion.

C. Flex the left elbow to 90° and place the affected hand in a palm down position.

D. Avoid using a pillow under the head, neck, and upper shoulders.

E. Maintain the affected hip in extension and the knee in slight flexion.

F. Use a pillow between the torso and upper arm to slightly adduct the left shoulder.

Correct Answers: A, B, E

RATIONALE:
Using these techniques to properly position the client will promote alignment, limit the effect of a flexor synergy pattern, and support normalization of muscle tone.

Reference:
Early, M.B. (2013). *Physical dysfunction practice skills for the occupational therapy assistant* (3rd ed., p. 427). St. Louis, MO: Elsevier Mosby.

53. A client who sustained an irreversible radial nerve injury had a tendon transfer of the pronator teres to extensor carpi radialis brevis muscle 8 weeks ago. The client has difficulty activating the muscle for its newly intended function of wrist extension. Which technique would be **MOST BENEFICIAL** to use for recruiting the donor muscle to extend the wrist?

Select the 3 best choices.

A. Gently tap along the antagonist muscles during ROM exercises.

B. **Instruct the client to simultaneously perform wrist extension with both hands.**

C. **Apply vibration to the pronator teres prior to the start of active wrist extension exercises.**

D. Fabricate an immobilization orthosis to support the wrist and digits in extension.

E. Encourage the client to extend the wrist in an ulnar direction as much as possible.

F. **Ask the client to imagine completing a simple task using the involved hand.**

Correct Answers: B, C, F

RATIONALE:
These facilitation techniques encourage wrist extension and the intended function of the newly transferred tendon.

Reference:
Cooper, C. (2014). *Fundamentals of hand therapy: Clinical reasoning and treatment guidelines for common diagnoses of the upper extremity* (2nd ed., p. 445). St. Louis, MO: Mosby Elsevier.

54. A child who has spastic hemiplegic cerebral palsy wants to independently play with toy cars on a mat placed on the floor. Which position is **MOST EFFECTIVE** for reducing the child's muscle tone to meet this objective?

    A. Side lying on the affected side supported by pillows

    B. Long-sitting on the floor while leaning against a wall

    C. Prone over a firm cylindrical bolster

Correct Answer: A

RATIONALE:
Supporting the affected side on pillows will assist the child in assuming and maintaining the side-lying position.

Reference:
Solomon, J. W., & O'Brien, J. C. (2016). *Pediatric skills for occupational therapy assistants* (4th ed., pp. 341-342). St. Louis, MO: Mosby Elsevier.

55. Which technique would be **MOST EFFECTIVE** for a client to use for managing the symptoms of COPD during a functional task at home?

    A. Breathing out when pushing items and breathing in when pulling items

    B. Inhaling through the mouth and exhaling through the nose when lifting

    C. Taking shallow, quick breaths whenever shortness of breath occurs

    D. Crossing both arms across the chest when breathing becomes difficult

Correct Answer: A

RATIONALE:
Using this breathing technique during exertion would be **MOST EFFECTIVE** in reducing demands on the lungs and cardiovascular system.

Reference:
Early, M.B. (2013). *Physical dysfunction practice skills for the occupational therapy assistant* (3rd ed., pp. 686-687). St. Louis, MO: Elsevier Mosby.

56. A client with relapsing-remitting multiple sclerosis is 7 days postpartum. The client requires minimal assistance for unsupported sitting balance, has mild incoordination of the upper extremity, and is able to independently complete self-care in a seated position. The client wants to learn how to safely hold the infant. Which positions should the COTA teach the client to use for supporting this goal?

    Select the 3 best choices.

    A. **Side lying on a bed with the client and the infant facing each other**

    B. Supine in a bed with the infant in a nearby baby seat secured to a raised safety frame

    C. **Supported in an arm chair with the infant in an over-the-shoulder sling baby carrier**

    D. Seated on the edge of the bed with the infant placed on a C-shaped nursing pillow

    E. **Propped against a 45° wedge cushion with the infant held on the chest**

    F. Semi-reclined in a gliding rocking chair with the infant supported in supine on the client's lap

Correct Answers: A, C, E

RATIONALE:
These positions support progress toward the goal identified by the client and promote a position of safety for both the client and the infant.

References:
Gillen, G. (2016). *Stroke rehabilitation: A function-based approach* (4th ed., pp. 268-270). St. Louis, MO: Elsevier.

Radomski, M. V., & Trombly Latham, C. A. (Eds.). (2014). *Occupational therapy for physical dysfunction* (7th ed., p. 858). Philadelphia, PA: Lippincott Williams & Wilkins.

57. A COTA is using a pediatric constraint-induced movement therapy (P-CIMT) approach during intervention for a 5-year-old child who has hemiplegic cerebral palsy. Which elements, when used together, are **MOST IMPORTANT** to incorporate into the overall intervention strategy when using the P-CIMT approach?

Select the 3 best choices.

A. Apply a mitt to the child's unaffected upper extremity at the start of an activity.

B. Engage the child in familiar play activities using only the affected upper extremity.

C. Implement the intervention activities in the clinic environment as much as possible.

D. Limit the use of the intervention approach to a maximum of 2 hours per day.

E. Provide the child's parents with activity suggestions for encouraging bilateral play.

F. Teach the child's parents how to implement this strategy as part of the child's typical daily tasks.

Correct Answers: A, B, F

RATIONALE:
Components of P-CIMT include immobilization of the unaffected or less affected upper extremity, repetitive training of the affected upper extremity, and integration of motor abilities into ADL performance.

References:
Early, M.B. (2013). *Physical dysfunction practice skills for the occupational therapy assistant* (3rd ed., p. 474). St. Louis, MO: Elsevier Mosby.

Solomon, J. W., & O'Brien, J. C. (2016). *Pediatric skills for occupational therapy assistants* (4th ed., p. 559). St. Louis, MO: Mosby Elsevier.

58. A 5-year-old child has moderate hypertonicity secondary to cerebral palsy. Increased muscle tone interferes with the child's ability to complete dressing independently. Which technique would be **MOST EFFECTIVE** for reducing the child's muscle tone prior to initiating a dressing task?

A. Bouncing the child up and down on a large therapy ball

B. **Having the child gently rock forward and backward in quadruped**

C. Using quick tapping to the spastic muscle bellies

D. Applying heavy joint compression to both arms

Correct Answer: B

RATIONALE:
Inhibitory therapeutic handling techniques such as slow rocking or rolling are used to influence hypertonicity that interfere with functional performance.

Reference:
Solomon, J. W., & O'Brien, J. C. (2016). *Pediatric skills for occupational therapy assistants* (4th ed., p. 349). St. Louis, MO: Mosby Elsevier.

59. A COTA is preparing to fabricate a thermoplastic anti-spasticity hand orthosis for a school-age child. Which orthotic material characteristics would be **BEST** for this type of orthosis?

   A. Bonds to itself

   B. High rigidity

   C. Stretches easily

Correct Answer: B

RATIONALE:
Thermoplastic material with high rigidity and strength is recommended for an anti-spasticity orthosis to tolerate the forces and maintain optimal alignment of the hand.

References:
Solomon, J. W., & O'Brien, J. C. (2016). *Pediatric skills for occupational therapy assistants* (4th ed., p. 549). St. Louis, MO: Mosby Elsevier.

Jacobs, M.A., & Austin, N.M. (2014). *Orthotic intervention for the hand and upper extremity: Splinting principles and processes* (2nd ed., pp. 89-92). Philadelphia, PA: Lippincott Williams & Wilkins.

60. An OTR and a COTA are collaborating to select a thermoplastic material to use when fabricating a long-arm posterior elbow immobilization orthosis for a client who sustained a proximal radius fracture. What material characteristics are **OPTIMAL** for this type of orthosis?

Select the 3 best choices.

A. Low conformability

B. High rigidity

C. High drapability

D. High conformability

E. 1/8" thickness material

F. 1/16" thickness material

Correct Answers: A, B, E

RATIONALE:
Strong thermoplastic materials with high rigidity and low conformability are recommended for immobilizing a large surface area, such as when fabricating a long-arm posterior elbow orthosis.

References:
Jacobs, M.A., & Austin, N.M. (2014). *Orthotic intervention for the hand and upper extremity: Splinting principles and processes* (2nd ed., pp. 89-90, 208-209). Philadelphia, PA: Lippincott Williams & Wilkins.

Solomon, J. W., & O'Brien, J. C. (2016). *Pediatric skills for occupational therapy assistants* (4th ed., pp. 549-550). St. Louis, MO: Mosby Elsevier.

61. A 5-year-old child has poor wrist stability and decreased fine motor coordination secondary to spastic cerebral palsy. One of the intervention goals is to fabricate a wrist orthosis to improve functional use of the hands to support independence with self-feeding. Which of the following options represent challenges associated with fabricating the orthosis for this child?

Select the 3 best choices.

A. Inconsistent nature of the child's hypertonicity

B. Child's fear of the unfamiliar clinic environment

C. Limitations in types and colors of thermoplastics

D. Inability to protect vulnerable areas of the hand

E. Lack of commercially available stretch resistant materials

F. Length of time to completely cool the material

Correct Answers: A, B, F

RATIONALE:
To create a positive experience for the child and to achieve the optimal therapeutic outcome, the COTA must consider these factors when planning the session.

Reference:
Jacobs, M.A., & Austin, N.M. (2014). *Orthotic intervention for the hand and upper extremity: Splinting principles and processes* (2nd ed., pp. 596-602). Philadelphia, PA: Lippincott Williams & Wilkins.

62. A patient sustained a complete C_6 spinal cord injury several weeks ago. One of the intervention goals is to maximize independence with self-feeding. Which assistive device would be **MOST BENEFICIAL** for the patient to use during meals to support this goal?

   A. Switch-operated feeder

   B. Mobile arm support

   C. **Tenodesis orthosis**

   D. Wrist cock-up splint

Correct Answer: C

RATIONALE:
A patient who sustained a complete C6 spinal cord injury typically has innervation of the radial wrist extensors. This will allow a weak tenodesis grasp. A tenodesis splint enables the patient to transfer power of active wrist extension to enable a stronger pinch. This is **MOST BENEFICIAL** for enabling the patient to hold eating utensils.

Reference:
Early, M.B. (2013). *Physical dysfunction practice skills for the occupational therapy assistant* (3rd ed., pp. 542-543, 548). St. Louis, MO: Elsevier Mosby.

63. A preschool student who has spastic diplegia cerebral palsy wants to play with peers during floor-time activities in the classroom. The COTA assists the student to sit on the floor, but tight hamstring muscles make it difficult for the student to sit comfortably. Which intervention is **MOST EFFECTIVE** for enabling the student to sit on the floor to participate in play activities with peers?

   A. Positioning a triangular-shaped wedge under the knees

   B. Placing lateral supports beside the student

   C. Strapping a small pillow under the student's ankles

Correct Answer: A

RATIONALE:
A triangular-shaped wedge placed under the student's knees encourages skeletal alignment and supports the shortened hamstrings in a position of comfort.

Reference:
Solomon, J. W., & O'Brien, J. C. (2016). *Pediatric skills for occupational therapy assistants* (4th ed., pp. 337, 342-344). St. Louis, MO: Mosby Elsevier.

64. An OTR and a COTA are selecting a manual wheelchair for a client who has flaccid hemiplegia and will be using a wheelchair for most mobility. Which of the following features are **OPTIMAL** to include in the wheelchair specifications for this client?

    Select the 3 best choices.

    A. Standard sling seat

    B. **Detachable arm rests**

    C. **Swing-away footrests**

    D. Elevating leg rests

    E. Adjustable recline

    F. **Wheel with two hand rims**

    Correct Answers: B, C, F

    RATIONALE:
    This client, who has hemiplegia, requires wheelchair features and accessories that will support the ability to complete transfers safely and allow for self-propulsion.

    Reference:
    Early, M.B. (2013). *Physical dysfunction practice skills for the occupational therapy assistant* (3rd ed., pp. 302-303, 310-311). St. Louis, MO: Elsevier Mosby.

65. A COTA is working with a resident in a skilled nursing facility during mealtime in the dining room. One of the resident's goals is to independently self-feed. The COTA determines that the resident initially sits upright in the wheelchair, but throughout the meal leans laterally to one side and slides forward in the chair. Which action would be **MOST BENEFICIAL** to include as part of the positioning recommendation for supporting the self-feeding goal?

A. **Use wheelchair accessories to support the resident's hips, knees, and ankles in 90° of flexion.**

B. Position the resident approximately 30 inches (76.2 cm) from the plate and utensils at the table.

C. Modify the chair by measuring the width of the resident's hips and adding 2 inches (5.08 cm).

Correct Answer: A

RATIONALE:
The optimal position to promote safe and independent self-feeding is for the resident to maintain an upright position with the head positioned 10 to 15 inches from the plate throughout the duration of the meal.

Reference:
Barney, K. F., & Perkinson, M. A. (2016). *Occupational therapy with aging adults: Promoting quality of life through collaboration* (p. 183). St. Louis, MO: Elsevier Mosby.

66. An adolescent sustained a C_8 spinal cord injury several months ago. One of the outpatient intervention goals is for the adolescent to be independent in functional mobility on all indoor surfaces and level outdoor terrain. What type of mobility equipment would be **MOST BENEFICIAL** for supporting this goal?

A. **Lightweight folding wheelchair with modified rims**

B. Power wheelchair with reclining back and chin control

C. Adjustable wheeled stander with sip and puff switch

D. Standard wheelchair with removable arms and leg rests

Correct Answer: A

RATIONALE:
A client who has a C_8 spinal cord injury has the ability to propel a manual lightweight folding wheelchair with modified rims.

Reference:
Early, M.B. (2013). *Physical dysfunction practice skills for the occupational therapy assistant* (3rd ed., pp. 545-549). St. Louis, MO: Elsevier Mosby.

67. A resident has poor motor control and incoordination of the dominant upper extremity secondary to cerebellar ataxia. One of the goals is to help the resident independently self-feed. Which assistive device would be **MOST BENEFICIAL** for the resident to use for supporting this goal?

    A. Plastic-coated, angled spoon

    B. Eating utensil with a built-up handle

    C. Scoop dish with a suction cup base

Correct Answer: C

RATIONALE:
This option stabilizes the food to allow the resident to scoop food onto the eating utensil and prevents food from sliding off the dish.

Reference:
Early, M.B. (2013). *Physical dysfunction practice skills for the occupational therapy assistant* (3rd ed., pp. 108-110, 251-255) St. Louis, MO: Elsevier Mosby.

68. An older adult who has osteoarthritis sits on a shower seat while in the tub but is unable to reach all body parts when bathing. Which adaptive equipment would be **MOST BENEFICIAL** to promote independence when bathing?

Select the 3 best choices.

A. Long-handled sponge

B. Laminated visual cue cards

C. Hand-held shower

D. Anti-slip shower mat

E. Water temperature control device

F. Suction cup soap holder

Correct Answers: A, C, F

RATIONALE:
These options offer a solution directly associated with the client's difficulties with limited reach.

Reference:
Mahle, A. J., & Ward, L. W. (2019). *Adult physical conditions: Intervention strategies for occupational therapy assistants* (pp. 345-347). Philadelphia, PA: F.A. Davis.

69. A student who is in the third grade has illegible handwriting due to a mild sensory processing disorder. The student does not space letters and words uniformly on the paper. What is the **FIRST** handwriting solution the COTA should use to help improve the student's handwriting?

    A. Encourage the teacher to allow the student extra time to complete desktop activities.

    B. Provide the student with a keyboard and computer to use for written assignments.

    C. Have the student write on paper with raised lines and use a finger to guide spacing.

Correct Answer: C

RATIONALE:
For this student, the COTA should **FIRST** offer a low-technology solution before progressing to a high-technology option or classroom accommodations.

Reference:
Solomon, J. W., & O'Brien, J. C. (2016). *Pediatric skills for occupational therapy assistants* (4th ed., p. 444). St. Louis, MO: Mosby Elsevier.

70. An inpatient has Fair minus (3-/5) functional muscle strength of the dominant upper extremity and of the dominant hand. One of the patient's goals is to independently brush teeth. Which assistive device would be **CONTRAINDICATED** for the patient to use for supporting this goal?

    A. Toothbrush with a built-up handle

    B. Weighted electric toothbrush

    C. Automatic toothpaste dispenser

Correct Answer: B

RATIONALE:
A patient with Fair minus (3-/5) muscle strength will not benefit from a weighted electric toothbrush.

Reference:
Early, M.B. (2013). *Physical dysfunction practice skills for the occupational therapy assistant* (3rd ed., p. 255). St. Louis, MO: Elsevier Mosby.

71. During a self-feeding session, the COTA teaches a client to use the adaptive utensil pictured below. What is the **PRIMARY** reason for recommending a client use this type of device?

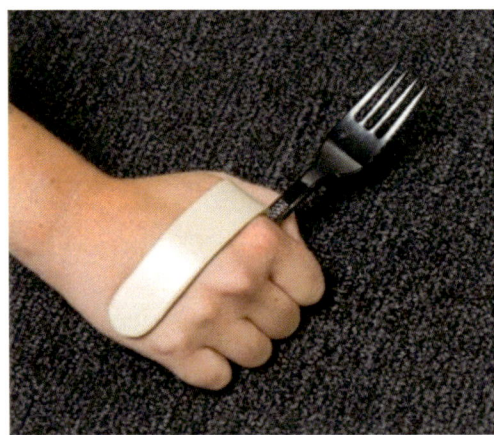

A. Impaired gross motor coordination

B. Weak hand and grasp strength

C. Limited upper extremity AROM

Correct Answer: B

RATIONALE:
A universal cuff is a low-technology assistive device that can be used by clients with limited strength to promote independence with functional tasks.

References:
Early, M.B. (2013). *Physical dysfunction practice skills for the occupational therapy assistant* (3rd ed., pp. 271-272). St. Louis, MO: Elsevier Mosby.

Pendleton, H. M., & Schultz-Krohn, W. (Eds.). (2018). *Pedretti's occupational therapy: Practice skills for the physical dysfunction* (8th ed., p. 197). St. Louis, MO: Mosby Elsevier.

72. An inpatient sustained an incomplete T_2 spinal cord injury (ASIA C) several weeks ago. One of the intervention goals is for the patient to be independent with wheelchair transfers. The patient is able to transfer without assistive devices from the bed to the wheelchair but requires moderate assistance when completing transfers from the wheelchair to a standard toilet. What is the **NEXT** action the COTA should take to support the patient's progress with this transfer skill?

A. Encourage the patient to use a bedside commode instead of the bathroom toilet.

B. Teach the patient to use a sliding board transfer to a raised toilet seat.

C. Complete a manual muscle test to determine the patient's triceps strength.

D. Evaluate the difference in height between the wheelchair and the toilet.

Correct Answer: D

RATIONALE:
The difference in height between the toilet and the wheelchair may cause the patient to have difficulty with the transfer at the initial stages of transfer training. The COTA should assess the height of the toilet in relation to the height of the wheelchair seat. This would give the COTA information needed to make necessary environmental modifications to support the patient's ability to complete the transfer.

Reference:
Early, M.B. (2013). *Physical dysfunction practice skills for the occupational therapy assistant* (3rd ed., pp. 318, 536, 550). St. Louis, MO: Elsevier Mosby.

73. A client in a home health setting has stage 2 Parkinson's disease. The client had a recent decline in function and is now learning to use a walker for mobility in the home. The COTA is teaching the client how to transport food items in the kitchen using the walker with an attached tray. What information should the COTA include as part of the instructions for minimizing fall risk during this task?

    A. **Stand inside the frame of the walker and turn slowly.**

    B. Turn the walker to the desired direction then move the legs.

    C. Move the walker to one side and use the counter for support.

    D. Place one hand on the counter and the other on the walker to move it.

Correct Answer: A

RATIONALE:
Clients who have stage 2 Parkinson's disease typically have difficulty shifting their weight to take steps. When using a walker, the safest way for the client to turn is to stay close to the walker, stand with a wide base of support, and move slowly. The client should also be taught to use a proper gait pattern to minimize fall risk.

Reference:
Early, M.B. (2013). *Physical dysfunction practice skills for the occupational therapy assistant* (3rd ed., pp. 299-300, 522-524). St. Louis, MO: Elsevier Mosby.

74. A client sustained a complete T_2 spinal cord injury several months ago. The client is learning compensatory strategies to use for promoting independence and safety during homemaking activities. One of the client's goals is to be able to prepare family meals independently. Which environmental modification would promote progress toward this goal?

A. Positioning an angled mirror above the stove

B. Replacing stove knobs with larger handles

C. Using smaller pans with extended handles

D. Stirring hot liquids with rubber-coated cooking utensils

Correct Answer: A

RATIONALE:
A client who has a complete T_2 spinal cord injury depends on a wheelchair for mobility. When preparing meals while seated in a wheelchair, it is difficult to see the contents of pots and pans on the stovetop. Placing a mirror over the stove enables the client to see food as it is cooking and determine the temperature from observation.

Reference:
Early, M.B. (2013). *Physical dysfunction practice skills for the occupational therapy assistant* (3rd ed., pp. 267-269, 550). St. Louis, MO: Elsevier Mosby.

75. A COTA is recommending home modifications for an inpatient who has general debility secondary to pneumonia. Currently, the patient independently performs ADL but needs a rest break every 5 minutes. The patient is preparing for discharge to live with a spouse in a single-level apartment with 3 stairs to enter. Which adaptations should be included as part of the discharge recommendations?

- **A.** Post safety reminders on the wall in a clearly visible location.
- **B.** Install a ramp with no more than a 5° incline.
- **C. Remove clutter and loose rugs in commonly used living areas.**

Correct Answer: C

RATIONALE:
Precautionary adaptations to minimize risk of falling should be recommended for this patient who is independent in ADL but has low activity tolerance.

Reference:
Lohman, H., Byers-Connon, S., & Padilla, R. L. (2019). *Occupational therapy with elders: Strategies for the COTA* (4th ed., pp. 202-203). Maryland Heights, MO: Mosby Elsevier.

NOTES

Chapter 12

Domain 3: Multiple Choice Sample Questions

Practice questions with answer key and references

The following multiple choice items are samples related to Domain 3.

Upholding Professional Standards and Responsibilities

Uphold professional standards and responsibilities by achieving service competence and applying evidence-based interventions to promote quality in practice.

1. An OTR and a COTA are collaborating to search for evidence about the effectiveness of constraint-induced movement therapy for stroke patients. Based on the hierarchy of evidence, which option is considered the highest level of evidence?

   A. Opinions of expert practitioners working in neurological rehabilitation

   B. Descriptive studies using a single-subject research design

   C. Meta-analyses of randomized controlled trials

2. A COTA plans to use the PICO method to search a database for practice-relevant information. What is the **PRIMARY** purpose for using this method to search for evidence?

   A. To identify a clinically relevant, answerable question

   B. To locate client-centered and occupation-based methods

   C. To filter the search for randomized controlled trials

3. A COTA is planning to lead a discussion about the first step in the evidence-based practice process during a rehabilitation team meeting. What information should the COTA include in the discussion when summarizing the first step in the evidence-based practice process?

   A. Asking a clinical question based on clients seen at the clinic

   B. Synthesizing several articles found in a scholarly database

   C. Applying research evidence when making practice decisions

4. A COTA works in an outpatient setting. A client who recently had a CVA and is on the COTA caseload asks the COTA about trying a new treatment technique for increasing movement in the affected upper extremity. The COTA has heard of the technique but does not know how beneficial it would be. In addition to informing the OTR, what actions should the COTA take based on the client's inquiry?

   Select the 3 best choices.

   A. Identify the value of using the new intervention instead of the current intervention.

   B. Ask if the client is willing to participate in a single-subject case study related to the technique.

   C. Tell the client that there are many well-accepted alternatives that should be tried before using this technique.

   D. Search online databases to identify best practice trends for the client's current condition.

   E. Read articles in peer-reviewed journals to determine if research supports the use of this intervention.

   F. Obtain intervention protocols from other clinics currently using the technique with clients.

5. An inpatient OT department recently completed a retrospective chart audit to determine staff compliance with the documentation policy. Over 60% of the charts that were reviewed had incomplete signatures or non-approved abbreviations. What is the **NEXT** action the OT department should take based on this information?

   A. Initiate a performance improvement program.

   B. Schedule a staff meeting to discuss the findings.

   C. Repeat the audit in 30 days to compare results.

6. A COTA and an OTR work in a hospital setting and are collaborating on the first step of a quality improvement initiative. The goal of the initiative is to review archived clinical documentation records to determine the presence of patient-specific discharge instructions. What is the **PRIMARY** purpose for completing this step of the quality initiative?

   A. To determine if change is needed to the department documentation policy for discharge instructions

   B. To provide the supervisor with names of staff members who frequently do not document discharge information

   C. To ensure the patient successfully transitioned from the hospital to home with minimal risk of readmission

7. A newly certified COTA recently started working at an inpatient rehabilitation facility. The supervising OTR wants the COTA to assist with administering standardized manual muscle tests as part of patient reevaluations. The COTA has only administered this test to classmates when in school and received an excellent score on the final laboratory exam. After confirming that state licensure regulations permit the COTA to administer standardized tests, what is the **NEXT** action the COTA should take?

   A. Review class notes on the proper administration procedures for the test.

   B. Ask the OTR to clarify the specific muscles included in the test.

   C. Talk with the OTR about establishing service competency for the test.

   D. Arrange for an OT colleague to observe so inter-rater reliability can be established.

8. A COTA worked in an outpatient hand therapy clinic for the past 5 years. The COTA recently obtained a new job and will start work as a COTA in an inpatient neuro-rehabilitation setting. What **INITIAL** step should the COTA take to develop service competency in the new job?

   A. Arrange a schedule to have close supervision when working with patients.

   B. Provide the OTR with verification of service-competent tasks from the previous job.

   C. Learn about clinical protocols by leading a staff discussion on the topic.

   D. Have the supervising OTR review and co-sign each patient contact note.

9. A newly certified COTA recently started a new job in a large rehabilitation clinic. Part of the essential job tasks include fabricating dynamic orthotics on a routine basis. The COTA received basic splinting instruction in school yet feels the need for further training. What action would be **MOST BENEFICIAL** for the COTA to take to establish service competency in this area?

   A. Register to attend an online professional development workshop on splinting.

   B. Arrange for structured mentorship that includes close supervision.

   C. Use a checklist of fabrication tips and techniques when making dynamic orthotics.

   D. Review school notes and read journal articles about splinting.

10. A school-based OTR and COTA are collaborating to evaluate a kindergarten student who has autism spectrum disorder. Which task can the COTA complete as part of this data gathering process?

    A. Score a sensory integration assessment.

    B. Select developmentally appropriate assessment tools.

    C. Analyze evaluation results.

    D. Administer a developmental skills checklist.

11. A COTA working in an inpatient rehabilitation clinic is assigned to supervise a newly hired therapy aide. What information **MUST** the COTA know prior to assigning job tasks to the aide?

    A. State OT practice act guidelines for service provision

    B. Critical demands listed in the aide's job description

    C. Previous experience the aide has had working with patients

    D. Aide's knowledge of occupational therapy interventions

12. A student in the first grade has difficulty forming letters and shapes and copying from the board at the front of the classroom. This interferes with the student's ability to complete grade-level tasks. The OTR and COTA are collaborating to gather information about client factors influencing the student's handwriting development. Which information gathering methods are within the scope of practice for a service-competent COTA to complete as part of this process?

    Select the 3 best choices.

    A. Describe the student's posture when seated at the desk.

    B. Determine the student's grade-level handwriting function.

    C. Note the type of grasp the student uses to hold a pencil.

    D. Compare the student's at-desk work to classmates' work.

    E. Administer and interpret the Sensory Processing Measure.

    F. Collect a sample of the student's in-class writing assignments.

13. A COTA has service competence for a specific standardized assessment. Which task related to the assessment can the COTA be expected to complete independently?

    A. Administering each of the subtests

    B. Interpreting the test results

    C. Selecting which client should be tested

14. An OTR and a service-competent COTA work in an outpatient pediatric setting and are collaborating to evaluate an adolescent who recently had a TBI. Which tasks are within the scope of practice for the COTA to complete as part of this data gathering process?

    Select the 3 best choices.

    A. Administer a standardized cognitive test.

    B. Analyze data from an occupational role history.

    C. Identify a performance-based outcome measure.

    D. Interpret results of the occupational profile.

    E. Perform an interview about daily routines.

    F. Record observations during a functional task.

15. A COTA is preparing an in-service about injury prevention for employees at a data-entry and computer software company. What information is **MOST IMPORTANT** to include in this presentation?

    A. Symptoms associated with cumulative trauma

    B. Isokinetic exercises for reducing painful symptoms

    C. Impact of work-related injuries on the company

    D. Methods for reducing work-related risk factors

16. A COTA is preparing to give a presentation about fall prevention strategies for community-dwelling older adults. The objective of the presentation is to reduce the participants' risk of falling. In addition to providing information on how to create a safe home environment, which topics would be **MOST BENEFICIAL** to teach in the presentation to meet this goal?

Select the 3 best choices.

- A. List of medical diagnoses that place a person at high risk for falling
- B. Resources to enhance social involvement in the community
- C. Reviews of healthy eating habits and nutritional information on prepared foods
- D. Advantages of routinely completing an exercise program
- E. Purpose of having a regular vision examination
- F. Benefits of a health-care provider to review a list of prescribed medications

17. The multidisciplinarny team at a community-based program is developing a substance use relapse program. The focus of the program is to promote healthy alternatives for at-risk clients. What is the **PRIMARY** contribution of the COTA during the initial phase of program development?

- A. To recommend program topics unrelated to triggers that lead to misuse
- B. To identify resources for determining barriers to participation
- C. To suggest program activities related to leisure skill development
- D. To determine specific outcome measures for the program

18. A COTA is preparing to give a presentation for an arthritis support group. The goal of the presentation is to communicate the role of occupational therapy in assisting individuals who have systemic lupus. Which communication method would be **MOST BENEFICIAL** to use in the presentation to meet this goal?

    A. Describe specific OT assessments typically used with individuals who have lupus.

    B. Discuss OT interventions and service options for individuals who have lupus.

    C. Simulate a typical OT session by including one of the participants as an example.

    D. Demonstrate a range of exercises for individuals who have lupus.

19. A COTA believes that several residents on the OT caseload no longer qualify for OT services, but the supervisor and the employer expect intervention should continue for the duration of the residents' length of stay. What is the **FIRST** action the COTA should take based on this concern?

    A. Seek input from colleagues on various social media platforms.

    B. Use a decision-making framework to develop a plan of action.

    C. File a formal complaint with the state regulatory board.

20. An inpatient is participating in a rehabilitation program after experiencing an exacerbation of relapsing-remitting multiple sclerosis. The patient is making steady progress toward the intervention goal of resuming independence with homemaking tasks. While completing personal laundry tasks during a session, the patient reports being extremely tired from not sleeping well the previous night and asks to take a brief rest. What **INITIAL** action should the COTA take in response to the patient's report?

    A. Ensure that the patient uses energy conservation techniques for the remainder of the session.

    B. Allow the patient to take a short break and encourage pursed-lip breathing.

    C. Discontinue the session and notify the charge nurse about the patient's fatigue.

    D. Demonstrate additional work simplification techniques to use during laundry tasks.

21. A client who has atrial fibrillation is taking a prescribed blood-thinning medication. The client attends college and wants to participate in leisure activities offered on the campus. Which preventive strategy should the COTA teach the client to minimize the risk of injury associated with common side effects of blood thinners?

    A. Ask the client not to attend events with flashing lights.

    B. Suggest that the client select sedentary activities.

    C. Advise the client to avoid contact sports.

22. A COTA who works in an intensive care unit is preparing to assist a patient, who had surgery for a coronary artery bypass graft, with completing BADL while seated in a bedside chair. What action is **MOST IMPORTANT** for the COTA to take as part of the intervention during this phase of the patient's rehabilitation?

    A. Discuss work simplification and pacing with the patient.

    B. Place grooming and bathing supplies within reach of the patient.

    C. Monitor the patient's heart rate and blood pressure during self-care.

23. An older adult who has emphysema was admitted to an acute care hospital 3 days ago with pneumonia. One of the intervention goals is for the patient to resume independence in ADL. During a session, the patient brushes teeth in a standing position. The COTA measures the patient's vital signs and notes oxygen saturation level is 92%, blood pressure is 101/65 mmHg, and heart rate is 98 bpm. Based on this information, what is the **NEXT** action the COTA should take?

    A. Advise the patient to put on a nasal cannula and discontinue the intervention session.

    B. Have the patient sit in a chair and teach the patient to use pursed-lip breathing.

    C. Proceed with the intervention activity and monitor the patient's vital signs periodically.

24. A COTA is scheduled to complete a transfer training session with an inpatient who has stage 4 Parkinson's disease. Admission notes indicate the patient has experienced several recent falls as a result of syncope and was using a walker for mobility prior to admission. The COTA plans to transfer the patient from the bed to a bedside commode during the session. To reduce fall risk, what information should the COTA gather about the patient prior to initiating the transfer training session?

    Select the 3 best choices.

    A. Cognitive function

    B. Oxygen levels

    C. Fluidity of movement

    D. Perceived exertion

    E. Depth perception

    F. Visual acuity

25. A COTA is teaching compensatory techniques for facial shaving to a client who has mild choreiform movements of bilateral upper extremities. The COTA wants to be sure standard precautions are followed during this BADL task. Which action should the COTA have the client do as part of this process?

   A. Clean the razor with alcohol after completing the shaving activity.

   B. Practice with an electric shaver borrowed from the OT self-care room.

   C. Bring in a personal electric shaver to use during the session.

   D. Purchase a bag of disposable straight-edge razors.

26. During a session in the home, a client who has dementia unexpectedly is incontinent of urine. While using personal protective barriers, the COTA works with the caregiver to clean the client and the area. What is the **NEXT** action the COTA should take?

   A. Wash hands for 15 seconds using a mild soap.

   B. Terminate therapy session and reschedule.

   C. Document occurrence in the electronic medical record.

27. During an ADL group session, an inpatient with quadriplegia reports a sudden onset of a pounding headache, begins to perspire excessively, and has chills. What **INITIAL** action should the COTA take in response to these symptoms?

   A. Activate the facility medical alert system.

   B. Transport the patient to their room to rest.

   C. Stop the activity until the patient's vital signs stabilize.

28. A client who has diabetes mellitus is participating in a BADL session. When sitting on the shower chair, the COTA notes that the client's skin is pale, breathing is shallow, and the client's hands are trembling. The client reports feeling hungry and confused. What **IMMEDIATE** action should the COTA take in this situation?

    A. Have the client administer an insulin injection.

    B. Check the client's blood glucose level.

    C. Provide the client with half a glass of fruit juice.

29. A COTA is fabricating an orthosis for a client who recently had a deep partial thickness burn to the dorsum of the hand. When the COTA removes the bulky dressing, the patient becomes lightheaded and begins to sweat. What **INITIAL** action should the COTA take in response to this occurrence?

    A. Break open an ammonia ampule and slowly pass it under the client's nose.

    B. Assist the client to a supine position and elevate the client's legs.

    C. Ask the client to rest their head on the table or between their knees.

    D. Moisten a cloth with cool water and hold it across the client's forehead.

30. During a community outing to a sporting event, a client chokes on a bite of food. The client is conscious and able to verbalize sounds but is having difficulty dislodging the food. In addition to calling for emergency assistance and helping the client stay calm, what **IMMEDIATE** action should the COTA take?

    A. Assist the client to a supine position.

    B. Perform the Heimlich maneuver.

    C. Encourage the client to cough forcefully.

31. During an intervention session, a resident in a skilled nursing facility reports that earlier in the day, a dizzy spell occurred with sharp headache pain and blurred vision. The COTA informs the resident that the medical staff needs to be informed, but the resident states, "I feel fine now, just a little tired. I want to keep working." In addition to reporting this occurrence to the OTR, how should the COTA respond in this situation?

    A. Continue the session while emphasizing safety precautions during mobility and transfers.

    B. Stop the activity and report the situation to the nurse prior to proceeding with the session.

    C. Respect the resident's wishes and plan to document the resident's symptoms in the progress note.

32. A COTA who works in an acute care hospital is providing intervention for an inpatient who has an intravenous (IV) line connected to an infusion pump. During the session, the auditory alarm of the infusion pump begins to sound. What action **MUST** the COTA take in response to the activation of the alarm system?

    A. Ask the patient to rate current pain level using a numerical rating scale.

    B. Press the nurse call button and alert the staff about the alarm.

    C. Locate the button to silence the alarm and turn down the volume.

33. A COTA is planning an in-service to instruct the nursing staff at a long-term care facility about safety techniques to use when transferring patients. What is the **PRIMARY** objective of this type of in-service?

    A. To identify injury risk factors and minimize hazards

    B. To reduce workers' compensation claims within the facility

    C. To comply with legal mandates for staff safety training

    D. To decrease facility liability for job-related injuries

34. An older adult patient is recovering from pneumonia in a subacute setting. The patient has generalized weakness and ambulates independently with a cane in physical therapy sessions. The COTA is scheduled to supervise the patient during self-care sessions. Which risk management technique would be **MOST BENEFICIAL** to use when walking the patient from the bed to the bathroom during the initial session in the patient's room?

    A. Have the patient wear a transfer belt and use a walker.

    B. Ask a caregiver to provide additional stand-by assistance.

    C. Have the patient wear well-fitting non-skid footwear.

    D. Ask the patient to walk with a slow, shuffling gait.

35. A COTA working in a long-term psychiatric facility is supervising a craft group for residents who have schizophrenia and are functioning at Allen Cognitive Level 3 (Manual actions). Which action should the COTA ensure takes place prior to the end of the session?

    A. Equipment and supplies used during the session are collected and counted.

    B. Residents wipe the tabletops clean with an antibacterial solution.

    C. Projects are labeled in bold print on a contrasting color background.

    D. Each resident signs an attendance sheet for therapy minutes verification.

36. A resident has moderate cognitive decline secondary to dementia and lives in the memory care unit of a skilled nursing facility. The resident is considered an elopement risk but is permitted to leave the unit to attend an OT gardening group. What preventive measure should the COTA take to ensure the resident's safety when participating in the group?

    A. Include residents of similar level of cognitive abilities in the group.

    B. Store materials needed for the group in a secure location.

    C. Schedule the group to occur in a secure, enclosed courtyard.

37. A COTA observes that an inpatient has used a lancing device to measure blood glucose level and has discarded it on the floor near the bed. What preventive measure **MUST** the COTA take when disposing of a used lancing device?

   A. Dispose in a trash can marked for hazardous waste.

   B. Place in a secure plastic bag in a trash receptacle.

   C. Insert into a wall-mounted or mobile sharps container box.

38. The special education team of a public school has verified that a student with Angelman syndrome requires an augmentative and alternative communication device to communicate with teachers and peers. According to the Individuals with Disabilities Education Act, which criteria **MUST** the school meet with regard to this device?

   Select the 3 best choices.

   A. Customize the device to the student's specific needs.

   B. Require the vendor to provide an extended maintenance agreement for the device.

   C. Purchase or lease the device for the student.

   D. Require the parents to finance the device for the student.

   E. Ensure the student and family receive training to operate the device.

   F. Teach the parents how to integrate the device into home activities.

39. An inpatient has provided the COTA with contact information for a family member who will be the primary caregiver for the patient after discharge from the hospital. The COTA plans to contact the family member to discuss recommendations for durable medical equipment and to schedule a time for the family member to attend a therapy session to participate in caregiver education. To be in compliance with the Health Insurance Portability and Accountability Act (HIPAA), which task **MUST** the COTA complete?

    A. Ensure the patient signs a release of information document in the presence of a witness and place it in the medical record.

    B. Have the patient review and approve the recommendations for durable medical equipment and the outline for the education session.

    C. Document the patient's consent in the medical record and use precautions to ensure communication is occurring with the intended family member.

40. Which federal law in the United States regulates how special education and related services are provided to school-aged children with disabilities?

    A. Individuals with Disabilities Education Act (IDEA) Part B

    B. Section 504 of the Vocational Rehabilitation Act

    C. Individuals with Disabilities Education Act (IDEA) Part C

41. A COTA and an OTR working in a skilled nursing facility are collaborating to complete an initial intervention plan for a patient who sustained a hip and wrist fracture 5 days ago. What information **MUST** be included in this patient's documentation to meet Medicare requirements for reimbursement of services?

    A. Pain level and expected changes to strength and ROM by time of discharge

    B. Activities the COTA will be responsible for providing during sessions

    C. Long-term functional goals that are medically necessary for the patient

    D. Specific techniques and activities that will be used during sessions

42. What information should be evident in the client contact notes to justify the need for additional OT services to a client's insurance company?

    A. Subjective reports of progress in therapy

    B. Progress as it relates to the initial functional goals

    C. Comments on anticipated function at discharge

    D. Rate of progress as compared to other patients

43. A COTA is working in a skilled nursing facility that operates under Medicare regulations. What information **MUST** the COTA document after each intervention session to meet reimbursement requirements of the prospective payment system (PPS)?

    A. Patient's response to specific treatment techniques

    B. Supplies and equipment used during the session

    C. Total number of minutes spent treating the patient

    D. Day and time of the next scheduled treatment session

44. In addition to documenting function-based, skilled interventions using professional terminology, what is the **MOST IMPORTANT** action the COTA must take to facilitate reimbursement for occupational therapy services?

   A. Document evidence to support intervention methods

   B. Obtain pre-authorization prior to each session

   C. Provide an accurate billing code

45. A COTA is preparing to write a SOAP progress note for an inpatient who has a complete C_7 spinal cord injury and has been participating in OT for one week to increase independence in upper extremity dressing. The patient is now able to independently sit up in bed and put on a pullover shirt but still requires caregiver assistance to get the shirt from the closet. Which statement about the patient would be **BEST** to include in the "A" section of the note?

   A. The patient is learning compensatory strategies and is moving toward the long-term dressing goal as stated in the initial plan.

   B. The patient will require assistive devices and assistance from a caregiver for most self-care tasks after discharge.

   C. The patient wants to learn how to use additional adaptive devices for lower body dressing and bathing.

   D. The patient scored a "3" (moderate assist) on the dressing section of the Functional Independence Measure (FIM™).

46. A patient who had a total knee replacement 3 days ago is being discharged from an acute care facility to an inpatient rehabilitation program. The COTA is contributing outcome information for the OTR to include in the discharge summary. What information would be **MOST BENEFICIAL** to use for this purpose?

   A. Types of assistive devices used during this phase of recovery

   B. Level of the patient's occupational function prior to hospitalization

   C. Objective information on functional goals achieved

   D. Statements about the patient's participation in goal setting

47. An inpatient is preparing for discharge from an acute mental health setting after undergoing treatment for major depression. The patient will receive follow-up services at a community mental health program. The COTA is contributing outcome information to the OTR for inclusion in the patient's discharge summary. What information would be **MOST BENEFICIAL** to use for this purpose?

  A. Description of job-related skills the patient used during activities

  B. Patient's functional potential based on current rate of progress

  C. Subjective impressions of the patient's functional independence

  D. Current self-care abilities compared to initial evaluation results

48. After a client participates in a session to learn how to access public transportation, the COTA documents in the medical record, "The client demonstrates difficulty navigating crowds at the train station due to the noise level triggering flashbacks to a traumatic event." In which section of the SOAP note should this statement appear?

  A. Subjective

  B. Objective

  C. Assessment

  D. Plan

49. A COTA who works in a hospital setting is documenting a cancellation note for a patient who was unavailable for therapy due to having a scheduled MRI. When documenting in the medical record, what information is **BEST** for the COTA to include in the cancellation note?

  A. Upon arrival at the patient's room today, the patient was not present. The occupational therapy session scheduled for today is canceled.

  B. Patient did not attend therapy today. Recommend placing the patient on medical hold until further orders are received from the physician.

  C. Attempted to provide intervention today, but the patient was unavailable due to having an MRI. Will attempt to see patient again tomorrow.

50. A COTA is providing services to an inpatient who recently had a brain injury and has impaired attention. One of the intervention goals is to increase the length of time the patient attends to paying bills online. When documenting the patient's progress toward this goal, what information is **BEST** to include in the "O" section of the SOAP note?

A. The patient often looks around the room and requires redirection to complete bill payment.

B. The patient is able to attend to paying bills for 10 minutes without getting distracted.

C. The patient frequently stops the bill payment task and reads emails during the session.

Answer Key

Domain 3 Sample Items

Item Number	Key
1.	C
2.	A
3.	A
4.	A, D, E
5.	A
6.	A
7.	C
8.	A
9.	B
10.	D
11.	A
12.	A, C, F
13.	A
14.	A, E, F
15.	D
16.	D, E, F
17.	C
18.	B
19.	B
20.	C
21.	C
22.	C
23.	B
24.	A, C, F
25.	C

Item Number	Key
26.	A
27.	A
28.	C
29.	B
30.	C
31.	B
32.	B
33.	A
34.	C
35.	A
36.	C
37.	C
38.	A, C, E
39.	C
40.	A
41.	C
42.	B
43.	C
44.	C
45.	A
46.	C
47.	D
48.	C
49.	C
50.	B

Multiple Choice Answers, Rationales, and References

1. An OTR and a COTA are collaborating to search for evidence about the effectiveness of constraint-induced movement therapy for stroke patients. Based on the hierarchy of evidence, which option is considered the highest level of evidence?

   A. Opinions of expert practitioners working in neurological rehabilitation

   B. Descriptive studies using a single-subject research design

   C. Meta-analyses of randomized controlled trials

Correct Answer: C

RATIONALE:
Systematic reviews and meta-analyses of randomized controlled trials are considered level 1 evidence, the highest level of evidence.

Reference:
Wagenfeld, A. (2016). *Foundations of theory and practice for the occupational therapy assistant* (pp. 56-57). Baltimore, MD: Lippincott Williams & Wilkins.

2. A COTA plans to use the PICO method to search a database for practice-relevant information. What is the **PRIMARY** purpose for using this method to search for evidence?

   A. **To identify a clinically relevant, answerable question**

   B. To locate client-centered and occupation-based methods

   C. To filter the search for randomized controlled trials

Correct Answer: A

RATIONALE:
The PICO method is an approach used to identify a clinically relevant, answerable question when searching for evidence.
P – Populations/People/Patient/Problem
I – Intervention(s)
C – Comparison
O – Outcome

Reference:
Jacobs, K. (Ed.). (2016). *Management and administration for the OTA: Leadership and application skills.* (pp. 152-153). Thorofare, NJ: SLACK, Inc.

3. A COTA is planning to lead a discussion about the first step in the evidence-based practice process during a rehabilitation team meeting. What information should the COTA include in the discussion when summarizing the first step in the evidence-based practice process?

   A. Asking a clinical question based on clients seen at the clinic

   B. Synthesizing several articles found in a scholarly database

   C. Applying research evidence when making practice decisions

Correct Answer: A

RATIONALE:
The first step in the evidence-based practice process is for the COTA to reflect on situations and issues associated with clients on the caseload and formulate a question based on clinical need.

References:
Smith-Gabai, H., & Holm, S. (Eds.). (2017). *Occupational therapy in acute care* (2nd ed., p. 28). Bethesda, MD: AOTA Press.

Sladyk, K., & Ryan, S. E. (Eds.). (2015). *Ryan's occupational therapy assistant: Principles, practice issues, and techniques* (5th ed., pp. 545-547). Thorofare, NJ: SLACK, Inc.

4. A COTA works in an outpatient setting. A client who recently had a CVA and is on the COTA caseload asks the COTA about trying a new treatment technique for increasing movement in the affected upper extremity. The COTA has heard of the technique but does not know how beneficial it would be. In addition to informing the OTR, what actions should the COTA take based on the client's inquiry?

Select the 3 best choices.

A. Identify the value of using the new intervention instead of the current intervention.

B. Ask if the client is willing to participate in a single-subject case study related to the technique.

C. Tell the client that there are many well-accepted alternatives that should be tried before using this technique.

D. Search online databases to identify best practice trends for the client's current condition.

E. Read articles in peer-reviewed journals to determine if research supports the use of this intervention.

F. Obtain intervention protocols from other clinics currently using the technique with clients.

Correct Answers: A, D, E

RATIONALE:
Using these principles of evidence-based practice, the COTA can work toward an increased understanding of the benefits associated with the intervention technique.

Reference:
Sladyk, K., & Ryan, S. E. (Eds.). (2015). *Ryan's occupational therapy assistant: Principles, practice issues, and techniques* (5th ed., pp. 545-553). Thorofare, NJ: SLACK, Inc.

5. An inpatient OT department recently completed a retrospective chart audit to determine staff compliance with the documentation policy. Over 60% of the charts that were reviewed had incomplete signatures or non-approved abbreviations. What is the **NEXT** action the OT department should take based on this information?

   A. **Initiate a performance improvement program.**

   B. Schedule a staff meeting to discuss the findings.

   C. Repeat the audit in 30 days to compare results.

Correct Answer: A

RATIONALE:
The chart audit has identified that there is a problem with staff compliance regarding the documentation policy. The **NEXT** step is to develop a systematic approach to improve and measure compliance with the policy.

References:
Early, M. B. (2017). *Mental health concepts & techniques for the occupational therapy assistant* (5th ed., pp. 468-470). Philadelphia, PA: Lippincott Williams & Wilkins.

Jacobs, K. (Ed.). (2016). *Management and administration for the OTA: Leadership and application skills.* (pp. 80-84). Thorofare, NJ: SLACK, Inc.

6. A COTA and an OTR work in a hospital setting and are collaborating on the first step of a quality improvement initiative. The goal of the initiative is to review archived clinical documentation records to determine the presence of patient-specific discharge instructions. What is the **PRIMARY** purpose for completing this step of the quality initiative?

   A. **To determine if change is needed to the department documentation policy for discharge instructions**

   B. To provide the supervisor with names of staff members who frequently do not document discharge information

   C. To ensure the patient successfully transitioned from the hospital to home with minimal risk of readmission

Correct Answer: A

RATIONALE:
The first step of a quality improvement initiative is to collect data related to the goal of the initiative to determine the need for process, procedural, or policy change.

Reference:
Jacobs, K. (Ed.). (2016). *Management and administration for the OTA: Leadership and application skills.* (pp. 80-84). Thorofare, NJ: SLACK, Inc.

7. A newly certified COTA recently started working at an inpatient rehabilitation facility. The supervising OTR wants the COTA to assist with administering standardized manual muscle tests as part of patient reevaluations. The COTA has only administered this test to classmates when in school and received an excellent score on the final laboratory exam. After confirming that state licensure regulations permit the COTA to administer standardized tests, what is the **NEXT** action the COTA should take?

   A. Review class notes on the proper administration procedures for the test.

   B. Ask the OTR to clarify the specific muscles included in the test.

   C. Talk with the OTR about establishing service competency for the test.

   D. Arrange for an OT colleague to observe so inter-rater reliability can be established.

Correct Answer: C

RATIONALE:
If the state OT practice act permits the COTA to administer standardized tests, then the COTA should collaborate with the OTR to establish service competency before independently administering a manual muscle test to a client.

Reference:
Early, M. B. (2013). *Physical dysfunction practice skills for the occupational therapy assistant* (3rd ed., p. 132). St. Louis, MO: Mosby Elsevier.

8. A COTA worked in an outpatient hand therapy clinic for the past 5 years. The COTA recently obtained a new job and will start work as a COTA in an inpatient neuro-rehabilitation setting. What **INITIAL** step should the COTA take to develop service competency in the new job?

   A. **Arrange a schedule to have close supervision when working with patients.**

   B. Provide the OTR with verification of service-competent tasks from the previous job.

   C. Learn about clinical protocols by leading a staff discussion on the topic.

   D. Have the supervising OTR review and co-sign each patient contact note.

   Correct Answer: A

   RATIONALE:
   Since the COTA does not have recent experience in this practice setting, the COTA should have close supervision until service competency is established.

   Reference:
   Early, M. B. (2013). *Physical dysfunction practice skills for the occupational therapy assistant* (3rd ed., pp. 56-57). St. Louis, MO: Mosby Elsevier.

9. A newly certified COTA recently started a new job in a large rehabilitation clinic. Part of the essential job tasks include fabricating dynamic orthotics on a routine basis. The COTA received basic splinting instruction in school yet feels the need for further training. What action would be **MOST BENEFICIAL** for the COTA to take to establish service competency in this area?

   A. Register to attend an online professional development workshop on splinting.

   B. Arrange for structured mentorship that includes close supervision.

   C. Use a checklist of fabrication tips and techniques when making dynamic orthotics.

   D. Review school notes and read journal articles about splinting.

Correct Answer: B

RATIONALE:
Supervision and structured learning provide an effective means for establishing service competency with splinting.

References:
Early, M. B. (2013). *Physical dysfunction practice skills for the occupational therapy assistant* (3rd ed., pp. 56-57). St. Louis, MO: Mosby Elsevier.

Solomon, J. W., & O'Brien, J. C. (2016). *Pediatric skills for occupational therapy assistants* (4th ed., pp. 6-7). St. Louis, MO: Mosby Elsevier.

10. A school-based OTR and COTA are collaborating to evaluate a kindergarten student who has autism spectrum disorder. Which task can the COTA complete as part of this data gathering process?

   A. Score a sensory integration assessment.

   B. Select developmentally appropriate assessment tools.

   C. Analyze evaluation results.

   D. **Administer a developmental skills checklist.**

Correct Answer: D

RATIONALE:
Administering a developmental skills checklist after establishing service competency is a typical responsibility for a COTA. This task is within the scope of practice for a newly certified COTA.

Reference:
Solomon, J. W., & O'Brien, J. C. (2016). *Pediatric skills for occupational therapy assistants* (4th ed., pp. 6-7, 51-52). St. Louis, MO: Mosby Elsevier.

11. A COTA working in an inpatient rehabilitation clinic is assigned to supervise a newly hired therapy aide. What information **MUST** the COTA know prior to assigning job tasks to the aide?

   A. **State OT practice act guidelines for service provision**

   B. Critical demands listed in the aide's job description

   C. Previous experience the aide has had working with patients

   D. Aide's knowledge of occupational therapy interventions

Correct Answer: A

RATIONALE:
The COTA is obligated to provide supervision to an OT aide in accordance with specific state practice acts and governing laws.

Reference:
Pendleton, H. M., & Schultz-Krohn, W. (Eds.). (2018). *Pedretti's occupational therapy: Practice skills for the physical dysfunction* (8th ed., p. 35). St. Louis, MO: Mosby Elsevier.

12. A student in the first grade has difficulty forming letters and shapes and copying from the board at the front of the classroom. This interferes with the student's ability to complete grade-level tasks. The OTR and COTA are collaborating to gather information about client factors influencing the student's handwriting development. Which information gathering methods are within the scope of practice for a service-competent COTA to complete as part of this process?

Select the 3 best choices.

A. Describe the student's posture when seated at the desk.

B. Determine the student's grade-level handwriting function.

C. Note the type of grasp the student uses to hold a pencil.

D. Compare the student's at-desk work to classmates' work.

E. Administer and interpret the Sensory Processing Measure.

F. Collect a sample of the student's in-class writing assignments.

Correct Answers: A, C, F

RATIONALE:
In collaboration with the OTR, classroom observations of handwriting performance are within the scope of practice for a service-competent COTA.

References:
Solomon, J. W., & O'Brien, J. C. (2016). *Pediatric skills for occupational therapy assistants* (4th ed., pp. 436-439). St. Louis, MO: Mosby Elsevier.

Wagenfeld, A., Kaldenberg, J., & Honaker, D. (Eds.). (2017). *Foundations of pediatric practice for the occupational therapy assistant* (2nd ed., p. 292). Thorofare, NJ: SLACK, Inc.

13. A COTA has service competence for a specific standardized assessment. Which task related to the assessment can the COTA be expected to complete independently?

   A. **Administering each of the subtests**

   B. Interpreting the test results

   C. Selecting which client should be tested

Correct Answer: A

RATIONALE:
Administering the subtests of a standardized assessment after establishing service competency is within the scope of practice for a COTA.

Reference:
Jacobs, K., & MacRae, N. (Eds.). (2017). *Occupational therapy essentials for clinical competence* (3rd ed., p. 768). Thorofare, NJ: SLACK, Inc.

14. An OTR and a service-competent COTA work in an outpatient pediatric setting and are collaborating to evaluate an adolescent who recently had a TBI. Which tasks are within the scope of practice for the COTA to complete as part of this data gathering process?

    Select the 3 best choices.

    A. **Administer a standardized cognitive test.**

    B. Analyze data from an occupational role history.

    C. Identify a performance-based outcome measure.

    D. Interpret results of the occupational profile.

    E. **Perform an interview about daily routines.**

    F. **Record observations during a functional task.**

Correct Answers: A, E, F

RATIONALE:
As part of the data gathering process, it is within the scope of practice for the service-competent COTA to complete these tasks in collaboration with the OTR.

Reference:
Jacobs, K., & MacRae, N. (Eds.). (2017). *Occupational therapy essentials for clinical competence* (3rd ed., p. 768). Thorofare, NJ: SLACK, Inc.

15. A COTA is preparing an in-service about injury prevention for employees at a data-entry and computer software company. What information is **MOST IMPORTANT** to include in this presentation?

- **A.** Symptoms associated with cumulative trauma
- **B.** Isokinetic exercises for reducing painful symptoms
- **C.** Impact of work-related injuries on the company
- **D. Methods for reducing work-related risk factors**

Correct Answer: D

RATIONALE:
It is **MOST IMPORTANT** to educate employees about work-related risk factors. Of the options presented, this has the greatest impact on preventing injuries, which is the purpose of the in-service.

Reference:
Early, M. B. (2013). *Physical dysfunction practice skills for the occupational therapy assistant* (3rd ed., pp. 346-349). St. Louis, MO: Mosby Elsevier.

16. A COTA is preparing to give a presentation about fall prevention strategies for community-dwelling older adults. The objective of the presentation is to reduce the participants' risk of falling. In addition to providing information on how to create a safe home environment, which topics would be **MOST BENEFICIAL** to teach in the presentation to meet this goal?

Select the 3 best choices.

A. List of medical diagnoses that place a person at high risk for falling

B. Resources to enhance social involvement in the community

C. Reviews of healthy eating habits and nutritional information on prepared foods

D. **Advantages of routinely completing an exercise program**

E. **Purpose of having a regular vision examination**

F. **Benefits of a health-care provider to review a list of prescribed medications**

Correct Answers: D, E, F

RATIONALE:
These options represent methods that are within the scope of occupational therapy practice to decrease the risk of falling.

References:
Early, M. B. (2013). *Physical dysfunction practice skills for the occupational therapy assistant* (3rd ed., p. 382). St. Louis, MO: Mosby Elsevier.

Smith-Gabai, H., & Holm, S. (Eds.). (2017). *Occupational therapy in acute care* (2nd ed., p. 110). Bethesda, MD: AOTA Press.

17. The multidisciplinary team at a community-based program is developing a substance use relapse program. The focus of the program is to promote healthy alternatives for at-risk clients. What is the **PRIMARY** contribution of the COTA during the initial phase of program development?

   A. To recommend program topics unrelated to triggers that lead to misuse

   B. To identify resources for determining barriers to participation

   C. To suggest program activities related to leisure skill development

   D. To determine specific outcome measures for the program

Correct Answer: C

RATIONALE:
The substance abuse program emphasizes improving clients' function and providing them with skill development.

Reference:
Early, M. B. (2017). *Mental health concepts & techniques for the occupational therapy assistant* (5th ed., p. 172). Philadelphia, PA: Lippincott Williams & Wilkins.

18. A COTA is preparing to give a presentation for an arthritis support group. The goal of the presentation is to communicate the role of occupational therapy in assisting individuals who have systemic lupus. Which communication method would be **MOST BENEFICIAL** to use in the presentation to meet this goal?

   A. Describe specific OT assessments typically used with individuals who have lupus.

   B. Discuss OT interventions and service options for individuals who have lupus.

   C. Simulate a typical OT session by including one of the participants as an example.

   D. Demonstrate a range of exercises for individuals who have lupus.

Correct Answer: B

RATIONALE:
An interactive discussion is not only informative but can be tailored to the participants' interests and concerns.

Reference:
Early, M. B. (2013). *Physical dysfunction practice skills for the occupational therapy assistant* (3rd ed., pp. 181-184, 574-575). St. Louis, MO: Mosby Elsevier.

19. A COTA believes that several residents on the OT caseload no longer qualify for OT services, but the supervisor and the employer expect intervention should continue for the duration of the residents' length of stay. What is the **FIRST** action the COTA should take based on this concern?

   A. Seek input from colleagues on various social media platforms.

   B. Use a decision-making framework to develop a plan of action.

   C. File a formal complaint with the state regulatory board.

Correct Answer: B

RATIONALE:
The **FIRST** action a COTA should take when faced with an ethical dilemma is to use a decision-making framework to develop a plan of action.

Reference:
Jacobs, K. (Ed.). (2016). *Management and administration for the OTA: Leadership and application skills.* (pp. 136-137). Thorofare, NJ: SLACK, Inc.

20. An inpatient is participating in a rehabilitation program after experiencing an exacerbation of relapsing-remitting multiple sclerosis. The patient is making steady progress toward the intervention goal of resuming independence with homemaking tasks. While completing personal laundry tasks during a session, the patient reports being extremely tired from not sleeping well the previous night and asks to take a brief rest. What **INITIAL** action should the COTA take in response to the patient's report?

    A. Ensure that the patient uses energy conservation techniques for the remainder of the session.

    B. Allow the patient to take a short break and encourage pursed-lip breathing.

    C. Discontinue the session and notify the charge nurse about the patient's fatigue.

    D. Demonstrate additional work simplification techniques to use during laundry tasks.

Correct Answer: C

RATIONALE:
The COTA should stop the activity for the day and alert the charge nurse of the patient's symptoms. Extreme fatigue can trigger an exacerbation of multiple sclerosis.

References:
Early, M. B. (2013). *Physical dysfunction practice skills for the occupational therapy assistant* (3rd ed., pp. 517-519). St. Louis, MO: Mosby Elsevier.

Pendleton, H. M., & Schultz-Krohn, W. (Eds.). (2018). *Pedretti's occupational therapy: Practice skills for the physical dysfunction* (8th ed., pp. 890-893). St. Louis, MO: Mosby Elsevier.

21. A client who has atrial fibrillation is taking a prescribed blood-thinning medication. The client attends college and wants to participate in leisure activities offered on the campus. Which preventive strategy should the COTA teach the client to minimize the risk of injury associated with common side effects of blood thinners?

    A. Ask the client not to attend events with flashing lights.

    B. Suggest that the client select sedentary activities.

    C. Advise the client to avoid contact sports.

Correct Answer: C

RATIONALE:
A common side effect of blood-thinning medication is a greater risk of bruising and bleeding. A client who is taking blood-thinning medication should avoid participation in leisure pursuits that are associated with risk of falling or direct physical contact.

Reference:
Lohman, H., Byers-Connon, S., & Padilla, R. L. (2019). *Occupational therapy with elders: Strategies for the COTA* (4th ed., p. 173). Maryland Heights, MO: Mosby Elsevier.

22. A COTA who works in an intensive care unit is preparing to assist a patient, who had surgery for a coronary artery bypass graft, with completing BADL while seated in a bedside chair. What action is **MOST IMPORTANT** for the COTA to take as part of the intervention during this phase of the patient's rehabilitation?

   A. Discuss work simplification and pacing with the patient.

   B. Place grooming and bathing supplies within reach of the patient.

   C. Monitor the patient's heart rate and blood pressure during self-care.

Correct Answer: C

RATIONALE:
To ensure patient safety in a critical care setting, it is important to monitor vital signs throughout the intervention session.

References:
Early, M. B. (2013). *Physical dysfunction practice skills for the occupational therapy assistant* (3rd ed., pp. 678-680). St. Louis, MO: Mosby Elsevier.

Smith-Gabai, H., & Holm, S. (Eds.). (2017). *Occupational therapy in acute care* (2nd ed., pp. 244-245, 251). Bethesda, MD: AOTA Press.

23. An older adult who has emphysema was admitted to an acute care hospital 3 days ago with pneumonia. One of the intervention goals is for the patient to resume independence in ADL. During a session, the patient brushes teeth in a standing position. The COTA measures the patient's vital signs and notes oxygen saturation level is 92%, blood pressure is 101/65 mmHg, and heart rate is 98 bpm. Based on this information, what is the **NEXT** action the COTA should take?

    A. Advise the patient to put on a nasal cannula and discontinue the intervention session.

    B. Have the patient sit in a chair and teach the patient to use pursed-lip breathing.

    C. Proceed with the intervention activity and monitor the patient's vital signs periodically.

Correct Answer: B

RATIONALE:
The normal range for pulse oximetry (SpO_2) is 95% - 100%; however, an abnormal reading of 92% does not warrant an emergency response. The blood pressure and heart rate measurements are within a normal range. The COTA should assist the patient to a position of safety and teach breathing techniques to encourage a rise in the level of oxygen saturation.

Reference:
Smith-Gabai, H., & Holm, S. (Eds.). (2017). *Occupational therapy in acute care* (2nd ed., pp. 116-118, 162, 278-279, 286). Bethesda, MD: AOTA Press.

24. A COTA is scheduled to complete a transfer training session with an inpatient who has stage 4 Parkinson's disease. Admission notes indicate the patient has experienced several recent falls as a result of syncope and was using a walker for mobility prior to admission. The COTA plans to transfer the patient from the bed to a bedside commode during the session. To reduce fall risk, what information should the COTA gather about the patient prior to initiating the transfer training session?

    Select the 3 best choices.

    A. Cognitive function

    B. Oxygen levels

    C. Fluidity of movement

    D. Perceived exertion

    E. Depth perception

    F. Visual acuity

Correct Answers: A, C, F

RATIONALE:
The COTA is responsible for understanding the client factors associated with fall risk in order to take necessary precautions to ensure the client's safety throughout the intervention session.

References:
Early, M. B. (2013). *Physical dysfunction practice skills for the occupational therapy assistant* (3rd ed., pp. 522-524). St. Louis, MO: Mosby Elsevier.

Lohman, H., Byers-Connon, S., & Padilla, R. L. (2019). *Occupational therapy with elders: Strategies for the COTA* (4th ed., pp. 197-200). Maryland Heights, MO: Mosby Elsevier.

25. A COTA is teaching compensatory techniques for facial shaving to a client who has mild choreiform movements of bilateral upper extremities. The COTA wants to be sure standard precautions are followed during this BADL task. Which action should the COTA have the client do as part of this process?

   A. Clean the razor with alcohol after completing the shaving activity.

   B. Practice with an electric shaver borrowed from the OT self-care room.

   C. **Bring in a personal electric shaver to use during the session.**

   D. Purchase a bag of disposable straight-edge razors.

Correct Answer: C

RATIONALE:
To minimize infection risk, the client should use a personal shaver. The client should use an electric razor to decrease risk of cuts from choreiform movements.

Reference:
Early, M. B. (2013). *Physical dysfunction practice skills for the occupational therapy assistant* (3rd ed., pp. 42-43, 45-46, 255-256). St. Louis, MO: Mosby Elsevier.

26. During a session in the home, a client who has dementia unexpectedly is incontinent of urine. While using personal protective barriers, the COTA works with the caregiver to clean the client and the area. What is the **NEXT** action the COTA should take?

   A. **Wash hands for 15 seconds using a mild soap.**

   B. Terminate therapy session and reschedule.

   C. Document occurrence in the electronic medical record.

Correct Answer: A

RATIONALE:
The **NEXT** action the COTA should take is to follow standard infection control procedures and use effective hand-washing techniques to reduce the spread of germs.

Reference:
Jacobs, K., & MacRae, N. (Eds.). (2017). *Occupational therapy essentials for clinical competence* (3rd ed., p. 165). Thorofare, NJ: SLACK, Inc.

27. During an ADL group session, an inpatient with quadriplegia reports a sudden onset of a pounding headache, begins to perspire excessively, and has chills. What **INITIAL** action should the COTA take in response to these symptoms?

   A. **Activate the facility medical alert system.**

   B. Transport the patient to their room to rest.

   C. Stop the activity until the patient's vital signs stabilize.

Correct Answer: A

RATIONALE:
These symptoms are consistent with autonomic dysreflexia, which is life-threatening. The COTA's **INITIAL** action should be to obtain emergency medical assistance.

Reference:
Early, M. B. (2013). *Physical dysfunction practice skills for the occupational therapy assistant* (3rd ed., p. 539). St. Louis, MO: Mosby Elsevier.

28. A client who has diabetes mellitus is participating in a BADL session. When sitting on the shower chair, the COTA notes that the client's skin is pale, breathing is shallow, and the client's hands are trembling. The client reports feeling hungry and confused. What **IMMEDIATE** action should the COTA take in this situation?

A. Have the client administer an insulin injection.

B. Check the client's blood glucose level.

C. **Provide the client with half a glass of fruit juice.**

Correct Answer: C

RATIONALE:
Drinking a small amount of a glucose-rich beverage, such as fruit juice, can reduce the effects of an insulin reaction.

Reference:
Early, M. B. (2013). *Physical dysfunction practice skills for the occupational therapy assistant* (3rd ed., p. 47). St. Louis, MO: Mosby Elsevier.

29. A COTA is fabricating an orthosis for a client who recently had a deep partial thickness burn to the dorsum of the hand. When the COTA removes the bulky dressing, the patient becomes lightheaded and begins to sweat. What **INITIAL** action should the COTA take in response to this occurrence?

   A. Break open an ammonia ampule and slowly pass it under the client's nose.

   B. Assist the client to a supine position and elevate the client's legs.

   C. Ask the client to rest their head on the table or between their knees.

   D. Moisten a cloth with cool water and hold it across the client's forehead.

Correct Answer: B

RATIONALE:
Intense pain or an unpleasant experience may cause a temporary autonomic vasovagal response. As a result, the heart rate and blood pressure drop, which reduces blood flow to the brain. This results in a feeling of warmth, lightheadedness, dimming vision and hearing, and even fainting (vasovagal syncope). The client must be quickly reclined with the legs elevated for the blood pressure to return to normal.

Reference:
Early, M. B. (2013). *Physical dysfunction practice skills for the occupational therapy assistant* (3rd ed., p. 47). St. Louis, MO: Mosby Elsevier.

30. During a community outing to a sporting event, a client chokes on a bite of food. The client is conscious and able to verbalize sounds but is having difficulty dislodging the food. In addition to calling for emergency assistance and helping the client stay calm, what **IMMEDIATE** action should the COTA take?

   A. Assist the client to a supine position.

   B. Perform the Heimlich maneuver.

   C. Encourage the client to cough forcefully.

Correct Answer: C

RATIONALE:
Initial first aid for a client who is choking but is conscious, can breathe, and speak is to encourage the client to independently clear the blockage.

Reference:
Pendleton, H. M., & Schultz-Krohn, W. (Eds.). (2018). *Pedretti's occupational therapy: Practice skills for the physical dysfunction* (8th ed., p. 151). St. Louis, MO: Mosby Elsevier.

31. During an intervention session, a resident in a skilled nursing facility reports that earlier in the day, a dizzy spell occurred with sharp headache pain and blurred vision. The COTA informs the resident that the medical staff needs to be informed, but the resident states, "I feel fine now, just a little tired. I want to keep working." In addition to reporting this occurrence to the OTR, how should the COTA respond in this situation?

   A. Continue the session while emphasizing safety precautions during mobility and transfers.

   B. **Stop the activity and report the situation to the nurse prior to proceeding with the session.**

   C. Respect the resident's wishes and plan to document the resident's symptoms in the progress note.

Correct Answer: B

RATIONALE:
The symptoms reported by the resident could be indicative of a medical incident that needs further follow-up by the medical staff.

References:
Early, M. B. (2013). *Physical dysfunction practice skills for the occupational therapy assistant* (3rd ed., p. 55). St. Louis, MO: Mosby Elsevier.

Sladyk, K., & Ryan, S. E. (Eds.). (2015). *Ryan's occupational therapy assistant: Principles, practice issues, and techniques* (5th ed., pp. 586-587). Thorofare, NJ: SLACK, Inc.

32. A COTA who works in an acute care hospital is providing intervention for an inpatient who has an intravenous (IV) line connected to an infusion pump. During the session, the auditory alarm of the infusion pump begins to sound. What action **MUST** the COTA take in response to the activation of the alarm system?

   A. Ask the patient to rate current pain level using a numerical rating scale.

   B. Press the nurse call button and alert the staff about the alarm.

   C. Locate the button to silence the alarm and turn down the volume.

Correct Answer: B

RATIONALE:
It is essential to prioritize informing nursing staff about the activation of the alarm to ensure the patient receives necessary medical care and to reduce risk of harm to the patient.

References:
Early, M. B. (2013). *Physical dysfunction practice skills for the occupational therapy assistant* (3rd ed., pp. 45-46). St. Louis, MO: Mosby Elsevier.

Smith-Gabai, H., & Holm, S. (Eds.). (2017). *Occupational therapy in acute care* (2nd ed., pp. 109, 202). Bethesda, MD: AOTA Press.

33. A COTA is planning an in-service to instruct the nursing staff at a long-term care facility about safety techniques to use when transferring patients. What is the **PRIMARY** objective of this type of in-service?

   A. **To identify injury risk factors and minimize hazards**

   B. To reduce workers' compensation claims within the facility

   C. To comply with legal mandates for staff safety training

   D. To decrease facility liability for job-related injuries

Correct Answer: A

RATIONALE:
In-service training as a preventive strategy benefits both staff and clients. Identifying risk factors and reducing hazards will decrease the likelihood of work-related injuries during patient transfers.

Reference:
Jacobs, K., & MacRae, N. (Eds.). (2017). *Occupational therapy essentials for clinical competence* (3rd ed., pp. 483, 497). Thorofare, NJ: SLACK, Inc.

34. An older adult patient is recovering from pneumonia in a subacute setting. The patient has generalized weakness and ambulates independently with a cane in physical therapy sessions. The COTA is scheduled to supervise the patient during self-care sessions. Which risk management technique would be **MOST BENEFICIAL** to use when walking the patient from the bed to the bathroom during the initial session in the patient's room?

   A. Have the patient wear a transfer belt and use a walker.

   B. Ask a caregiver to provide additional stand-by assistance.

   C. **Have the patient wear well-fitting non-skid footwear.**

   D. Ask the patient to walk with a slow, shuffling gait.

Correct Answer: C

RATIONALE:
Non-skid footwear will help the patient obtain a more secure footing and minimize the risk of falling.

Reference:
Early, M. B. (2013). *Physical dysfunction practice skills for the occupational therapy assistant* (3rd ed., pp. 298-299). St. Louis, MO: Mosby Elsevier.

35. A COTA working in a long-term psychiatric facility is supervising a craft group for residents who have schizophrenia and are functioning at Allen Cognitive Level 3 (Manual actions). Which action should the COTA ensure takes place prior to the end of the session?

   A. Equipment and supplies used during the session are collected and counted.

   B. Residents wipe the tabletops clean with an antibacterial solution.

   C. Projects are labeled in bold print on a contrasting color background.

   D. Each resident signs an attendance sheet for therapy minutes verification.

Correct Answer: A

RATIONALE:
Residents functioning at this cognitive level should be monitored at all times. All equipment and supplies must be returned to a storage area and accounted for prior to allowing the residents to leave the room.

Reference:
Early, M. B. (2017). *Mental health concepts & techniques for the occupational therapy assistant* (5th ed., pp. 352-353). Philadelphia, PA: Lippincott Williams & Wilkins.

36. A resident has moderate cognitive decline secondary to dementia and lives in the memory care unit of a skilled nursing facility. The resident is considered an elopement risk but is permitted to leave the unit to attend an OT gardening group. What preventive measure should the COTA take to ensure the resident's safety when participating in the group?

   A. Include residents of similar level of cognitive abilities in the group.

   B. Store materials needed for the group in a secure location.

   C. Schedule the group to occur in a secure, enclosed courtyard.

Correct Answer: C

RATIONALE:
Using the contextual features of the enclosed courtyard will support the resident in safely participating in the gardening group while minimizing the risk of elopement.

References:
Early, M. B. (2017). *Mental health concepts & techniques for the occupational therapy assistant* (5th ed., pp. 334-35). Philadelphia, PA: Lippincott Williams & Wilkins.

Lohman, H., Byers-Connon, S., & Padilla, R. L. (2019). *Occupational therapy with elders: Strategies for the COTA* (4th ed., p. 287). Maryland Heights, MO: Mosby Elsevier.

37. A COTA observes that an inpatient has used a lancing device to measure blood glucose level and has discarded it on the floor near the bed. What preventive measure **MUST** the COTA take when disposing of a used lancing device?

A. Dispose in a trash can marked for hazardous waste.

B. Place in a secure plastic bag in a trash receptacle.

C. **Insert into a wall-mounted or mobile sharps container box.**

Correct Answer: C

RATIONALE:
It is essential to place all sharps in a designated sharps container box to prevent the risk of accidental needle sticks or punctures.

Reference:
Smith-Gabai, H., & Holm, S. (Eds.). (2017). *Occupational therapy in acute care* (2nd ed., pp. 202-203). Bethesda, MD: AOTA Press.

38. The special education team of a public school has verified that a student with Angelman syndrome requires an augmentative and alternative communication device to communicate with teachers and peers. According to the Individuals with Disabilities Education Act, which criteria **MUST** the school meet with regard to this device?

Select the 3 best choices.

A. **Customize the device to the student's specific needs.**

B. Require the vendor to provide an extended maintenance agreement for the device.

C. **Purchase or lease the device for the student.**

D. Require the parents to finance the device for the student.

E. **Ensure the student and family receive training to operate the device.**

F. Teach the parents how to integrate the device into home activities.

Correct Answers: A, C, E

RATIONALE:
These options represent the school system's responsibility to provide assistive technology services and devices to students with disabilities under the Individuals with Disabilities Education Act (IDEA).

Reference:
Solomon, J. W., & O'Brien, J. C. (2016). *Pediatric skills for occupational therapy assistants* (4th ed., p. 540). St. Louis, MO: Mosby Elsevier.

39. An inpatient has provided the COTA with contact information for a family member who will be the primary caregiver for the patient after discharge from the hospital. The COTA plans to contact the family member to discuss recommendations for durable medical equipment and to schedule a time for the family member to attend a therapy session to participate in caregiver education. To be in compliance with the Health Insurance Portability and Accountability Act (HIPAA), which task **MUST** the COTA complete?

A. Ensure the patient signs a release of information document in the presence of a witness and place it in the medical record.

B. Have the patient review and approve the recommendations for durable medical equipment and the outline for the education session.

C. **Document the patient's consent in the medical record and use precautions to ensure communication is occurring with the intended family member.**

Correct Answer: C

RATIONALE:
Once consent to communicate with the family members is obtained, the COTA should document this in the patent's medical record. Additionally, the COTA **MUST** take necessary precautions to ensure communication is occurring with the intended family member.

References:
Barney, K. F., & Perkinson, M. A. (2016). *Occupational therapy with aging adults: Promoting quality of life through collaborative practice* (pp. 20-21). St. Louis, MO: Elsevier Mosby.

Early, M. B. (2013). *Physical dysfunction practice skills for the occupational therapy assistant* (3rd ed., p. 78). St. Louis, MO: Mosby Elsevier.

Lohman, H., Byers-Connon, S., & Padilla, R. L. (2019). *Occupational therapy with elders: Strategies for the COTA* (4th ed., pp. 138-139). Maryland Heights, MO: Mosby Elsevier.

40. Which federal law in the United States regulates how special education and related services are provided to school-aged children with disabilities?

    A. Individuals with Disabilities Education Act (IDEA) Part B

    B. Section 504 of the Vocational Rehabilitation Act

    C. Individuals with Disabilities Education Act (IDEA) Part C

Correct Answer: A

RATIONALE:
Part B of the Individuals with Disabilities Education Act (IDEA) mandates the provision of special education services to children with disabilities ages 3 through 21 years of age.

Reference:
Case-Smith, J., & O'Brien, J. C. (2015). *Occupational therapy for children and adolescents* (7th ed., p. 665). St. Louis, MO: Mosby Elsevier.

41. A COTA and an OTR working in a skilled nursing facility are collaborating to complete an initial intervention plan for a patient who sustained a hip and wrist fracture 5 days ago. What information **MUST** be included in this patient's documentation to meet Medicare requirements for reimbursement of services?

A. Pain level and expected changes to strength and ROM by time of discharge

B. Activities the COTA will be responsible for providing during sessions

C. Long-term functional goals that are medically necessary for the patient

D. Specific techniques and activities that will be used during sessions

Correct Answer: C

RATIONALE:
To qualify for Medicare reimbursement, the documentation **MUST** indicate that the services provided are functional and medically necessary.

References:
Morreale, M. J., & Borcherding, S. (2017). *The OTA's guide to documentation: Writing SOAP notes* (4th ed., p. 234). Thorofare, NJ: SLACK, Inc.

Lohman, H., Byers-Connon, S., & Padilla, R. L. (2019). *Occupational therapy with elders: Strategies for the COTA* (4th ed., pp. 73-75). Maryland Heights, MO: Mosby Elsevier.

42. What information should be evident in the client contact notes to justify the need for additional OT services to a client's insurance company?

    A. Subjective reports of progress in therapy

    B. Progress as it relates to the initial functional goals

    C. Comments on anticipated function at discharge

    D. Rate of progress as compared to other patients

Correct Answer: B

RATIONALE:
Progress notes should provide evidence about the client's progress in relation to the established functional goals.

References:
Early, M. B. (2013). *Physical dysfunction practice skills for the occupational therapy assistant* (3rd ed., pp. 77-80, 90). St. Louis, MO: Mosby Elsevier.

Morreale, M. J., & Borcherding, S. (2017). *The OTA's guide to documentation: Writing SOAP notes* (4th ed., p. 28). Thorofare, NJ: SLACK, Inc.

43. A COTA is working in a skilled nursing facility that operates under Medicare regulations. What information **MUST** the COTA document after each intervention session to meet reimbursement requirements of the prospective payment system (PPS)?

A. Patient's response to specific treatment techniques

B. Supplies and equipment used during the session

C. Total number of minutes spent treating the patient

D. Day and time of the next scheduled treatment session

Correct Answer: C

RATIONALE:
Reimbursement from Medicare is determined by the number of "therapy minutes" that are documented in the minimum data set (MDS).

Reference:
Morreale, M. J., & Borcherding, S. (2017). *The OTA's guide to documentation: Writing SOAP notes* (4th ed., pp. 50-52). Thorofare, NJ: SLACK, Inc.

44. In addition to documenting function-based, skilled interventions using professional terminology, what is the **MOST IMPORTANT** action the COTA must take to facilitate reimbursement for occupational therapy services?

A. Document evidence to support intervention methods

B. Obtain pre-authorization prior to each session

C. Provide an accurate billing code

Correct Answer: C

RATIONALE:
Reimbursement for occupational therapy services is based on documentation and billing codes submitted by the provider. Accurate billing codes are essential to facilitate reimbursement for occupational therapy services.

References:
Jacobs, K. (Ed.). (2016). *Management and administration for the OTA: Leadership and application skills.* (p. 49). Thorofare, NJ: SLACK, Inc.

Wagenfeld, A. (2016). *Foundations of theory and practice for the occupational therapy assistant* (pp. 174-175). Baltimore, MD: Lippincott Williams & Wilkins.

45. A COTA is preparing to write a SOAP progress note for an inpatient who has a complete C_7 spinal cord injury and has been participating in OT for one week to increase independence in upper extremity dressing. The patient is now able to independently sit up in bed and put on a pullover shirt but still requires caregiver assistance to get the shirt from the closet. Which statement about the patient would be **BEST** to include in the "A" section of the note?

   A. **The patient is learning compensatory strategies and is moving toward the long-term dressing goal as stated in the initial plan.**

   B. The patient will require assistive devices and assistance from a caregiver for most self-care tasks after discharge.

   C. The patient wants to learn how to use additional adaptive devices for lower body dressing and bathing.

   D. The patient scored a "3" (moderate assist) on the dressing section of the Functional Independence Measure (FIM™).

Correct Answer: A

RATIONALE:
The "A" section of the SOAP note should reflect an assessment of the situation in relation to the established goal(s). In this case, the assessment is reflected **BEST** in option A.

References:
Morreale, M. J., & Borcherding, S. (2017). *The OTA's guide to documentation: Writing SOAP notes* (4th ed., pp. 133-136). Thorofare, NJ: SLACK, Inc.

Early, M. B. (2013). *Physical dysfunction practice skills for the occupational therapy assistant* (3rd ed., pp. 79-80, 92). St. Louis, MO: Mosby Elsevier.

46. A patient who had a total knee replacement 3 days ago is being discharged from an acute care facility to an inpatient rehabilitation program. The COTA is contributing outcome information for the OTR to include in the discharge summary. What information would be **MOST BENEFICIAL** to use for this purpose?

   A. Types of assistive devices used during this phase of recovery

   B. Level of the patient's occupational function prior to hospitalization

   C. Objective information on functional goals achieved

   D. Statements about the patient's participation in goal setting

Correct Answer: C

RATIONALE:
The discharge summary is a key document used when assessing outcomes. It must contain objective information about functional progress from initiation of OT to discharge.

References:
Early, M. B. (2013). *Physical dysfunction practice skills for the occupational therapy assistant* (3rd ed., pp. 77, 79, 80). St. Louis, MO: Mosby Elsevier.

Morreale, M. J., & Borcherding, S. (2017). *The OTA's guide to documentation: Writing SOAP notes* (4th ed., p. 222). Thorofare, NJ: SLACK, Inc.

47. An inpatient is preparing for discharge from an acute mental health setting after undergoing treatment for major depression. The patient will receive follow-up services at a community mental health program. The COTA is contributing outcome information to the OTR for inclusion in the patient's discharge summary. What information would be **MOST BENEFICIAL** to use for this purpose?

A. Description of job-related skills the patient used during activities

B. Patient's functional potential based on current rate of progress

C. Subjective impressions of the patient's functional independence

D. **Current self-care abilities compared to initial evaluation results**

Correct Answer: D

RATIONALE:
Emphasis of intervention in an acute mental health setting is on improving self-care skills. Progress and outcome are based on a comparison of skills from initiation of intervention to time of discharge.

References:
Early, M. B. (2013). *Physical dysfunction practice skills for the occupational therapy assistant* (3rd ed., pp. 77, 79, 80). St. Louis, MO: Mosby Elsevier.

Morreale, M. J., & Borcherding, S. (2017). *The OTA's guide to documentation: Writing SOAP notes* (4th ed., p. 222). Thorofare, NJ: SLACK, Inc.

48. After a client participates in a session to learn how to access public transportation, the COTA documents in the medical record, "The client demonstrates difficulty navigating crowds at the train station due to the noise level triggering flashbacks to a traumatic event." In which section of the SOAP note should this statement appear?

    A. Subjective

    B. Objective

    C. Assessment

    D. Plan

Correct Answer: C

RATIONALE:
This statement represents the "A" section of a SOAP note. It is a brief summary of the client's functional status based on the intervention provided during the session.

Reference:
Morreale, M. J., & Borcherding, S. (2017). *The OTA's guide to documentation: Writing SOAP notes* (4th ed., pp. 133-137). Thorofare, NJ: SLACK, Inc.

49. A COTA who works in a hospital setting is documenting a cancellation note for a patient who was unavailable for therapy due to having a scheduled MRI. When documenting in the medical record, what information is **BEST** for the COTA to include in the cancellation note?

   A. Upon arrival at the patient's room today, the patient was not present. The occupational therapy session scheduled for today is canceled.

   B. Patient did not attend therapy today. Recommend placing the patient on medical hold until further orders are received from the physician.

   C. Attempted to provide intervention today, but the patient was unavailable due to having an MRI. Will attempt to see patient again tomorrow.

Correct Answer: C

RATIONALE:
A cancellation note should include the reason for cancellation and relevant follow-up whenever possible.

Reference:
Morreale, M. J., & Borcherding, S. (2017). *The OTA's guide to documentation: Writing SOAP notes* (4th ed., p. 153). Thorofare, NJ: SLACK, Inc.

50. A COTA is providing services to an inpatient who recently had a brain injury and has impaired attention. One of the intervention goals is to increase the length of time the patient attends to paying bills online. When documenting the patient's progress toward this goal, what information is **BEST** to include in the "O" section of the SOAP note?

A. The patient often looks around the room and requires redirection to complete bill payment.

B. The patient is able to attend to paying bills for 10 minutes without getting distracted.

C. The patient frequently stops the bill payment task and reads emails during the session.

Correct Answer: B

RATIONALE:
The "O" section of the SOAP note includes quantitative information that the COTA measures from the patient's current performance abilities.

Reference:
Morreale, M. J., & Borcherding, S. (2017). *The OTA's guide to documentation: Writing SOAP notes* (4th ed., p. 93). Thorofare, NJ: SLACK, Inc.

Section 4
Appendices

Appendix A

Content Outline for the COTA Examination

	COTA DOMAIN DESCRIPTIONS	% OF EXAM
DOMAIN 01	**COLLABORATING AND GATHERING INFORMATION** Assist the OTR to acquire information regarding factors that influence occupational performance on an ongoing basis throughout the occupational therapy process.	28%
DOMAIN 02	**SELECTING AND IMPLEMENTING INTERVENTIONS** Implement interventions under the supervision of the OTR in accordance with the intervention plan and level of service competence to support client participation in areas of occupation throughout the occupational therapy process.	55%
DOMAIN 03	**UPHOLDING PROFESSIONAL STANDARDS AND RESPONSIBILITIES** Uphold professional standards and responsibilities by achieving service competence and applying evidence-based interventions to promote quality in practice.	17%

Appendix A • Content Outline for the COTA Examination

Validated Domain, Task, Knowledge Statements for the COTA Examination

DOMAIN 01	**COLLABORATING AND GATHERING INFORMATION** **Assist the OTR to acquire information regarding factors that influence occupational performance on an ongoing basis throughout the occupational therapy process.**

Task 0101	Recognize the influence of development; body functions and body structures; and values, beliefs, and spirituality on a client's occupational performance.

KNOWLEDGE OF:	
010101	Impact of typical development and aging on occupational performance, health, and wellness across the life span
010102	Expected patterns, progressions, and prognoses associated with conditions that limit occupational performance
010103	Impact of body functions, body structures, and values, beliefs, and spirituality on occupational performance

Task 0102	Acquire information by using available resources about a client's functional skills, roles, culture, performance context, and prioritized needs in order to contribute to the development and update of an occupational profile.

KNOWLEDGE OF:	
010201	Resources for acquiring information about the client's current condition and occupational performance
010202	Purpose, advantages, limitations, and service competency needs related to the administration of commonly used standardized assessments and non-standardized screening as a means of acquiring client information
010203	Internal and external factors influencing a client's meaningful engagement in occupation related to typical habits, roles, routines, and rituals, and the level and type of assistance required

Task 0103	Provide information regarding the influence of current conditions, contexts, and task demands on occupational performance in order to assist the OTR in planning interventions and monitoring progress as guided by the practice setting and theoretical construct.
	KNOWLEDGE OF:
	010301 — Influence of theoretical approaches, models of practice, and frames of reference on information-gathering and the intervention process
	010302 — Task analysis in relation to a client's performance skills, the occupational profile, practice setting, stage of occupational therapy process, areas of occupation, and activity demands

Task 0104	Collaborate with the client, the client's relevant others, occupational therapy colleagues, and other professionals and staff by using a culturally sensitive, client-centered approach and therapeutic use of self to provide quality services guided by evidence, scope of practice, service competence, and principles of best practice.
	KNOWLEDGE OF:
	010401 — Characteristics and functions of interprofessional teams for coordinating client care and providing efficient and effective services consistent with specific core competencies, expertise, unique contributions, team roles, and context of the organization
	010402 — Coordination of occupational therapy services related to collaborative client-centered intervention plans, Individualized Education Program plans, and transition plans based on client skills, abilities, and expected outcomes in relation to available resources, level of service delivery, and frequency and duration of intervention
	010403 — Collaborative processes and procedures for prioritizing intervention goals and activities based on client needs, wants, developmental skills, abilities, progress, and expected outcomes in relation to level of service delivery as well as frequency and duration of intervention
	010404 — Fundamental strategies used for addressing health literacy to enhance non-verbal and verbal interactions with a client and relevant others in order to promote positive health behaviors, enable informed decisions, maximize safety of care, and promote carry-over of the intervention to support positive outcomes

Appendix A • Content Outline for the COTA Examination

Task 0105	Monitor the intervention plan and progress toward goals in collaboration with the OTR by using clinical reasoning, therapeutic use of self, and cultural sensitivity to make decisions about the intervention approach, context, or goals based on client needs, priorities, response to intervention, status changes, reevaluation results, and targeted outcomes.	
	KNOWLEDGE OF:	
	010501	Factors related to determining the context and type of individual and group activities for effectively supporting intervention goals and objectives
	010502	Methods for monitoring the effectiveness of individual and group intervention in order to keep the OTR informed about continuation of skilled services or opportunities to modify the intervention, intervention approach, context, or goals based on client needs, responses to intervention, and progress toward goals
	010503	Clinical decision-making for implementing modifications to the intervention plan and prioritization of goals under the supervision of the OTR in response to physiological changes, behavioral reaction, emotion regulation, and developmental needs of the client

DOMAIN 02	SELECTING AND IMPLEMENTING INTERVENTIONS
	Implement interventions under the supervision of the OTR in accordance with the intervention plan and level of service competence to support client participation in areas of occupation throughout the occupational therapy process.

Task 0201	Incorporate methods and techniques as an adjunct to interventions in order to facilitate healing and enhance engagement in occupation-based activities.	
	KNOWLEDGE OF:	
	020101	Methods for selecting, preparing, and adapting the intervention technique and environment to support optimal engagement in the intervention and promote goal achievement
	020102	Technical level indications, contraindications, and precautions associated with wound management, considering the characteristics of a wound, the stage of wound healing, and the influence of the wound on engagement in occupation as guided by evidence, best practice standards, scope of practice, and state licensure practice acts in order to support functional outcomes
	020103	Technical level indications, contraindications, precautions, and appropriate clinical application of superficial thermal agents as guided by evidence, best practice standards, scope of practice, and state licensure practice acts
	020104	Technical level indications, contraindications, precautions, and appropriate clinical application of deep thermal, mechanical, and electrotherapeutic physical agent modalities as guided by evidence, best practice standards, scope of practice, and state licensure practice acts

Task 0202	Implement developmental, remedial, and adaptive occupation-based strategies to support participation in activities of daily living (ADL), instrumental activities of daily living (IADL), rest and sleep, education, work, play, leisure, and social participation across the life span.	
	KNOWLEDGE OF:	
	020201	Intervention methods for supporting leisure and play-based exploration and participation consistent with client interests, needs, goals, and context
	020202	Methods for grading an activity, task, or technique based on level of development, client status, response to intervention, and client needs
	020203	Methods for facilitating individual and group participation in shared tasks or activities consistent with the type, function, format, context, goals, and stage of the group
	020204	Intervention methods and activities to support optimal sensory arousal and visual motor, cognitive, or perceptual processing for supporting engagement in occupations based on current level of development, abilities, task characteristics, and environmental demands
	020205	Compensatory and remedial interventions for managing cognitive and perceptual deficits or intellectual disabilities
	020206	Adaptive and preventive interventions for optimal engagement in occupation consistent with developmental level, neuromotor status, and condition
	020207	Technical level intervention strategies and techniques used to facilitate oral motor skills for drinking, eating, and swallowing consistent with developmental level, client condition, caregiver interaction, and mealtime environment and context
	020208	Prevocational, vocational, and transitional services, options, and resources for supporting strengths, interests, employment, and lifestyle goals of the adolescent, middle-aged, and older adult client

Task 0203	**Implement interventions for improving range of motion, strength, activity tolerance, sensation, postural control, and balance based on neuromotor status, cardiopulmonary response, and current stage of recovery or condition in order to support occupational performance.**	
	KNOWLEDGE OF:	
	020301	Methods for grading various types of therapeutic exercise and conditioning programs consistent with indications and precautions for strengthening muscles, increasing endurance, improving range of motion and coordination, and increasing joint flexibility in relation to task demands
	020302	Technical level techniques for implementing sensory and motor reeducation, desensitization, pain management, edema reduction, and scar management programs
	020303	Technical level techniques and activities for promoting or improving postural stability, facilitating dynamic balance, and teaching proper body mechanics and efficient breathing patterns during functional tasks to support engagement in occupation

Task 0204	**Apply anatomical, physiological, biomechanical, and healing principles to select or fabricate orthotic devices, and provide training in the use of orthotic and prosthetic devices by using critical thinking and problem-solving as related to a specific congenital anomaly or type of injury, current condition, or disease process in order to support functional outcomes.**	
	KNOWLEDGE OF:	
	020401	Types and functions of immobilization, mobilization, restriction, and non-articular orthoses for managing specific conditions
	020402	Influence of general anatomical, physiological, biomechanical, and healing principles on orthotic selection, design, fabrication, and modification
	020403	Training methods regarding the safe and effective use of orthotic and prosthetic devices consistent with the client's prioritized needs, goals, and task demands in order to optimize or enhance function

Appendix A • Content Outline for the COTA Examination

Task 0205	Integrate assistive technology options, adaptive devices, mobility aids, and other durable medical equipment into the intervention, considering the client's developmental, physical, functional, cognitive, and mental health status; prioritized needs; task demands; and context to enable participation in meaningful occupation.	
	KNOWLEDGE OF:	
	020501	Factors related to measuring, selecting, monitoring fit of, and recommending modifications to seating systems, positioning devices, and mobility aids
	020502	Characteristics and features of commonly used high- and low-tech assistive technology for supporting engagement in meaningful occupation
	020503	Types of commonly used mobility options, vehicle adaptations, and alternative devices for supporting participation in community mobility
	020504	Training methods and other factors influencing successful use and maintenance of commonly used assistive technology options, adaptive devices, and durable medical equipment

Task 0206	Implement environmental modifications guided by an occupation-based model, disability discrimination legislation, and accessibility guidelines and standards to support participation in occupation consistent with a client's physical needs; cognitive, mental health, and developmental status; context; and task demands.	
	KNOWLEDGE OF:	
	020601	Fundamental principles of ergonomics and universal design for identifying, recommending, and implementing reasonable accommodations and features in the workplace, home, and public spaces in order to optimize accessibility and usability
	020602	Processes and procedures for identifying, recommending, and implementing modifications in the workplace, home, and public spaces, considering the interaction among client factors, contexts, roles, task demands, and resources

DOMAIN 03	UPHOLDING PROFESSIONAL STANDARDS AND RESPONSIBILITIES
	Uphold professional standards and responsibilities by achieving service competence and applying evidence-based interventions to promote quality in practice.

Task 0301	Engage in professional development and competency assessment activities by using evidence-based strategies and approaches to provide safe, effective, and efficient services relevant to the job role, practice setting, scope of practice, and professional certification standards.

KNOWLEDGE OF:	
030101	Methods for locating, reviewing, and interpreting scholarly research in occupational therapy to guide and support professional competence and practice-relevant decision-making
030102	Methods for contributing to continuous quality improvement processes and procedures related to occupational therapy service delivery
030103	Methods for identifying, documenting, and monitoring service competency and professional development needs based on scope of practice and certification standards for occupational therapy
030104	Types of evidence-based programming for advancing positive population health outcomes
030105	Application of ethical decision-making and professional behaviors guided by the NBCOT standards of practice and Code of Conduct

Task 0302	Incorporate risk management techniques at an individual and practice-setting level by using standard operating procedures, safety principles, best practice guidelines, and relevant compliance trainings to protect clients, self, and staff from injury or harm during interventions.

	KNOWLEDGE OF:
030201	Precautions or contraindications associated with a client condition or stage of recovery
030202	Standard infection control procedures and universal precautions for reducing transmission of contaminants
030203	Basic first aid in response to minor injuries and adverse reactions
030204	Essential safety procedures to integrate into the intervention activities
030205	Preventive measures for minimizing risk in the intervention environment

Task 0303	Provide occupational therapy service in accordance with laws, regulations, state occupational therapy practice acts, and accreditation guidelines in order to protect consumers and meet applicable reimbursement requirements in relation to the service delivery setting.

	KNOWLEDGE OF:
030301	Methods for identifying, locating, and integrating federal regulations, facility policies, and accreditation guidelines related to service delivery across occupational therapy practice settings
030302	Influence of reimbursement policies and guidelines related to skilled and medically necessary occupational therapy service delivery
030303	Accountability processes and procedures using relevant practice terminology, abbreviations, and information technology for justifying, tracking, and monitoring outcomes related to occupational therapy service delivery

Appendix B

An Illustrated Description of Entry-Level COTA® Practice

The *Illustrated Description of Entry-Level COTA® Practice* brings to life the results from the 2017 NBCOT practice analysis study. Practice analysis is the method used to establish a clearly delineated set of domains, tasks, and associated knowledge necessary for the entry-level certified occupational therapist assistant to provide safe and effective services to clients. The results of the practice analysis study are used to develop the content outline for the COTA certification examination.

Much like looking through the clinic window, the NBCOT's *Illustrated Description of Entry-Level COTA® Practice* presents sample scenarios across a variety of practice settings that depict the tasks COTAs complete in practice. Alongside each scenario* is a description of how the knowledge required to competently perform a task is applied throughout the occupational therapy process. Occupational therapy assistant students may use the sample **scenarios** and associated **application to practice** to support their understanding of entry-level practice, as described in the practice analysis study, and as a tool to prepare for the national certification examination.

Appendix B • An Illustrated Description of Entry-Level COTA® Practice

The following is an extract from the *Illustrated Description of Entry-Level COTA® Practice* that shows the related knowledge, scenario, and application to practice for the class code presented:

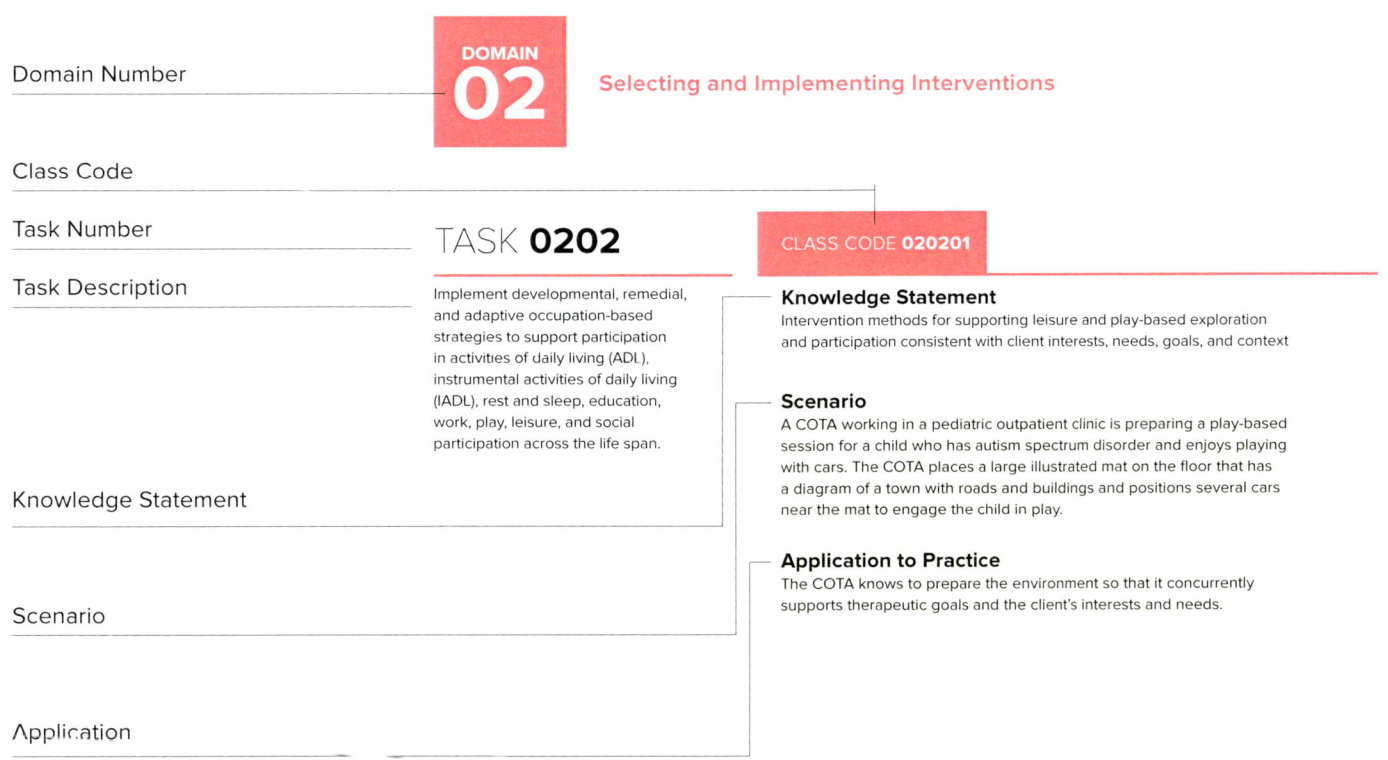

Domain Number — **DOMAIN 02** Selecting and Implementing Interventions

Class Code

Task Number — **TASK 0202** | **CLASS CODE 020201**

Task Description — Implement developmental, remedial, and adaptive occupation-based strategies to support participation in activities of daily living (ADL), instrumental activities of daily living (IADL), rest and sleep, education, work, play, leisure, and social participation across the life span.

Knowledge Statement
Intervention methods for supporting leisure and play-based exploration and participation consistent with client interests, needs, goals, and context

Scenario
A COTA working in a pediatric outpatient clinic is preparing a play-based session for a child who has autism spectrum disorder and enjoys playing with cars. The COTA places a large illustrated mat on the floor that has a diagram of a town with roads and buildings and positions several cars near the mat to engage the child in play.

Application to Practice
The COTA knows to prepare the environment so that it concurrently supports therapeutic goals and the client's interests and needs.

Knowledge Statement

Scenario

Application

*The content contained in the Illustrated Guide was developed to support your certification examination preparation activities. Please note, the scenarios presented in this document are single examples. They are condensed in focus and NOT intended to be inclusive of all the practice situations where you may use this knowledge or all of the knowledge you may be assessed on during the NBCOT certification examination. Using this resource alone or with other resources does not guarantee a passing score on your certification examination.

DOMAIN 01

Collaborating and Gathering Information

Assist the OTR to acquire information regarding factors that influence occupational performance on an ongoing basis throughout the occupational therapy process.

DOMAIN 01: Collaborating and Gathering Information

TASK 0101

Recognize the influence of development; body functions and body structures; and values, beliefs, and spirituality on a client's occupational performance.

CLASS CODE 010101

Knowledge Statement
Impact of typical development and aging on occupational performance, health, and wellness across the life span

Scenario
A COTA is observing a 3-year-old child playing at a sand table. While the child is engaged in building a sand castle, the COTA notes that another child is independently working on constructing a road in the sand.

Application to Practice
The COTA knows that in normal development, parallel play is a type of play where children play separately to each other while engaging in the same activity.

CLASS CODE 010102

Knowledge Statement
Expected patterns, progressions, and prognoses associated with conditions that limit occupational performance

Scenario
An outpatient who recently had a transradial amputation of the dominant upper extremity is in the pre-prosthetic phase of rehabilitation. The COTA asks the patient if there has been any evidence of sensitivity of the residual limb while completing personal hygiene activities.

Application to Practice
The COTA knows that hypersensitivity of the residual limb is associated with the pre-prosthetic phase of rehabilitation after amputation.

DOMAIN 01 — Collaborating and Gathering Information

TASK 0101

CLASS CODE 010103

Knowledge Statement
Impact of body functions, body structures, and values, beliefs, and spirituality on occupational performance

Scenario
A client who has osteoarthritis of both shoulders is participating in a grooming session and is standing at the sink combing their hair. The COTA observes that the client has limited shoulder flexion resulting in difficulty reaching hair on the back of the head.

Application to Practice
The COTA knows to observe the influence of available glenohumeral joint flexion on the client's ability to perform functional movements during everyday activities.

TASK 0102

Acquire information by using available resources about a client's functional skills, roles, culture, performance context, and prioritized needs in order to contribute to the development and update of an occupational profile.

CLASS CODE 010201

Knowledge Statement
Resources for acquiring information about the client's current condition and occupational performance

Scenario
An OTR and a COTA are collaborating to complete an initial evaluation of a kindergarten student who has autism spectrum disorder. The COTA provides the OTR with information on the frequency of the student's social interactions during outdoor recess on the playground.

Application to Practice
The COTA knows the importance of completing a naturalistic observation in order to collect information to contribute to the evaluation process.

DOMAIN 01

Collaborating and Gathering Information

TASK 0102

CLASS CODE 010202

Knowledge Statement
Purpose, advantages, limitations, and service competency needs related to the administration of commonly used standardized assessments and non-standardized screening as a means of acquiring client information

Scenario
A COTA and an OTR are collaborating to evaluate an inpatient recently admitted to a forensic mental health unit. The COTA follows the administration protocol for the Bay Area Functional Performance Evaluation (BaFPE) and provides the results to the OTR.

Application to Practice
The service competent COTA knows to adhere to the administration protocol for the BaFPE to contribute valid and reliable results to the evaluation process.

CLASS CODE 010203

Knowledge Statement
Internal and external factors influencing a client's meaningful engagement in occupation related to typical habits, roles, routines, and rituals, and the level and type of assistance required

Scenario
An outpatient client tells the COTA that they occasionally forget to take prescribed medication at night. The COTA consults with the OTR, then asks the client to explain daily routines related to the medication regimen.

Application to Practice
The COTA knows that daily habits and routines influence the client's ability to manage and adhere to the medication regimen.

Collaborating and Gathering Information

TASK 0103

Provide information regarding the influence of current conditions, contexts, and task demands on occupational performance in order to assist the OTR in planning interventions and monitoring progress as guided by the practice setting and theoretical construct.

CLASS CODE 010301

Knowledge Statement
Influence of theoretical approaches, models of practice, and frames of reference on information-gathering and the intervention process

Scenario
A COTA who works in an outpatient clinic is using the multicontext intervention approach to guide intervention planning for a client who has a mild TBI. The COTA first teaches the client to use a checklist to follow a recipe in the OT kitchen at the clinic, then instructs the client on how to use a similar checklist to follow simple recipes at home.

Application to Practice
The COTA is using tenets of the multicontext intervention approach to teach the client how to use a checklist strategy in the clinic setting that can later be generalized to similar activities that are completed in different settings.

CLASS CODE 010302

Knowledge Statement
Task analysis in relation to a client's performance skills, the occupational profile, practice setting, stage of occupational therapy process, areas of occupation, and activity demands

Scenario
A COTA who works in an outpatient setting, is observing a client who has fibromyalgia vacuum a carpet to determine which steps of the task could be adapted to reduce symptoms.

Application to Practice
The COTA knows to complete an activity analysis to guide task modifications and the selection of appropriate adaptations to meet the intervention goals established for the client.

DOMAIN 01

Collaborating and Gathering Information

TASK 0104

Collaborate with the client, the client's relevant others, occupational therapy colleagues, and other professionals and staff by using a culturally sensitive, client-centered approach and therapeutic use of self to provide quality services guided by evidence, scope of practice, service competence, and principles of best practice.

CLASS CODE 010401

Knowledge Statement
Characteristics and functions of interprofessional teams for coordinating client care and providing efficient and effective services consistent with specific core competencies, expertise, unique contributions, team roles, and context of the organization

Scenario
A COTA is working with a preschool student who has reactive attachment disorder and requires constant redirection in the classroom and on the playground. The COTA collaborates with the OTR to refer the student to the school psychologist.

Application to Practice
The COTA knows the role of the school psychologist on the interprofessional team.

CLASS CODE 010402

Knowledge Statement
Coordination of occupational therapy services related to collaborative client-centered intervention plans, Individualized Education Program plans, and transition plans based on client skills, abilities, and expected outcomes in relation to available resources, level of service delivery, and frequency and duration of intervention

Scenario
A COTA is working with an inpatient who has had a CVA. As part of the discharge planning process, the COTA meets with the patient, the social worker, and the medical equipment vendor to ensure necessary durable medical equipment is in the home prior to discharge.

Application to Practice
The COTA knows to collaborate with the interprofessional team members to facilitate a safe and effective discharge for the patient who is returning home.

DOMAIN 01
Collaborating and Gathering Information

TASK 0104

CLASS CODE 010403

Knowledge Statement
Collaborative processes and procedures for prioritizing intervention goals and activities based on client needs, wants, developmental skills, abilities, progress, and expected outcomes in relation to level of service delivery as well as frequency and duration of intervention

Scenario
A COTA is working with a 10-year-old child who has arthrogryposes and wants to play baseball. The COTA and the client work together to customize a catcher's mitt, then progress to throwing and catching the ball.

Application to Practice
The COTA knows to prioritize intervention activities based on the client's preferences and to grade the tasks to support progress toward the long-term goal.

CLASS CODE 010404

Knowledge Statement
Fundamental strategies used for addressing health literacy to enhance non-verbal and verbal interactions with a client and relevant others in order to promote positive health behaviors, enable informed decisions, maximize safety of care, and promote carry-over of the intervention to support positive outcomes

Scenario
A COTA is teaching fall prevention strategies to a group of community-dwelling older adults. As part of the education session, the COTA provides each person with a written handout containing clear illustrations, then engages the group in an interactive discussion.

Application to Practice
The COTA knows the principles of health literacy and facilitates the client's understanding of the information to encourage carryover of learning into daily routines.

DOMAIN 01: Collaborating and Gathering Information

TASK 0105

Monitor the intervention plan and progress toward goals in collaboration with the OTR by using clinical reasoning, therapeutic use of self, and cultural sensitivity to make decisions about the intervention approach, context, or goals based on client needs, priorities, response to intervention, status changes, reevaluation results, and targeted outcomes.

CLASS CODE 010501

Knowledge Statement
Factors related to determining the context and type of individual and group activities for effectively supporting intervention goals and objectives

Scenario
A COTA is preparing for a gardening group with residents who have dementia and are at-risk for wandering. The COTA plans for the group to occur in the facility's enclosed courtyard.

Application to Practice
The COTA knows to select a physical environment that concurrently meets the objectives for the group and the safety needs of the group members.

CLASS CODE 010502

Knowledge Statement
Methods for monitoring the effectiveness of individual and group intervention in order to keep the OTR informed about continuation of skilled services or opportunities to modify the intervention, intervention approach, context, or goals based on client needs, responses to intervention, and progress toward goals

Scenario
A COTA is leading a meal planning group for young adult clients who have anorexia nervosa. At the end of each session, the COTA completes a behavioral observation checklist and gives the checklists to the OTR.

Application to Practice
The COTA knows to observe and document each group member's behavior during the group process to allow for performance change to be monitored over time.

Domain 01
Collaborating and Gathering Information

TASK 0105

CLASS CODE 010503

Knowledge Statement
Clinical decision-making for implementing modifications to the intervention plan and prioritization of goals under the supervision of the OTR in response to physiological changes, behavioral reaction, emotion regulation, and developmental needs of the client

Scenario
A COTA collaborates with an OTR to update the intervention goals for a resident of a skilled nursing facility who has ankylosing spondylitis and has experienced a recent progression of symptoms. Previously, the resident was independent in self-feeding but now requires moderate assistance.

Application to Practice
The COTA knows to communicate with the OTR to update the intervention goals when a change in medical condition influences level of function.

Appendix B • An Illustrated Description of Entry-Level COTA® Practice

DOMAIN 02

Selecting and Implementing Interventions

Implement interventions under the supervision of the OTR in accordance with the intervention plan and level of service competence to support client participation in areas of occupation throughout the occupational therapy process.

305

DOMAIN 02: Selecting and Implementing Interventions

TASK 0201

Incorporate methods and techniques as an adjunct to interventions in order to facilitate healing and enhance engagement in occupation-based activities.

CLASS CODE 020101

Knowledge Statement
Methods for selecting, preparing, and adapting the intervention technique and environment to support optimal engagement in the intervention and promote goal achievement

Scenario
A COTA is modifying the intervention method for an active pediatric client, who has camptodactaly and refuses to follow the wearing schedule for the custom-fabricated orthosis. To increase wearing compliance, the COTA develops a sticker reward chart.

Application to Practice
The COTA knows to modify the intervention approach and employ an alternate strategy to increase wearing compliance for the orthosis.

CLASS CODE 020102

Knowledge Statement
Technical level indications, contraindications, and precautions associated with wound management, considering the characteristics of a wound, the stage of wound healing, and the influence of the wound on engagement in occupation as guided by evidence, best practice standards, scope of practice, and state licensure practice acts in order to support functional outcomes

Scenario
A COTA is working with an older adult inpatient who is significantly deconditioned and is recovering from reconstructive surgery to treat a sacral decubitus ulcer. While the patient is in a side-lying position in bed, the COTA teaches the patient to routinely check the surgical site using a skin inspection mirror with a long, flexible handle.

Application to Practice
The COTA knows that an integral part of preventing skin breakdown and managing decubitus ulcers is for the patient to routinely perform skin checks of the at-risk areas of the body.

DOMAIN 02: Selecting and Implementing Interventions

TASK 0201

CLASS CODE 020103

Knowledge Statement
Technical level indications, contraindications, precautions, and appropriate clinical application of superficial thermal agents as guided by evidence, best practice standards, scope of practice, and state licensure practice acts

Scenario
A service competent COTA, who has met local state regulatory requirements associated with physical agent modalities, is following the intervention plan for a client who has upper extremity flexor spasticity. The COTA applies a hot pack over the belly of the biceps before asking the client to reach for groceries on a shelf.

Application to Practice
The service competent COTA knows that neutral warmth influences muscle tone and prepares the client who has spasticity to perform a functional task using available ROM.

CLASS CODE 020104

Knowledge Statement
Technical level indications, contraindications, precautions, and appropriate clinical application of deep thermal, mechanical, and electrotherapeutic physical agent modalities as guided by evidence, best practice standards, scope of practice, and state licensure practice act

Scenario
An OTR and a COTA are providing intervention to an outpatient client who has complex regional pain syndrome (CRPS). The COTA observes the service competent OTR remove the transcutaneous electrical nerve stimulation (TENS) electrodes that are applied to the painful area and asks the client to rate current level of pain before initiating the planned functional activity.

Application to Practice
The service competent COTA knows that transcutaneous electrical nerve stimulation is a physical agent modality that delivers an electrical current that may influence the client's level of pain.

DOMAIN 02: Selecting and Implementing Interventions

TASK 0202

Implement developmental, remedial, and adaptive occupation-based strategies to support participation in activities of daily living (ADL), instrumental activities of daily living (IADL), rest and sleep, education, work, play, leisure, and social participation across the life span.

CLASS CODE 020201

Knowledge Statement
Intervention methods for supporting leisure and play-based exploration and participation consistent with client interests, needs, goals, and context

Scenario
A COTA working in a pediatric outpatient clinic is preparing a play-based session for a child who has autism spectrum disorder and enjoys playing with cars. The COTA places a large illustrated mat on the floor that has a diagram of a town with roads and buildings and positions several cars near the mat to engage the child in play.

Application to Practice
The COTA knows to prepare the environment so that it concurrently supports therapeutic goals and the client's interests and needs.

CLASS CODE 020202

Knowledge Statement
Methods for grading an activity, task, or technique based on level of development, client status, response to intervention, and client needs

Scenario
An inpatient who is recovering from a bilateral lung transplant independently brushes their hair and washes their face when supported in an upright sitting position in bed. The COTA increases the challenge of the activity by assisting the patient to sit on the edge of the bed to complete simple grooming tasks with the patient's feet positioned on the floor.

Application to Practice
The COTA knows to grade the level of difficulty of the grooming activity by progressing the patient from a supported sitting position in bed to an unsupported sitting position on the edge of the bed.

DOMAIN 02
Selecting and Implementing Interventions

TASK 0202

CLASS CODE 020203

Knowledge Statement
Methods for facilitating individual and group participation in shared tasks or activities consistent with the type, function, format, context, goals, and stage of the group

Scenario
When facilitating a life skills group for clients who have intellectual disabilities, the COTA leads the group members through a role-playing exercise to practice ordering food in a restaurant.

Application to Practice
The COTA knows that role-playing is an effective technique to promote and practice skills for independent living.

CLASS CODE 020204

Knowledge Statement
Intervention methods and activities to support optimal sensory arousal and visual motor, cognitive, or perceptual processing for supporting engagement in occupations based on current level of development, abilities, task characteristics, and environmental demands

Scenario
A COTA encourages a kindergarten student who has a sensory processing disorder to swing on a hanging hammock chair during recess to prepare for at-desk work in the classroom.

Application to Practice
The COTA knows that including movement in the student's sensory diet may assist the student in attending to written work during the school day.

DOMAIN 02: Selecting and Implementing Interventions

TASK 0202

CLASS CODE 020205

Knowledge Statement
Compensatory and remedial interventions for managing cognitive and perceptual deficits or intellectual disabilities

Scenario
A COTA is working with an inpatient who has right homonymous hemianopia. The COTA asks the patient to stand in front of a vending machine in the hospital's cafeteria and visually scan for items located in the patient's blind hemifield.

Application to Practice
The COTA knows that performing visual scanning during functional tasks will enhance the patient's awareness of visual field loss and teach visual compensatory strategies that the patient can use in everyday activities at home and in the community.

CLASS CODE 020206

Knowledge Statement
Adaptive and preventive interventions for optimal engagement in occupation consistent with developmental level, neuromotor status, and condition

Scenario
An inpatient who has flaccid hemiplegia is learning to put on a button-down shirt while sitting in a bedside chair. The COTA teaches the patient to use the unaffected hand to place the affected hand into the sleeve of the shirt then push the sleeve up toward the elbow.

Application to Practice
The COTA knows that teaching a one-handed dressing sequence that begins with dressing the affected upper extremity first will support a patient who has hemiplegia to independently put on a button-down shirt.

DOMAIN 02

Selecting and Implementing Interventions

TASK 0202

CLASS CODE 020207

Knowledge Statement
Technical level intervention strategies and techniques used to facilitate oral motor skills for drinking, eating, and swallowing consistent with developmental level, client condition, caregiver interaction, and mealtime environment and context

Scenario
During a mealtime session, a COTA teaches an inpatient who recently had a C_6 spinal cord injury how to apply a universal cuff to the dominant hand and load food onto a spoon before bringing the hand toward the mouth.

Application to Practice
The COTA knows that the expected functional outcomes for a patient who has a C_6 spinal cord injury includes independence in self-feeding with adapted equipment.

CLASS CODE 020208

Knowledge Statement
Prevocational, vocational, and transitional services, options, and resources for supporting strengths, interests, employment, and lifestyle goals of the adolescent, middle-aged, and older adult client

Scenario
A client who has a low back injury is preparing for discharge from a work hardening program. The COTA observes as the client, who works as a mail carrier, carries a mailbag loaded with letters and delivers them to several designated areas in the therapy space.

Application to Practice
The COTA knows that work hardening activities that simulate the demands of the job and incorporate equipment used at the client's job site will support the client's goal to return to work.

DOMAIN 02: Selecting and Implementing Interventions

TASK 0203

Implement interventions for improving range of motion, strength, activity tolerance, sensation, postural control, and balance based on neuromotor status, cardiopulmonary response, and current stage of recovery or condition in order to support occupational performance.

CLASS CODE 020301

Knowledge Statement
Methods for grading various types of therapeutic exercise and conditioning programs consistent with indications and precautions for strengthening muscles, increasing endurance, improving range of motion and coordination, and increasing joint flexibility in relation to task demands

Scenario
An outpatient has a second degree burn of the elbow and forearm. The COTA is teaching the client how to perform PROM exercises with a prolonged stretch to achieve full elbow extension.

Application to Practice
The COTA knows that an integral part of the rehabilitation phase after a burn injury is to prevent joint contracture and preserve ROM through an effective stretching program.

CLASS CODE 020302

Knowledge Statement
Technical level techniques for implementing sensory and motor reeducation, desensitization, pain management, edema reduction, and scar management programs

Scenario
An inpatient who is recovering from a CVA with hemiplegia has pitting edema on the dorsum of the affected hand. The COTA teaches the caregiver to elevate the patient's arm and massage the hand and forearm distally, then stroke it firmly and smoothly in a proximal direction.

Application to Practice
The COTA knows that retrograde massage will influence edema by manually moving fluid from the hand to be reabsorbed into the body.

DOMAIN 02 — Selecting and Implementing Interventions

TASK 0203

CLASS CODE 020303

Knowledge Statement
Technical level techniques and activities for promoting or improving postural stability, facilitating dynamic balance, and teaching proper body mechanics and efficient breathing patterns during functional tasks to support engagement in occupation

Scenario
An outpatient client, who has COPD, wants to get dressed while sitting on the edge of the bed but becomes short of breath during the activity. The COTA teaches the client to breath in through the nose and slowly exhale through pursed lips.

Application to Practice
The COTA knows that pursed lip breathing decreases the use of accessory muscles and increases the use of the diaphragm during respiration.

TASK 0204

Apply anatomical, physiological, biomechanical, and healing principles to select or fabricate orthotic devices, and provide training in the use of orthotic and prosthetic devices by using critical thinking and problem-solving as related to a specific congenital anomaly or type of injury, current condition, or disease process in order to support functional outcomes.

CLASS CODE 020401

Knowledge Statement
Types and functions of immobilization, mobilization, restriction, and non-articular orthoses for managing specific conditions

Scenario
A client with rheumatoid arthritis has a swan neck deformity of the 3rd digit. Under the direction of the OTR, the service competent COTA follows the intervention plan and provides the client with a three-point finger orthosis.

Application to Practice
The COTA knows that an anti-swan neck orthosis positions the PIP joint in slight flexion while limiting full PIP joint extension. This allows for full PIP flexion and full DIP ROM supporting the client to engage in functional activities.

Selecting and Implementing Interventions

TASK 0204

CLASS CODE 020402

Knowledge Statement
Influence of general anatomical, physiological, biomechanical, and healing principles on orthotic selection, design, fabrication, and modification

Scenario
An outpatient client, who is an amateur guitar player, has trigger finger of the 2nd digit. As part of the intervention plan, the service competent COTA teaches the client how to wear a trigger finger orthosis for nighttime use.

Application to Practice
The COTA knows that wearing this type of immobilization orthosis at night will support reduction in inflammation and pain associated with the condition.

CLASS CODE 020403

Knowledge Statement
Training methods regarding the safe and effective use of orthotic and prosthetic devices consistent with the client's prioritized needs, goals, and task demands in order to optimize or enhance function

Scenario
A COTA is teaching the parents of a child who has spastic cerebral palsy to correctly apply a hand-based orthosis to position the child's wrist in extension and thumb in abduction for self-feeding. After demonstrating how to put on the orthosis, the COTA observes the parents applying the orthosis.

Application to Practice
The COTA knows to teach family members the proper application of the orthosis to improve hand function prior to mealtime.

Appendix B • An Illustrated Description of Entry-Level COTA® Practice

Selecting and Implementing Interventions

TASK 0205

Integrate assistive technology options, adaptive devices, mobility aids, and other durable medical equipment into the intervention, considering the client's developmental, physical, functional, cognitive, and mental health status; prioritized needs; task demands; and context to enable participation in meaningful occupation.

CLASS CODE 020501

Knowledge Statement
Factors related to measuring, selecting, monitoring fit of, and recommending modifications to seating systems, positioning devices, and mobility aids

Scenario
A client who has a T_4 spinal cord injury needs to purchase a new cushion for the wheelchair. The COTA provides the client with information about the features and benefits of air-filled, foam, and gel cushions.

Application to Practice
The COTA knows the advantages and disadvantages of various types of wheelchair cushions and assists the client in selecting the optimal cushion for the client's needs.

CLASS CODE 020502

Knowledge Statement
Characteristics and features of commonly used high- and low-tech assistive technology for supporting engagement in meaningful occupation

Scenario
A COTA is teaching a patient who has amyotrophic lateral sclerosis how to use voice-activated technology to answer the phone and call a friend who is on the patient's contact list.

Application to Practice
The COTA knows how to select simple electronic aids to daily living (EADL) to support progress toward the patient's intervention goals.

DOMAIN 02: Selecting and Implementing Interventions

TASK 0205

CLASS CODE 020503

Knowledge Statement
Types of commonly used mobility options, vehicle adaptations, and alternative devices for supporting participation in community mobility

Scenario
An outpatient client recently stopped driving due to the progression of relapsing-remitting multiple sclerosis and is feeling socially isolated. After reviewing transportation options, the COTA assists the client in completing the application for paratransit bus service.

Application to Practice
The COTA is familiar with available transportation options within the client's local community and knows the importance of facilitating the client's need to engage in preferred activities outside the home.

CLASS CODE 020504

Knowledge Statement
Training methods and other factors influencing successful use and maintenance of commonly used assistive technology options, adaptive devices, and durable medical equipment

Scenario
A COTA asks an inpatient who recently had a total hip arthroplasty to show return demonstration of how to use a long-handled reacher to put on pants while maintaining post-operative hip precautions.

Application to Practice
The COTA knows to provide the patient with instruction and demonstration of a new skill and to ask the patient to perform the skill to ensure hip precautions are being followed.

DOMAIN 02

Selecting and Implementing Interventions

TASK 0206

Implement environmental modifications guided by an occupation-based model, disability discrimination legislation, and accessibility guidelines and standards to support participation in occupation consistent with a client's physical needs; cognitive, mental health, and developmental status; context; and task demands.

CLASS CODE 020601

Knowledge Statement
Fundamental principles of ergonomics and universal design for identifying, recommending, and implementing reasonable accommodations and features in the workplace, home, and public spaces in order to optimize accessibility and usability

Scenario
A COTA is making work station recommendations for a client who works as a data entry clerk and has low back pain. The COTA adjusts the client's office chair to ensure that the client's torso is properly supported by the back of the chair, thighs are parallel to the floor and feet are positioned on the ground.

Application to Practice
The COTA knows how to apply ergonomic principles to adjust the client's work station for optimal positioning and reduce the incidence of low back pain.

CLASS CODE 020602

Knowledge Statement
Processes and procedures for identifying, recommending, and implementing modifications in the workplace, home, and public spaces, considering the interaction among client factors, contexts, roles, task demands, and resources

Scenario
A COTA is making worksite recommendations for a client who uses a wheelchair for mobility and plans to return to work. The COTA measures the vertical rise of the stairs leading to the entryway to be 2 feet and calculates the minimum length of the ramp to be 24 feet.

Application to Practice
The COTA knows that the ADA recommends a 1:12 slope, which means that for every 1 foot of vertical rise, the ramp length should be a minimum of 12 feet.

DOMAIN 03

Upholding Professional Standards and Responsibilities

Uphold professional standards and responsibilities by achieving service competence and applying evidence-based interventions to promote quality in practice.

DOMAIN 03
Upholding Professional Standards and Responsibilities

TASK 0301
Engage in professional development and competency assessment activities by using evidence-based strategies and approaches to provide safe, effective, and efficient services relevant to the job role, practice setting, scope of practice, and professional certification standards.

CLASS CODE 030101

Knowledge Statement
Methods for locating, reviewing, and interpreting scholarly research in occupational therapy to guide and support professional competence and practice-relevant decision-making

Scenario
An outpatient client who has Parkinson's disease asks the COTA if attending dance lessons would be beneficial to improving balance for walking around the house and in the community. The COTA formulates a clinical question to search an online database.

Application to Practice
The COTA knows to use the principles of evidence-based practice to develop a clear clinical question and search for high-quality evidence to respond to the client's query.

CLASS CODE 030102

Knowledge Statement
Methods for contributing to continuous quality improvement processes and procedures related to occupational therapy service delivery

Scenario
A COTA who works in a rehabilitation hospital has been asked by the department supervisor to collect information for a hospital-wide initiative to improve patient satisfaction. At predetermined intervals during the patients' length of stay, the COTA asks each identified patient a series of questions related to satisfaction with occupational therapy services.

Application to Practice
The COTA knows that an important step in the continuous quality improvement process is to collect data.

DOMAIN 03

Upholding Professional Standards and Responsibilities

TASK 0301

CLASS CODE 030103

Knowledge Statement
Methods for identifying, documenting, and monitoring service competency and professional development needs based on scope of practice and certification standards for occupational therapy

Scenario
A COTA who recently started to work in a rehabilitation setting is unfamiliar with the administration protocol for a standardized assessment frequently used by the OTR. The OTR teaches the test protocol to the COTA and the COTA dedicates time to learn the administration procedure and subsequently administer the assessment several times under the supervision of the OTR until service competency is achieved.

Application to Practice
The COTA knows that acquiring adequate service competency for the administration of evaluation tools selected by the OTR is a professional responsibility.

CLASS CODE 030104

Knowledge Statement
Types of evidence-based programming for advancing positive population health outcomes

Scenario
A COTA is teaching a fall prevention class as part of a health and wellness program for community-dwelling older adults who are at-risk for falls. The COTA provides information and strategies to decrease the risk of falls in the home and the community.

Application to Practice
The COTA knows that fall prevention programming will promote the health and wellness of older adults and support aging in place.

Appendix B • An Illustrated Description of Entry-Level COTA® Practice

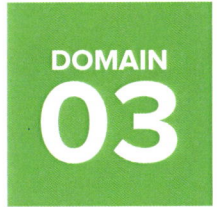

DOMAIN 03: Upholding Professional Standards and Responsibilities

TASK 0301

CLASS CODE 030105

Knowledge Statement
Application of ethical decision-making and professional behaviors guided by the NBCOT standards of practice and Code of Conduct

Scenario
An OTA student is preparing to apply for jobs after graduating and passing the certification exam. The supervising COTA reviews the OTA student's drafted resume but notices several inaccuracies related to job duties performed at the fieldwork site. The supervisor provides feedback to the OTA student, explains that misrepresenting information on a resume is unethical, and explains the principles of the NBCOT Code of Conduct.

Application to Practice
The COTA knows that misrepresenting information on the resume is a violation of Principle 3 of the NBCOT Code of Conduct, which states: "Certificants shall be accurate, truthful, and complete in any and all communications, direct or indirect, with any client, employer, regulatory agency, or other parties as they relate to their professional work, education, professional credentials, research and contributions to the field of occupational therapy."

TASK 0302

Incorporate risk management techniques at an individual and practice-setting level by using standard operating procedures, safety principles, best practice guidelines, and relevant compliance trainings to protect clients, self, and staff from injury or harm during interventions.

CLASS CODE 030201

Knowledge Statement
Precautions or contraindications associated with a client condition or stage of recovery

Scenario
A COTA is planning an ADL intervention session for an inpatient who had a total hip arthroplasty with a posterior approach 2 days ago. The focus of the intervention session is to teach the patient how to use assistive devices and adhere to hip precautions during lower body dressing and toilet transfers.

Application to Practice
The COTA knows that it is important to instruct the patient in the application of hip precautions during ADL at this stage of recovery to prevent the risk of hip dislocation and prepare the patient for discharge from the hospital.

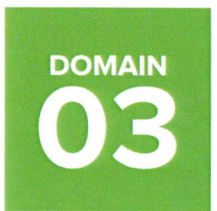

Upholding Professional Standards and Responsibilities

TASK 0302

CLASS CODE 030202

Knowledge Statement
Standard infection control procedures and universal precautions for reducing transmission of contaminants

Scenario
A COTA who works in a hospital setting puts on a pair of disposal gloves before working on toileting goals with a patient. During the session, the patient is incontinent, and requires assistance from the COTA for personal hygiene. After providing assistance and ensuring the client is safely situated, the COTA removes the gloves, washes hands with soap and water, and reapplies a clean pair of gloves to continue the session.

Application to Practice
The COTA knows standard infection control precautions, which requires healthcare personnel to wear gloves, follow hand hygiene protocol when there is contact with body fluid during a session, and change gloves before proceeding to the next intervention activity.

CLASS CODE 030203

Knowledge Statement
Basic first aid in response to minor injuries and adverse reactions

Scenario
An inpatient who recently had a C_5 spinal cord injury is participating in a grooming task. While sitting in a wheelchair in front of the bathroom mirror, the patient suddenly reports a pounding headache, has feelings of anxiety, and is sweating profusely. The COTA calls for immediate assistance while staying with the patient, checks the patient's vital signs, and removes any restrictive clothing the patient is wearing.

Application to Practice
The COTA knows that autonomic dysreflexia is a serious medical emergency associated with spinal cord injuries above T_6 and to seek immediate medical assistance while providing appropriate care to the patient.

DOMAIN 03
Upholding Professional Standards and Responsibilities

TASK 0302

CLASS CODE 030204

Knowledge Statement
Essential safety procedures to integrate into the intervention activities

Scenario
A COTA who is working in a memory care unit is assisting a client who has Alzheimer's disease to use scissors to clip coupons from a newspaper. At the end of the session, the COTA follows the department safety policy and checks that the scissors are returned to the inventory system and are secured in a locked location.

Application to Practice
The COTA knows the importance of following the department's safety policy to minimize risk of harm to the client and others who are attending the unit.

CLASS CODE 030205

Knowledge Statement
Preventive measures for minimizing risk in the intervention environment

Scenario
A COTA is teaching toilet transfers to an inpatient who has a progressive neurological condition. While the COTA and the patient are in the bathroom, housekeeping staff enter the patient's hospital room and wash the floor. The COTA is aware of the wet floor hazard and includes rest break in the session to allow time for the floor to dry before assisting the patient to the bedside.

Application to Practice
The COTA is aware of safety risks in the intervention environment and modifies the session to create a safe treatment space.

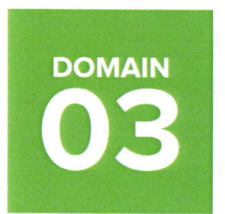

DOMAIN 03: Upholding Professional Standards and Responsibilities

TASK 0303

Provide occupational therapy service in accordance with laws, regulations, state occupational therapy practice acts, and accreditation guidelines in order to protect consumers and meet applicable reimbursement requirements in relation to the service delivery setting.

CLASS CODE 030301

Knowledge Statement
Methods for identifying, locating, and integrating federal regulations, facility policies, and accreditation guidelines related to service delivery across occupational therapy practice settings

Scenario
A friend asks a COTA about the progress of a prominent client who is being treated at the outpatient clinic where the COTA is employed The COTA immediately informs the friend that privacy laws forbid any discussion about the client's health care information and tells the friend not to ask about clients who are treated at the clinic.

Application to Practice
The COTA knows that the Health Insurance Portability and Accountability Act is a federal law that protects patients' personal health information and that providing client information to the friend would violate this law.

CLASS CODE 030302

Knowledge Statement
Influence of reimbursement policies and guidelines related to skilled and medically necessary occupational therapy service delivery

Scenario
During a team meeting at a skilled nursing facility, a COTA reports that skilled occupational therapy is provided to a resident who is a beneficiary of Medicare and is at-risk for falls. The COTA states that the resident is making progress toward the goal to use a tub transfer bench and adaptive equipment to decrease the risk of falls while bathing.

Application to Practice
The COTA knows that Medicare regulations require that occupational therapy services must be skilled, reasonable, and medically necessary to meet the qualification criteria for reimbursement.

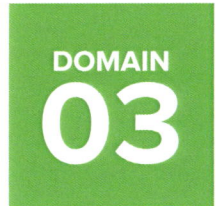

DOMAIN 03 — Upholding Professional Standards and Responsibilities

TASK 0303

CLASS CODE 030303

Knowledge Statement
Accountability processes and procedures using relevant practice terminology, abbreviations, and information technology for justifying, tracking, and monitoring outcomes related to occupational therapy service delivery

Scenario
A COTA is using an electronic documentation system to record objective information about a client's progress during an ADL intervention session. In addition to selecting the relevant assist levels from the drop-down menu, the COTA enters brief descriptors of the adaptive strategies used by the client in the available comment box.

Application to Practice
The COTA knows to accurately report objective data in the electronic health record.

Bibliography

Barney, K. F., & Perkinson, M. A. (2016). *Occupational therapy with aging adults: Promoting quality of life through collaboration.* St. Louis, MO: Elsevier Mosby.

Early, M. B. (2017). *Mental health concepts & techniques for the occupational therapy assistant (5th ed.).* Philadelphia, PA: Wolters Kluwer Lippincott Williams & Wilkins.

Early, M. B. (2013). *Physical dysfunction practice skills for the occupational therapy assistant (3rd ed.).* St. Louis, MO: Mosby Elsevier.

Gillen, G. (2016). *Stroke rehabilitation: A function-based approach (4th ed.).* St. Louis, MO: Elsevier Mosby.

Haertl, K. (Ed.). (2014). *Adults with intellectual and developmental disabilities: Strategies for occupational therapy.* Bethesda, MD: American Occupational Therapy Association, Inc.

Jacobs, K., MacRae, N., & Sladyk, K. (2014). *Occupational therapy essentials for clinical competence* (2nd ed.). Thorofare, NJ: SLACK, Inc.

Keough, J. L., Sain, S. J., & Roller, C. L. (2017). *Kinesiology for the occupational therapy assistant: Essential components of function and movement* (2nd ed.). Thorofare, NJ: SLACK, Inc.

Lane, S.J., & Bundy A.C. (2012). *KIDS can be kids: A childhood occupations approach.* Philadelphia, PA: F.A. Davis Company.

Manville, C.A. & Keough, J. L. (2016). *Mental health practice for the occupational therapy assistant.* Thorofare, NJ: SLACK Inc.

Morreale, M. J., & Borcherding, S. (2017). *The OTA's guide to documentation: Writing SOAP notes (4th ed.).* Thorofare, NJ: SLACK, Inc.

O'Brien, J.C., Solomon, J.W. (2013). *Occupational analysis group process.* St. Louis, MO: Elsevier Mosby.

Pendleton, H.M., & Schultz-Krohn, W. (Eds.). (2017). *Pedretti's occupational therapy practice skills for the physical dysfunction* (8th ed.). St. Louis, MO: Elsevier Mosby.

Radomski, M.V., & Trombly Latham, C.A. (2014). *Occupational therapy for physical dysfunction* (7th ed.). Philadelphia, PA: Lippincott Williams & Wilkins.

Sames, K.M. (2015). *Documenting occupational therapy practice* (3rd ed.). Upper Saddle River, NJ: Pearson Education, Inc.

Scaffa, M.E., Reitz, S.M., & Pizzi, M.A. (2010). *Occupational therapy in the promotion of health and wellness*. Philadelphia, PA: F.A. Davis Company.

Smith-Gabai, H. (2017). *Occupational therapy in acute care* (2nd ed.). Bethesda, MD: American Occupational Therapy Association, Inc.

Solomon, J. W., & O'Brien, J. C. (2016). *Pediatric skills for occupational therapy assistants (4th ed.)*. St. Louis, MO: Mosby Elsevier.

Wagenfeld, A. (2016). *Foundations of theory and practice for the occupational therapy assistant*. Baltimore, MD: Wolters Kluwer –Lippincott, Williams & Wilkins.

Appendix C

Worksheet: Illustrated Guide

Use the sample scenarios in each domain area to brainstorm your own examples of situations where you have seen a COTA use this knowledge in practice. From this, jot down your own list of study topics.

Appendix C • Worksheet: Illustrated Guide

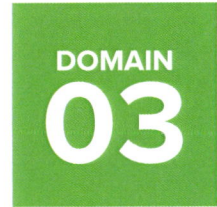

Appendix D

NBCOT COTA® Entry-Level Self-Assessment

Collaborating and Gathering Information

Assist the OTR to acquire information regarding factors that influence occupational performance on an ongoing basis throughout the occupational therapy process.

Task 1: Recognize the influence of development; body functions and body structures; and values, beliefs, and spirituality on a client's occupational performance.

When thinking about your knowledge and experience related to the following entry-level COTA skills, how would you rate your current level of competence?

Impact of typical development and aging on occupational performance, health, and wellness across the life span	○ 0 ○ 1 ○ 2 ○ 3
Expected patterns, progressions, and prognoses associated with conditions that limit occupational performance	○ 0 ○ 1 ○ 2 ○ 3
Impact of body functions, body structures, and values, beliefs, and spirituality on occupational performance	○ 0 ○ 1 ○ 2 ○ 3

Appendix D • Self Assessment

Task 2: Acquire information by using available resources about a client's functional skills, roles, culture, performance context, and prioritized needs in order to contribute to the development and update of an occupational profile.

When thinking about your knowledge and experience related to the following entry-level COTA skills, how would you rate your current level of competence?

Resources for acquiring information about the client's current condition and occupational performance	○ 0 ○ 1 ○ 2 ○ 3
Purpose, advantages, limitations, and service competency needs related to the administration of commonly used standardized assessments and non-standardized screening as a means of acquiring client information	○ 0 ○ 1 ○ 2 ○ 3
Internal and external factors influencing a client's meaningful engagement in occupation related to typical habits, roles, routines, and rituals, and the level and type of assistance required	○ 0 ○ 1 ○ 2 ○ 3

Task 3: Provide information regarding the influence of current conditions, contexts, and task demands on occupational performance in order to assist the OTR in planning interventions and monitoring progress as guided by the practice setting and theoretical construct.

When thinking about your knowledge and experience related to the following entry-level COTA skills, how would you rate your current level of competence?

Influence of theoretical approaches, models of practice, and frames of reference on information-gathering and the intervention process	○ 0 ○ 1 ○ 2 ○ 3
Task analysis in relation to a client's performance skills, the occupational profile, practice setting, stage of occupational therapy process, areas of occupation, and activity demands	○ 0 ○ 1 ○ 2 ○ 3

Task 4: Collaborate with the client, the client's relevant others, occupational therapy colleagues, and other professionals and staff by using a culturally sensitive, client-centered approach and therapeutic use of self to provide quality services guided by evidence, scope of practice, service competence, and principles of best practice.

When thinking about your knowledge and experience related to the following entry-level COTA skills, how would you rate your current level of competence?

Characteristics and functions of interprofessional teams for coordinating client care and providing efficient and effective services consistent with specific core competencies, expertise, unique contributions, team roles, and context of the organization	○ 0 ○ 1 ○ 2 ○ 3
Coordination of occupational therapy services related to collaborative client-centered intervention plans, Individualized Education Program plans, and transition plans based on client skills, abilities, and expected outcomes in relation to available resources, level of service delivery, and frequency and duration of intervention	○ 0 ○ 1 ○ 2 ○ 3
Collaborative processes and procedures for prioritizing intervention goals and activities based on client needs, wants, developmental skills, abilities, progress, and expected outcomes in relation to level of service delivery as well as frequency and duration of intervention	○ 0 ○ 1 ○ 2 ○ 3
Fundamental strategies used for addressing health literacy to enhance non-verbal and verbal interactions with a client and relevant others in order to promote positive health behaviors, enable informed decisions, maximize safety of care, and promote carry-over of the intervention to support positive outcomes	○ 0 ○ 1 ○ 2 ○ 3

Task 5: Monitor the intervention plan and progress toward goals in collaboration with the OTR by using clinical reasoning, therapeutic use of self, and cultural sensitivity to make decisions about the intervention approach, context, or goals based on client needs, priorities, response to intervention, status changes, reevaluation results, and targeted outcomes.

When thinking about your knowledge and experience related to the following entry-level COTA skills, how would you rate your current level of competence?

Factors related to determining the context and type of individual and group activities for effectively supporting intervention goals and objectives	○ 0 ○ 1 ○ 2 ○ 3
Methods for monitoring the effectiveness of individual and group intervention in order to keep the OTR informed about continuation of skilled services or opportunities to modify the intervention, intervention approach, context, or goals based on client needs, responses to intervention, and progress toward goals	○ 0 ○ 1 ○ 2 ○ 3
Clinical decision-making for implementing modifications to the intervention plan and prioritization of goals under the supervision of the OTR in response to physiological changes, behavioral reaction, emotion regulation, and developmental needs of the client	○ 0 ○ 1 ○ 2 ○ 3

Selecting and Implementing Interventions

implement interventions under the supervision of the OTR in accordance with the intervention plan and level of service competence to support client participation in areas of occupation throughout the occupational therapy process.

Task 1: Incorporate methods and techniques as an adjunct to interventions in order to facilitate healing and enhance engagement in occupation-based activities.

When thinking about your knowledge and experience related to the following entry-level COTA skills, how would you rate your current level of competence?

Methods for selecting, preparing, and adapting the intervention technique and environment to support optimal engagement in the intervention and promote goal achievement	○ 0 ○ 1 ○ 2 ○ 3
Technical level indications, contraindications, and precautions associated with wound management, considering the characteristics of a wound, the stage of wound healing, and the influence of the wound on engagement in occupation as guided by evidence, best practice standards, scope of practice, and state licensure practice acts in order to support functional outcomes	○ 0 ○ 1 ○ 2 ○ 3
Technical level indications, contraindications, precautions, and appropriate clinical application of superficial thermal agents as guided by evidence, best practice standards, scope of practice, and state licensure practice acts	○ 0 ○ 1 ○ 2 ○ 3
Technical level indications, contraindications, precautions, and appropriate clinical application of deep thermal, mechanical, and electrotherapeutic physical agent modalities as guided by evidence, best practice standards, scope of practice, and state licensure practice acts	○ 0 ○ 1 ○ 2 ○ 3

Task 2: Implement developmental, remedial, and adaptive occupation-based strategies to support participation in activities of daily living (ADL), instrumental activities of daily living (IADL), rest and sleep, education, work, play, leisure, and social participation across the life span.

When thinking about your knowledge and experience related to the following entry-level COTA skills, how would you rate your current level of competence?

Intervention methods for supporting leisure and play-based exploration and participation consistent with client interests, needs, goals, and context	○ 0 ○ 1 ○ 2 ○ 3
Methods for grading an activity, task, or technique based on level of development, client status, response to intervention, and client needs	○ 0 ○ 1 ○ 2 ○ 3
Methods for facilitating individual and group participation in shared tasks or activities consistent with the type, function, format, context, goals, and stage of the group	○ 0 ○ 1 ○ 2 ○ 3
Intervention methods and activities to support optimal sensory arousal and visual motor, cognitive, or perceptual processing for supporting engagement in occupations based on current level of development, abilities, task characteristics, and environmental demands	○ 0 ○ 1 ○ 2 ○ 3
Compensatory and remedial interventions for managing cognitive and perceptual deficits or intellectual disabilities	○ 0 ○ 1 ○ 2 ○ 3
Adaptive and preventive interventions for optimal engagement in occupation consistent with developmental level, neuromotor status, and condition	○ 0 ○ 1 ○ 2 ○ 3
Technical level intervention strategies and techniques used to facilitate oral motor skills for drinking, eating, and swallowing consistent with developmental level, client condition, caregiver interaction, and mealtime environment and context	○ 0 ○ 1 ○ 2 ○ 3
Prevocational, vocational, and transitional services, options, and resources for supporting strengths, interests, employment, and lifestyle goals of the adolescent, middle-aged, and older adult client	○ 0 ○ 1 ○ 2 ○ 3

Task 3: Implement interventions for improving range of motion, strength, activity tolerance, sensation, postural control, and balance based on neuromotor status, cardiopulmonary response, and current stage of recovery or condition in order to support occupational performance.

When thinking about your knowledge and experience related to the following entry-level COTA skills, how would you rate your current level of competence?

Methods for grading various types of therapeutic exercise and conditioning programs consistent with indications and precautions for strengthening muscles, increasing endurance, improving range of motion and coordination, and increasing joint flexibility in relation to task demands	○ 0 ○ 1 ○ 2 ○ 3
Technical level techniques for implementing sensory and motor reeducation, desensitization, pain management, edema reduction, and scar management programs	○ 0 ○ 1 ○ 2 ○ 3
Technical level techniques and activities for promoting or improving postural stability, facilitating dynamic balance, and teaching proper body mechanics and efficient breathing patterns during functional tasks to support engagement in occupation	○ 0 ○ 1 ○ 2 ○ 3

Appendix D • Self Assessment

Task 4: Apply anatomical, physiological, biomechanical, and healing principles to select or fabricate orthotic devices, and provide training in the use of orthotic and prosthetic devices by using critical thinking and problem-solving as related to a specific congenital anomaly or type of injury, current condition, or disease process in order to support functional outcomes.

When thinking about your knowledge and experience related to the following entry-level COTA skills, how would you rate your current level of competence?

Types and functions of immobilization, mobilization, restriction, and non-articular orthoses for managing specific conditions	○ 0 ○ 1 ○ 2 ○ 3
Influence of general anatomical, physiological, biomechanical, and healing principles on orthotic selection, design, fabrication, and modification	○ 0 ○ 1 ○ 2 ○ 3
Training methods regarding the safe and effective use of orthotic and prosthetic devices consistent with the client's prioritized needs, goals, and task demands in order to optimize or enhance function	○ 0 ○ 1 ○ 2 ○ 3

Task 5: Integrate assistive technology options, adaptive devices, mobility aids, and other durable medical equipment into the intervention, considering the client's developmental, physical, functional, cognitive, and mental health status; prioritized needs; task demands; and context to enable participation in meaningful occupation.

When thinking about your knowledge and experience related to the following entry-level COTA skills, how would you rate your current level of competence?

Factors related to measuring, selecting, monitoring fit of, and recommending modifications to seating systems, positioning devices, and mobility aids	○ 0 ○ 1 ○ 2 ○ 3
Characteristics and features of commonly used high- and low-tech assistive technology for supporting engagement in meaningful occupation	○ 0 ○ 1 ○ 2 ○ 3
Types of commonly used mobility options, vehicle adaptations, and alternative devices for supporting participation in community mobility	○ 0 ○ 1 ○ 2 ○ 3
Training methods and other factors influencing successful use and maintenance of commonly used assistive technology options, adaptive devices, and durable medical equipment	○ 0 ○ 1 ○ 2 ○ 3

Appendix D • Self Assessment

Task 6: Implement environmental modifications guided by an occupation-based model, disability discrimination legislation, and accessibility guidelines and standards to support participation in occupation consistent with a client's physical needs; cognitive, mental health, and developmental status; context; and task demands.

When thinking about your knowledge and experience related to the following entry-level COTA skills, how would you rate your current level of competence?

Fundamental principles of ergonomics and universal design for identifying, recommending, and implementing reasonable accommodations and features in the workplace, home, and public spaces in order to optimize accessibility and usability	○ 0 ○ 1 ○ 2 ○ 3
Processes and procedures for identifying, recommending, and implementing modifications in the workplace, home, and public spaces, considering the interaction among client factors, contexts, roles, task demands, and resources	○ 0 ○ 1 ○ 2 ○ 3

Upholding Professional Standards and Responsibilities

DOMAIN 03

Uphold professional standards and responsibilities by achieving service competence and applying evidence-based interventions to promote quality in practice.

Task 1: Engage in professional development and competency assessment activities by using evidence-based strategies and approaches to provide safe, effective, and efficient services relevant to the job role, practice setting, scope of practice, and professional certification standards.

When thinking about your knowledge and experience related to the following entry-level COTA skills, how would you rate your current level of competence?

Methods for locating, reviewing, and interpreting scholarly research in occupational therapy to guide and support professional competence and practice-relevant decision-making	○ 0	○ 1	○ 2	○ 3
Methods for contributing to continuous quality improvement processes and procedures related to occupational therapy service delivery	○ 0	○ 1	○ 2	○ 3
Methods for identifying, documenting, and monitoring service competency and professional development needs based on scope of practice and certification standards for occupational therapy	○ 0	○ 1	○ 2	○ 3
Types of evidence-based programming for advancing positive population health outcomes	○ 0	○ 1	○ 2	○ 3
Application of ethical decision-making and professional behaviors guided by the NBCOT standards of practice and Code of Conduct	○ 0	○ 1	○ 2	○ 3

Appendix D • Self Assessment

Task 2: Incorporate risk management techniques at an individual and practice-setting level by using standard operating procedures, safety principles, best practice guidelines, and relevant compliance trainings to protect clients, self, and staff from injury or harm during interventions.

When thinking about your knowledge and experience related to the following entry-level COTA skills, how would you rate your current level of competence?

Precautions or contraindications associated with a client condition or stage of recovery	○ 0 ○ 1 ○ 2 ○ 3
Standard infection control procedures and universal precautions for reducing transmission of contaminants	○ 0 ○ 1 ○ 2 ○ 3
Basic first aid in response to minor injuries and adverse reactions	○ 0 ○ 1 ○ 2 ○ 3
Essential safety procedures to integrate into the intervention activities	○ 0 ○ 1 ○ 2 ○ 3
Preventive measures for minimizing risk in the intervention environment	○ 0 ○ 1 ○ 2 ○ 3

Task 3: Provide occupational therapy service in accordance with laws, regulations, state occupational therapy practice acts, and accreditation guidelines in order to protect consumers and meet applicable reimbursement requirements in relation to the service delivery setting.

When thinking about your knowledge and experience related to the following entry-level COTA skills, how would you rate your current level of competence?

Methods for identifying, locating, and integrating federal regulations, facility policies, and accreditation guidelines related to service delivery across occupational therapy practice settings	○ 0 ○ 1 ○ 2 ○ 3
Influence of reimbursement policies and guidelines related to skilled and medically necessary occupational therapy service delivery	○ 0 ○ 1 ○ 2 ○ 3
Accountability processes and procedures using relevant practice terminology, abbreviations, and information technology for justifying, tracking, and monitoring outcomes related to occupational therapy service delivery	○ 0 ○ 1 ○ 2 ○ 3

Appendix E

References

Barney, K. F., & Perkinson, M. A. (2016). *Occupational therapy with aging adults: Promoting quality of life through collaboration*. St. Louis, MO: Elsevier Mosby.

Bonder, B. R. (2015). *Psychopathology and function* (5th ed.). Thorofare, NJ: SLACK, Inc.

Brown, C., & Stoffel V. C. (2011). *Occupational therapy in mental health: A vision for participation*. Philadelphia, PA: F.A. Davis Company.

Case-Smith, J., & O'Brien, J. C. (2015). *Occupational therapy for children and adolescents* (7th ed.). St. Louis, MO: Mosby Elsevier.

Cooper, C. (2014). *Fundamentals of hand therapy: Clinical reasoning and treatment guidelines for common diagnoses of the upper extremity* (2nd ed.). St. Louis, MO: Mosby Elsevier.

DeLany, J.V., & Pendzick, M.J. (2009). *Working with children and adolescents: A guide for the occupational therapy assistant*. Upper Saddle River, N.J.: Pearson Prentice Hall.

Early, M. B. (2017). *Mental health concepts & techniques for the occupational therapy assistant* (5th ed.). Philadelphia, PA: Lippincott Williams & Wilkins.

Early, M.B. (2013). *Physical dysfunction practice skills for the occupational therapy assistant* (3rd ed.). St. Louis, MO: Elsevier Mosby.

Gillen, G. (2016). *Stroke rehabilitation: A function-based approach* (4th ed.). St. Louis, MO: Elsevier.

Jacobs, K. (Ed.). (2016). *Management and administration for the OTA: Leadership and application skills*. Thorofare, NJ: SLACK, Inc.

Jacobs, M.A., & Austin, N.M. (2014). *Orthotic intervention for the hand and upper extremity: Splinting principles and processes* (2nd ed.). Philadelphia, PA: Lippincott Williams & Wilkins.

Jacobs, K., & MacRae, N. (Eds.). (2017). *Occupational therapy essentials for clinical competence* (3rd ed.). Thorofare, NJ: SLACK, Inc.

Keough, J. L., Sain, S. J., & Roller, C. L. (2017). *Kinesiology for the occupational therapy assistant: Essential components of function and movement* (2nd ed.). Thorofare, NJ: SLACK, Inc.

Lohman, H., Byers-Connon, S., & Padilla, R. L. (2019). *Occupational therapy with elders: Strategies for the COTA* (4th ed.). Maryland Heights, MO: Mosby Elsevier.

Mahle, A. J., & Ward, L. W. (2019). *Adult physical conditions: Intervention strategies for occupational therapy assistants*. Philadelphia, PA: F.A.Davis.

Manville, C. A., & Keough, J. L. (2016). *Mental health practice for the occupational therapy assistant.* (p.70). Thorofare, NJ: SLACK Inc.

Morreale, M. J., & Borcherding, S. (2017). *The OTA's guide to documentation: Writing SOAP notes* (4th ed.). Thorofare, NJ: SLACK, Inc.

Pendleton, H. M., & Schultz-Krohn, W. (Eds.). (2018). *Pedretti's occupational therapy: Practice skills for the physical dysfunction* (8th ed.). St. Louis, MO: Mosby Elsevier.

Radomski, M. V., & Trombly Latham, C. A. (Eds.). (2014). *Occupational therapy for physical dysfunction* (7th ed.). Philadelphia, PA: Lippincott Williams & Wilkins.

Sladyk, K., & Ryan, S. E. (Eds.). (2015). *Ryan's occupational therapy assistant: Principles, practice issues, and techniques* (5th ed.). Thorofare, NJ: SLACK, Inc.

Smith-Gabai, H., & Holm, S. (Eds.). (2017). *Occupational therapy in acute care* (2nd ed.). Bethesda, MD: AOTA Press.

Solomon, J. W., & O'Brien, J. C. (2016). *Pediatric skills for occupational therapy assistants* (4th ed.). St. Louis, MO: Mosby Elsevier.

Wagenfeld, A. (2016). *Foundations of theory and practice for the occupational therapy assistant*. Baltimore, MD: Wolters Kluwer-Lippincott, Williams & Wilkins.

Wagenfeld, A., Kaldenberg, J., & Honaker, D. (Eds.). (2017). *Foundations of pediatric practice for the occupational therapy assistant* (2nd ed.). Thorofare, NJ: SLACK, Inc.